ACCESSIBLE GOLF

Making It a Game Fore All

Ladies Professional Golf Association

with

Dan Drane, PhD
University of Southern Mississippi

Martin E. Block, PhD
University of Virginia

Human Kinetics

Library of Congress Cataloging-in-Publication Data

Accessible golf : making it a game fore all / Ladies Professional Golf Association ; with Dan Drane, Martin E. Block.
   p. cm.
   Includes bibliographical references.
   ISBN 0-88011-979-9 (soft cover)
   1. Golf for people with disabilities. 2. People with disabilities--Education. I. Drane, Dan. II. Block, Martin E.,
1958- III. Ladies Professional Golf Association.
   GV965.5.A22 2005
   796.352'087--dc22

                                  2005015290

ISBN: 0-88011-979-9

The Web addresses cited in this text were current as of July 15, 2005, unless otherwise noted.

Acquisitions Editor: Bonnie Pettifor; **Developmental Editor:** Amy Stahl; **Assistant Editors:** Bethany J. Bentley and Kathleen Bernard; **Copyeditor:** Alisha Jeddeloh; **Proofreader:** Julie Marx Goodreau; **Permission Manager:** Carly Breeding; **Graphic Designer:** Fred Starbird; **Graphic Artist:** Denise Lowry; **Photo Manager:** Sarah Ritz; **Cover Designer:** Keith Blomberg; **Photograph (cover):** © Corbis; **Art Manager:** Kelly Hendren; **Illustrator:** Roberta Polfus; **Printer:** Versa Press

Human Kinetics books are available at special discounts for bulk purchase. Special editions or book excerpts can also be created to specification. For details, contact the Special Sales Manager at Human Kinetics.

Printed in the United States of America   10 9 8 7 6 5 4 3 2 1

Human Kinetics
Web site: www.HumanKinetics.com

United States: Human Kinetics, P.O. Box 5076, Champaign, IL 61825-5076
800-747-4457
e-mail: humank@hkusa.com

Canada: Human Kinetics, 475 Devonshire Road Unit 100, Windsor, ON N8Y 2L5
800-465-7301 (in Canada only)
e-mail: orders@hkcanada.com

Europe: Human Kinetics, 107 Bradford Road, Stanningley, Leeds LS28 6AT, United Kingdom
+44 (0) 113 255 5665
e-mail: hk@hkeurope.com

Australia: Human Kinetics, 57A Price Avenue, Lower Mitcham, South Australia 5062
08 8277 1555
e-mail: liaw@hkaustralia.com

New Zealand: Human Kinetics, Division of Sports Distributors NZ Ltd., P.O. Box 300 226 Albany, North Shore City, Auckland
0064 9 448 1207
e-mail: info@humankinetics.co.nz

"People are the focus of all golf instruction . . . what is most important is to always remember that you are working with a valuable, unique individual each time you teach."

DeDe Owens, EdD

Proceeds from the sale of *Accessible Golf* will be donated to the LPGA Foundation's DeDe Owens Education and Research Fund.

Contents

A Note From the LPGA

Accessible Golf: Making It a Game Fore All is an education initiative of the Ladies Professional Golf Association (LPGA) that was spearheaded by Dr. DeDe Owens just months before her untimely death in 1999. DeDe was a consummate professional, a former LPGA Tour player, and an LPGA Master Teaching Professional. Her real love was her work with people as a golf educator. In 1984 she published her first book focusing on teaching golf to people with disabilities, *Teaching Golf to Special Populations*. By 1998 DeDe and I knew it was time to update the publication and to encourage the golf industry to support initiatives that would bring all people into the game of golf. We connected with Rainer Martens at Human Kinetics and launched the concept and the task of updating the material, the resources, and the references of the original text to best meet the needs of people with disabilities who want to get into the game of golf or get back into the game. We also considered the need for integrated training between golf professionals and allied health and rehabilitation specialists.

Between our initial conversations with Human Kinetics representatives in 1998 and now, much has happened to lend support to bringing people with disabilities into the game. In 1999, shortly after DeDe's death, the LPGA hosted an Accessible Golf Teacher Education Program and brought golf professionals, allied health professionals, and rehabilitation specialists together for a comprehensive three-day program focusing on integrated golf education training. By 2002 the National Alliance for Accessible Golf, an industry-wide alliance bringing the golf industry and rehabilitation organizations together, was formed. Soon after that the Alliance developed and implemented Project GAIN, a community-based program that focuses on helping people with disabilities learn the game and play the game. The Americans with Disabilities Act (ADA) has also enhanced opportunities for play and continues to evaluate its policies regarding access to sport and recreation for people with disabilities. The National Center on Accessibility (NCA) and the United States Golf Association (USGA), the governing body of golf in America, established comprehensive Web sites to assist people with disabilities with golf resources and references.

The LPGA is proud to be a contributing member of industry-wide efforts to bring all people into the game of golf through *Accessible Golf*. We are thankful for the years and foresight that DeDe Owens gave us as an LPGA member and educator. We continue to broaden our reach to all and hope this book will help you do the same.

Dr. Betsy Clark
Vice President of
Professional Development,
LPGA

Preface

The game of golf provides a wonderful recreational opportunity for all. It is a source of tremendous challenge and fulfillment as new golfers master the fundamentals and easily see improvement with practice. Of all the sport experiences in our culture, golf provides one of the best avenues for players of various skill levels to participate together. It is not uncommon to see a family with children or a group of adults whose skills vary markedly having a wonderful time together, or serious competitors matching their skills against the skills of others.

The purpose of this book is to provide crucial information for those who wish to help all people, regardless of physical or cognitive abilities, learn the game of golf and participate successfully in all of its aspects. This book was written to help golf professionals, teachers, coaches, rehabilitation specialists, and allied health professionals feel comfortable teaching golf to a wide variety of people. The underlying premise is that golf diminishes our differences and should be available to anyone who chooses to participate. It is an ideal sport for people with disabilities because the range of accommodations to help meet their needs is almost infinite. Golf is also a game that can be played informally, socially, or competitively.

Accessible Golf presents specific strategies for understanding individuals with disabilities and providing golf instruction and play that emphasize a team approach. Our goals are twofold. First, *Accessible Golf* is designed to provide fundamental information about golf instruction to teachers and health care workers who work with individuals with disabilities. Second, *Accessible Golf* is designed to provide basic information about individuals with disabilities to golf professionals who are already knowledgeable about golf and who are proficient instructors.

A behavioral framework is the foundation of this book and emphasizes the importance of focusing on individual motivations and capabilities. Most chapters include a case study followed by specific, practical content that will help individuals provide golfing opportunities to people with disabilities.

The process begins by understanding the potential of golf to enhance people's lives. Part I, Making Golf Accessible to All, emphasizes the role of golf in players' lives and the importance of providing equal access for all golfers. The first four chapters contain information about protecting the rights of all to play golf (chapter 1), improving access at golf facilities (chapter 2), meeting the needs in your community (chapter 3), and understanding the value of golf in the lives of individuals with disabilities (chapter 4). These chapters will be particularly useful to golf professionals and club owners who want to make their programs and facilities more accessible to people with disabilities.

Part II, Learning and Playing With a Disability, includes information about teaching the game of golf and will be particularly important for teachers and health care providers who wish to know more about teaching golf. It focuses on the LPGA Student-Centered Model for instruction (chapter 5) and includes fundamental information about teaching golf. These materials have been developed over the years and were especially influenced by the work of Dr. DeDe Owens, who devoted much of her professional career to teaching individuals with disabilities. Chapter 6 includes the fundamental rules of golf and how modifications to the rules can help accommodate the needs of golfers with disabilities. Chapter 7 focuses on creating safe learning environments, including designing effective practice spaces, understanding the psychological needs of learners, and minimizing golf injuries. Chapter 8 focuses on understanding individual learners and suggests strategies for assessing the motivations and skills of each golfer.

Part III, Understanding the Needs of Golfers With Disabilities, includes background information about specific disabilities as well as suggestions for teachers, therapists, and golf professionals to accommodate golfers with disabilities through unique teaching strategies, rule modifications, and adaptive equipment. Because each person's disability is complex, this section is organized by the nature of the disability: cognitive impairments and learning disabilities (chapter 9); attentional impairments (chapter 10); visual impairments (chapter 11); hearing impairments (chapter 12); and physical disabilities (chapter 13). It was impossible to cover every type of disability, so we chose to highlight the more common types of disabilities seen in children and adults.

Part IV, Developing a Full-Participation Golf Program, provides practical information about developing and delivering golf programs for individuals with disabilities. Chapter 14 discusses adaptive equipment and techniques to improve participation at all levels. Chapter 15 includes information about identifying people who can benefit from golf programs and strategies for recruiting their participation, and chapter 16 provides specific information about creating a team of professionals and interested citizens to foster golf programs for individuals with disabilities.

The book also includes four appendixes. Appendix A contains modified rules for golfers with disabilities, while appendix B includes an extensive list of materials to assist you in providing quality programs for golfers with disabilities. Written publications and video and Internet resources are identified and described. In addition, model programs and clinics are identified. Numerous resources that can provide adaptive equipment, advice about the design of facilities, and instructional expertise are also listed. Appendix C contains etiquette tips for golfers with disabilities and golf course operators. Finally, appendix D provides guidelines for making your facility accessible to golfers with disabilities.

The underlying tenet of the LPGA Teaching and Club Professional certification is to teach teachers how to teach all people the game of golf. *Accessible Golf* provides a comprehensive model and a unique student-centered approach to teaching and learning based on the LPGA's model. This book is just one resource, a starting point for those who wish to enhance the lives of others through the game of golf.

Acknowledgments

Accessible Golf: Making it a Game Fore All would not have been realized without the dedication of many individuals and the support of the Ladies Professional Golf Association (LPGA) and the LPGA Teaching and Club Professional membership. In particular, the late Dr. DeDe Owens, LPGA Master Teaching Professional and former chairperson of the LPGA National Education Advisory Committee for Accessible Golf, gave birth to this book and recruited the support of Human Kinetics, which has consistently supported the best of professional practice in fields related to sport and physical education. There have also been many individuals who have contributed over the years, including (but not limited to) the leadership of the LPGA, especially Dr. Betsy Clark, vice president of professional development, and dedicated professionals, including Dr. Larry Allen, Dr. Linda Bunker, Noel Jablonski, and Dr. Gary Robb. In addition, we appreciate the opportunity to tell the stories of individuals who serve as role models for golfers with disabilities and of organizations dedicated to providing opportunities for all individuals to enjoy the wonderful game of golf. This book, *Accessible Golf*, is much better because of their stories and contributions, and we are forever grateful.

Part I

Making Golf Accessible to All

Chapter 1

Protecting the Rights of All to Play Golf

Jerry was a pretty good golfer before his accident. A 12 handicapper who played two or three times per week, he loved playing golf. He had a regular outing scheduled on Thursdays and Saturdays with three buddies from work, and on Tuesday afternoons he enjoyed driving around the countryside looking for golf courses he had never played before. Work was the only thing that kept Jerry from playing golf every day, but he figured that would change in five years when he retired. All that changed suddenly when Jerry fell off his roof trying to clean out his gutters. The doctors said that he was actually lucky that he broke his back where he did. He had full movement of his arms and his trunk, but all Jerry focused on was the fact that he could not move his legs. He would be using a wheelchair for the rest of his life. While others in similar situations thought about how paralysis might affect their work, their ability to drive a car, or their ability to live on their own, Jerry focused on never being able to play golf again.

After all, he thought that people couldn't play golf from wheelchairs.

Jerry went through six months of rehabilitation that included attempts by therapeutic recreation and physical therapy personnel to get Jerry interested in sports. Jerry simply said

(continued)

(continued)

that he only liked to play golf, and he knew he could not do that anymore. One day Sarah, one of the physical therapists at the rehabilitation center, brought in a set of golf clubs. Jerry thought it was some kind of cruel joke, but the physical therapist assured Jerry that this was for real. First, she told Jerry to wheel himself over to the VCR and TV. She put in a short video showing people in single-rider golf cars playing golf. Jerry was amazed at how well they actually played. Then the physical therapist told Jerry to wheel himself over to the gymnasium. Jerry found a mini-practice facility set up with an Astroturf tee area and several plastic golf balls. The physical therapist gave Jerry a 9-iron and said, "Let's see what you got!" Jerry wheeled himself over to the makeshift tee box, lined himself up as well as he could, and took a swing. It was awkward, and he topped the ball, but he hit it. The next attempt went a little better, and before he knew it, Jerry had hit 100 golf balls. He was sweaty and tired, but he was happier than he had been in months. It was easy to track down Jerry after that: He

spent hour after hour in the gym or out in the athletic field hitting golf balls.

He actually got pretty good, and he was excited when one of the therapists suggested they go to a local golf course to play a round of golf. They arrived at the club and went into the clubhouse. The staff at the golf course had a copy of the document titled *National Alliance for Accessible Golf: Toolkit for Golf Course Owners and Operators,* which assists staff at golf courses in making the courses more accessible for golfers with disabilities. The assistant pro had gone through a training session only two weeks earlier and knew just what to do. She told Jerry that he could take his single-rider golf car on all the tees and greens, to let her know if he needed any other help, and to go have fun. Jerry was surprised that the clerk didn't give him a hard time about driving the single-rider car on the course, especially the greens. In fact, the clerk treated Jerry just as she would treat any other customer. It was one of the most enjoyable days of Jerry's life.

On July 26, 1990, President George Bush signed into law the Americans with Disabilities Act (ADA). The ADA has been called the most sweeping piece of civil rights legislation since the Civil Rights Act of 1964. Its protection of individuals with disabilities spans a variety of public and private services such as education, transportation, housing, employment, and recreation (Carpenter, 2000; Epstein, McGovern, & Moon, 1994; Fried, 1998; Sullivan, Lantz, & Zirkel, 2000). Sport and recreation facilities, including golf courses, are covered under the ADA. Thus, golf course owners and employees need to understand the ADA and its implications for golfers with disabilities. This chapter reviews the basic provisions and titles of ADA and discusses what golf course owners and staff need to do to meet the mandate of the ADA.

What Is the ADA?

The ADA provides a national mandate for basic civil rights protection for persons with disabilities. The ADA was designed to prevent people with disabilities from being treated differently solely because of their disabilities. The ADA also serves to abolish discrimination against people with disabilities and allows them to participate in all aspects of life that most of us consider basic rights of human beings. It extended previous civil rights legislation such as the Architectural Barriers Act of 1968 and Section 504 of the Rehabilitation Act of 1973 (Imber & van Geel, 2001; Sullivan, Lantz, & Zirkel, 2000; U.S. Department of Justice, 2001). Although these previous acts laid the foundation for antidiscriminatory practice, they covered only federal agencies and those agencies and businesses that received federal assistance (e.g., public universities, federal offices, federal contractors). Testimony before Congress in the late 1980s showed that while these acts had some effect on the lives of people with disabilities, there continued to be widespread inequity toward people with disabilities in such everyday activities as employment, housing, and recreation (Block, 1994; U.S. Department of Justice, 2001; U.S. Department of Justice, 2002). For example, entities such as small businesses, restaurants, movie theaters, and recreation facilities that were private (i.e., did not receive federal funding) but were open to the public were not covered. Thus, the ADA was passed into law.

Note that the ADA was not designed to be a statute of affirmative action. There are no quotas stating that a certain number of employees or club members in a business or organization must have disabilities. Rather, it ensures equality of opportunity and full participation. As such, the law prohibits persons with disabilities from being excluded from jobs, services, activities, or benefits based solely on their disabilities (Stein, 1993; U.S. Department of Justice, 2002). For example, an employer would be in violation of the ADA for denying employment to someone who has a hearing impairment if that person could meet all the requirements of the job. Similarly, a golf course that was open to the public would be in violation of the ADA if it denied a person like Jerry who uses a specially designed wheelchair or people with other disabilities from using the course solely because of a disability.

Who Is Protected?

The ADA does not identify specific disabilities. The ADA does, however, provide a general description of who is covered. This description includes an otherwise qualified person who has a physical or mental impairment that substantially limits one or more of the major life activities of that person (e.g., seeing, hearing, speaking, walking, breathing, performing manual tasks, learning, caring for oneself, and working); who has a record of such an impairment (e.g., a person who is recovering from cancer, mental illness, or an alcohol problem); or who is regarded as having such an impairment (e.g., limits major life activities as the result of negative attitudes of others toward the disabilities such as severe burns, HIV/AIDS, epilepsy, facial abnormalities, or alcoholism) (Americans with Disabilities Act, 1990; U.S. Department of Justice, 2001; U.S. Department of Justice, 2002). People with minor conditions that can be corrected, such as vision problems that can be corrected with glasses or mild hearing impairments that can be corrected with hearing aids, are not generally covered in the act. Similarly, nonchronic conditions that disable a person for a short period (e.g., sprain, broken limb, or flu) are not considered disabling conditions under this act (U.S. Department of Justice, 2002).

The ADA does not cover an individual who is a direct threat to the health or safety of others and whose condition cannot be alleviated by appropriate modifications or aids (Appenzeller, 2000; Block, 1994; Imber & van Geel, 2001). Three criteria must be met before one can exclude a person based on health or safety factors: The threat must be real; the treatment should be based on objective and unbiased information; and attempts must be made to reduce or eliminate the risk (Appenzeller, 2000). For example, an adult with a severe mental illness who has violent tendencies signs up for group instruction at your golf course. If this person's violent outbursts are clearly documented, cannot be controlled with support from a health professional (e.g., a clinical psychologist), and medication and modifications are not feasible (even working with this person one on one will not reduce the risk for the golf instructor), then the golf course has the right to not allow this person to join the group lesson. On the other hand, an individual with HIV/AIDS is not dangerous to others if those around this person take proper precautions when handling blood products.

Note that a person with a disability cannot be denied participation in an activity because the activity is perceived to be dangerous for that person. It is the right of all Americans to choose activities, including those that involve a certain level of risk (Block, 1994). While golf course staff can suggest that a particular person not participate in certain golf activities, it ultimately is the decision of the golfer. For example, a golfer with multiple sclerosis who has poor balance might be at risk of falling into another player's area at the practice facility. Although the risk of harm is possible, the golfer has the right to make an informed decision if he wants to hit a bucket of balls.

Five Major Titles of the ADA

The ADA is divided into five major titles. These titles and their coverage are as follows:

• Title I: Employment. Employers cannot discriminate against a qualified individual with a disability because of the disability in regard to job application procedures, hiring, advancement, or discharge of employees. This employment provision applies to all golf courses, including public and privately owned clubs. Additionally, an employer may not ask an applicant about the nature of his or her disability. However, an employer can ask about the applicant's abilities to perform job-related functions and may even ask for a demonstration (Carpenter, 2000; U.S. Department of Justice, 2002). For example, a golf course owner can ask a potential golf instructor who has only one arm to demonstrate her ability to teach golf. Please note that this criterion should be applied to all applicants with or without disability.

Employers must make reasonable accommodations for qualified individuals with disabilities. Such accommodations might be ramps for those who use wheelchairs, signs in Braille for those who are blind, and nonvoice telephone terminals for those who are Deaf. (See discussion of reasonable accommodations later in this chapter.) But employers do not have to provide preferential treatment to applicants with disabilities (U.S. Department of Justice, 2002). For example, in the case of a potential snack bar employee who uses a wheelchair, the manager of the club may need to make reasonable accommodations to ensure accessibility to the snack bar area. However, the owner of the club may choose to hire a person with more experience working in food service. The owner is within his legal rights if he made the decision based on individual qualifications and not disability. Note also that eligibility criteria for a particular job cannot be developed with the intent of screening out people with disabilities unless the criteria are needed for the job (U.S. Department of Justice, 2002).

• Title II: Public Services and Transportation. It is not legal to discriminate against a person with a disability by denying benefits of state and local government, transportation, activities, programs, and services (U.S. Department of Justice, 2001). This title covers publicly funded golf programs such as those sponsored by local communities. These locally supported programs must provide people with disabilities access to all activities, programs, and services. For example, a child who uses a wheelchair (using an appropriate adapted chair or cart) should be allowed to participate in a community-sponsored golf camp. This includes accessible transportation (if provided to other golfers), facilities, and access to the course. Public agencies can provide separate programs for individuals with disabilities (e.g., golf programs for those who use wheelchairs, Special Olympics golf for individuals with cognitive impairment). However, a person with a disability has the right under the ADA to choose integrated programs rather than separate programs (Block, 1994).

• Title III: Public Accommodations. It is illegal to discriminate against a person with a disability by denying the full and equal enjoyment of goods, services, facilities, privileges, advantages, or accommodations that are available to the general public. This includes hotels, restaurants, banks, business offices, convention centers, retail stores, libraries, schools, and recreation facilities (U.S. Department of Justice, 2001). Management at a golf course must change its policies and practices in all programs, provide assistance as needed, and improve accessibility unless that would impose undue hardship (see later discussion of undue burden) (Paciorek & Jones, 2001).

For example, a privately sponsored residential golf school is open to the public, which means that no special skills or qualifications are required for enrollment in the golf school. A Deaf participant enrolls in the golf school. The golf school cannot deny this person enrollment solely because of his disability. In addition, the golf school must make reasonable accommodations to ensure safe and successful participation. In this case, the golf school might need to provide an interpreter for the Deaf if that is the only way this person can successfully participate in the program. Similarly, this golf school would have to make reasonable modifications to its facilities to accommodate a participant who uses a wheelchair (e.g., make the bathrooms wheelchair accessible, find a hotel with accessible rooms).

- Title IV: Telecommunications. This refers to telephone services for the Deaf (nonvoice terminals) as well as access to federally funded TV message services (close-captioned television). In terms of golf courses, nonvoice terminals or other accommodations to allow a Deaf person to use the telephone should be available (U.S. Department of Justice, 2001). *Nonvoice terminals,* or text telephones, is a generic term for devices that provide access to real-time telephone communications for persons with hearing or speech impairments. Like computers with modems, text telephones provide some form of keyboard input and visual display output to callers and receiving parties connected over standard telephone lines and networks. Title IV also mandated establishment of the Telecommunication Relay Service (TRS), which is a national service in which two-way translation between spoken word and typed text is provided by relay operators. To access the TRS, simply dial 7-1-1 and you are automatically connected.

- Title V: Other Provisions. This title covers the Access Board that issues accessibility standards. In addition, this title discusses such matters as attorneys' fees and the availability of technical assistance by the federal government. The Access Board is responsible for creating regulations and standards regarding accessibility issues, including making recreation facilities accessible.

Reasonable Accommodation and Undue Hardship

Two important tenets of the ADA are reasonable accommodations and undue hardships. The ADA defines a reasonable accommodation as an adaptation to a program, facility, or workplace that allows a person with a disability to participate in the program or service or perform a job. Accommodations also may consist of changes in policies, practices, or services and the use of auxiliary aids. Examples of reasonable accommodations include qualified interpreters for the Deaf, qualified readers and taped texts for people who are blind, acquisition or modification of equipment or devices for people with physical disabilities, making a facility more accessible, adding more staff, and providing extra training for staff. Reasonable accommodations apply to qualified individuals with disabilities (Carpenter, 2000; Imber & van Geel, 2001). In other words, if the individual is not qualified for an activity, then accommodations are not necessary. For example, a local golf tournament that is open only to a select few with a USGA handicap of 10 or lower does not have to make accommodations to a golfer who is blind and whose golf handicap is 14. On the other hand, another golfer who is blind and has a golf handicap of 8 would qualify. Accommodations would then be necessary for this golfer (e.g., she would be allowed to have a coach line her up, someone could describe the layout of the course to her, and she could use auditory cues when putting). Note that these accommodations do not fundamentally alter the nature of the game of golf, give the golfer with a disability an unfair advantage, or cause undue hardship on the club or tournament staff (Paciorek & Jones, 2001; USGA, 2001).

Undue hardship refers to an action requiring significant difficulty or expense when considered in light of certain factors. This would be an action that is unduly costly, extensive, or disruptive or that fundamentally alters the nature of the program. The following are factors to be considered: nature and cost of the accommodation; overall financial resources of the facility involved in the provision of the reasonable accommodation, including number of persons employed; overall financial resources of the covered entity; overall size of the business; and the type of operation of covered entity, including the composition, structure, and function of its workforce (U.S. Department of Justice, 2002). For example, it may be an undue hardship for a golf school to make a golf course totally accessible for a participant who uses a wheelchair unless the player has a modified golf car that can move around without damaging the course. On the other hand, it would be reasonable (known as "readily achievable," according to the ADA) to allow this person to use a regular golf car to get around the course and facilities; allow the person to hit from the golf car; and allow the golfer some modifications to rules, such as grounding crutches in the sand or hitting from the forward tees. Determining what

is an undue hardship or what fundamentally alters the nature of a game can be difficult (see appendix A).

This concept was at the heart of a case filed with the United States Department of Justice against Sun City Summerlin Community Association. The plaintiff alleged that the association refused requests to modify rules restricting use of golf cars to allow persons with disabilities to use accessible cars that would permit them to play on the course and enjoy the same goods, services, facilities, and privileges that nondisabled players enjoy. It was ruled that allowing accessible cars on the golf course was not an undue hardship, and their use is now permitted (United States Department of Justice, 2002). This concept was also an issue in the case of Casey Martin versus the PGA Tour. Casey Martin argued that riding a golf car would not fundamentally alter the game of golf, while the PGA Tour argued that walking was fundamental to competitive golf, and use of a car would give Casey an advantage. The Supreme Court ruled in favor of Casey Martin (Lane, 2001; Paciorek & Jones, 2001; Walsh, 2001).

Meeting the Mandate of the ADA

The preceding sections contain background information on ADA and its five major titles. The focus is now on what golf courses and instructional schools must do to meet the mandate of the ADA.

Opportunity to Participate

Publicly or privately owned golf courses that are open to the general public must provide individuals with disabilities the opportunity to participate in their regular programs that have no other criteria (e.g., no skill requirements). Staff at golf courses must provide auxiliary aid and services unless such services would cause undue hardship. That is, support must be provided unless it would be significantly difficult to do, based on objective criteria. Privately owned clubs not currently open to the public would be responsible for meeting the

© Associated Press

Casey Martin caused controversy in the PGA Tour when he argued that riding a golf car would not alter his game of golf.

requirements of the ADA only if the person were otherwise qualified (e.g., could pay the initiation fee and lived in the community in which the golf course was located).

Publicly or privately sponsored golf tournaments or schools that have special skill criteria but are open to the general public must provide opportunity to try out or qualify for a place in the tournament or school (Block, 1994). Auxiliary aid and services must be available during tryouts to give all participants equal opportunity. For example, officials at a qualifying tournament for a state amateur event would be required to allow a person with paraplegia to play from a single-rider golf car or a player with a visual impairment to have a coach to assist the player in addressing the ball and aligning herself before the stroke (USGA, 2001). If either of these players then shoots a qualifying score, she cannot be denied an opportunity to participate in the tournament (using modifications just described). In other words, officials at a golf tournament cannot deny an individual participation in the tournament based solely on disability.

Even if a specialized golf program is offered in a particular community or by a particular agency, the community or agency still must provide opportunity for someone with a disability to participate in its regular programs. For example, a community might offer a Special Olympics golf program for people with cognitive impairment or a specific tournament for people with amputations. However, if a person with cognitive impairment or an amputation chooses to participate in any of the community's golf programs, then the community must make provisions to include that person. (Note that a person with a disability can choose to participate in both the program or tournament specifically developed for people with disabilities *and* other programs or tournaments offered to the public.)

Facilities

Publicly or privately owned golf courses that are open to the general public must make facilities accessible to individuals with disabilities if such accommodations are readily achievable and do not cause an undue hardship to the owners or staff (Paciorek & Jones, 2001). In most cases reasonable accommodations mean that a portion of existing facilities need to be made accessible. For example, it would be reasonable to have one accessible stall in the rest room rather than change all the stalls. Similarly, just one or two tables, not all the tables, in the club's dining room or snack bar would need to be accessible for people who use wheelchairs. Proprietors of golf facilities do need to make efforts to make key areas accessible so that golfers with disabilities can be integrated into as many activities as possible. For example, it might be reasonable for staff at a golf school to bring in a temporary ramp to get golfers who use wheelchairs to the practice facility rather than build an expensive, permanent ramp. (See Fried, 1998, for simple, inexpensive ways to modify facilities to meet the mandate of the ADA.) Note that any structure built after 1993 must be fully accessible to individuals with disabilities. ADA regulations contain a range of relatively moderate measures that proprietors may take in order to remove barriers, including installing ramps, making curb cuts, repositioning shelves, rearranging tables, repositioning telephones, adding Braille markings on doorways and elevators, and creating designated parking spaces (U.S. Department of Justice, 2002).

Transportation

Publicly or privately sponsored golf programs that are open to the general public must make transportation and telecommunication available to golfers with disabilities if such services are provided to golfers without disabilities. Vehicles with a seating capacity of 16 passengers or fewer do not necessarily have to be accessible for people with disabilities, but at least one vehicle within the fleet must be accessible. All vehicles with a seating capacity in excess of 16 passengers must be accessible (U.S. Department of Justice, 2002). Again, reasonable accommodations for a small golf school with one bus might be as simple as hiring (on an as-needed basis) a driver and bus with a hydraulic lift for the golfer who uses a wheelchair rather than making expensive alterations to its bus. However, it would be ideal if any new vehicles that the golf school purchased were accessible to people with disabilities.

Enforcement of the ADA

The Equal Employment Opportunity Commission enforces the employment section of the ADA, the Department of Justice enforces the public accommodation section (public and private facilities that are open to the general public), and the Department of Transportation enforces the transportation section (U.S. Department of Justice, 2001). In most cases remedies include injunctive relief in the form of changes in facilities, programs, and policies to make facilities and programs more accessible. Disputes in employment also can result in back pay and attorneys' fees (U.S. Department of Justice, 2002).

Assisting Golf Courses and Programs in Complying With the ADA

Hypes, Himmelstein, and Falardeau (2002) and Stein (1993) list several steps that organizations can take to implement the ADA in recreation and sport settings. These steps have been adapted here to apply to golf courses and programs.

1. Have an available copy of, and be familiar with, the Americans with Disabilities Act. Create simple ADA compliance documents and procedures for employees and volunteers.
2. Set up an advisory committee that includes people with disabilities. Solicit other resources such as families of board members with disabilities, social and educational professionals, and medical professionals.
3. Review current programs and protocol of the golf school and other golf programs and determine whether they meet the mandate of the ADA. Look for policies or practices that may be discriminatory.
4. Educate boards of directors about the ADA through preservice and in-service training.
5. Train golf course and golf school staff to eliminate discriminatory remarks and practices and to heighten their awareness of golfers with disabilities. If a golfer with a specific disability is definitely coming to your golf course or golf school, then train staff to meet the unique needs of this golfer.
6. For other questions, refer to the National Alliance for Accessible Golf's toolkit for golf course operators. It provides a wealth of information and can be accessed at www.accessgolf.org/operator-toolkit.shtml.
7. Review current program applications, health care statements, and other documents to ensure that the language is not discriminatory.
8. If you are not sure of the accessibility of your golf course or golf school, seek advice before responding.
9. Review safety considerations and emergency procedures to ensure that individuals with disabilities can take part safely and are warned of the inherent risks of the activity.

The goal of the ADA is to provide opportunities for individuals with disabilities to participate in all aspects of everyday life. This includes access to public and private golf courses and golf schools that are open to the general public. The ADA mandates that golf courses and golf schools that provide golf programs and facilities to individuals without disabilities make these same programs and facilities available to qualified individuals with disabilities. Fried (1998) cautioned that the U.S. Department of Justice is past the point of educating businesses (including recreation facilities such as golf courses). Rather, the department is now aggressively enforcing the law and pursuing violators. With relatively simple modifications, many more golfers with disabilities can experience all the joy and excitement of participation in golf programs with their peers without disabilities.

Adapted, by permission, from M.G. Hypes, C. Himmelstein, and J. Falardeau, 2002, "Athletic eligibility and the Americans with Disabilities Act," *Journal of Physical Education, Recreation and Dance* 73(1):11-14; adapted, by permission, from J.U. Stein, 1993, "The Americans with Disabilities Act: Implications for recreation and leisure." In *Leisure opportunities for individuals with disabilities: Legal issues,* edited by S.J. Grosse, (Reston, VA: AAHPERD), 1-11.

Chapter 2

Improving Access at Your Facility

Joe is the golf professional and general manager at a public golf course that his family owns. Recently, some larger companies have come into the area and built golf courses. The new courses have been cutting into Joe's family's market share, and profits are down. Joe tried to come up with solutions to their cash-flow problems, but nothing seemed to work. He had heard of the efforts of organizations such as the National Alliance for Accessible Golf to increase golf participation for people with disabilities, but he was skeptical. After he looked into it, Joe realized that it wouldn't take much for their course to become more accessible to golfers with disabilities. Joe instructed his staff to make some minor changes such as adding an accessible parking spot near the clubhouse, cutting passageways in the railings that kept golf cars from entering some fairways, and providing cups at the drinking fountain that was inaccessible. They also made changes in some of their policies, such as allowing single-rider golf cars to maneuver on greens and tees. Pretty soon, the word got out and more golfers with disabilities started showing up at Joe's course. The amount of play at the course began to increase dramatically. Even golfers without disabilities told Joe they appreciated his efforts. Joe's experiment with making the course accessible to golfers with disabilities was a huge success. Now there is a weekly league for golfers with disabilities, and revenue at the course is better than ever. Play in

(continued)

(continued)

the existing leagues has also increased because some golfers with disabilities feel more comfortable playing golf and have joined them.

Joe is happy that he didn't let his preconceived notions get in the way of making changes that have benefited everyone.

Golf is a game that should be enjoyed by all, including people with disabilities. Many golf course operators think that making a course accessible for golfers with disabilities will require a large investment of time and money. Some also think that it will take away from the quality of the golf course. However, these are misconceptions. Making a golf course accessible does not take a great deal of effort and can actually save money in the long run. If the course is accessible for golfers with disabilities then it will also be accessible for maintenance equipment, which could save on labor costs. If done correctly, making a golf course accessible is not even noticeable and may have other advantages such as increasing the pace of play. This chapter will provide an overview of the Americans with Disabilities Act (ADA) requirements for golf courses and guidelines for making them accessible for golfers with disabilities.

The Need for Golf Course and Golf Program Accessibility

The legal and ethical principle is that all golf programs and facilities should be uniformly accessible to all people. An opportunity to participate in golf activities is not an opportunity for a person with a disability if the facility is not accessible. Proprietors of golf courses and golf professionals also have an ethical responsibility to make certain that programs are accessible to all, regardless of any legal loopholes that may not require them to comply with certain standards.

Accessibility applies to golf opportunities in three ways. The most generally understood

kind is physical accessibility, which normally refers to the physical environment within which a golf program is offered. A physical barrier is a circumstance that limits or complicates access, mobility, or participation. Physical barriers include more than just architectural impediments, such as steps, curbs, and narrow hallways; they also consist of natural physical barriers such as steep hills, thick plots of grass, and other obstacles for many people with limited mobility. These physical obstacles could make it difficult or impracticable for people with certain disabilities to participate in golf activities.

The second kind of accessibility involves administrative policies and procedures, which are also part of the environment within which golf programs are offered and can sometimes be considered attitudinal barriers to participation. Negative attitudes of the golf staff and "car path only" policies are examples of these types of barriers. Such barriers seem to constitute a major problem in fulfilling the mandate that people with disabilities receive equal opportunities for participation in golf activities. Attitudinal barriers also involve perceptions and resulting mind-sets of the nondisabled public toward people who are disabled as well as the views and attitudes of people who are disabled themselves. Eliminating these attitudinal barriers is essential to achieving equal opportunity for people with disabilities in the golf community.

The third kind of accessibility is programmatic. Golf programs and activities must be planned so that people with various disabilities can participate fully and have enjoyable experiences. Program accessibility means that any standards for participation are applied to all prospective participants; the standards are uniformly based on skill levels or reasonable safety considerations and not on characteristics such as sex, race, religion, national origin, or handicap (Miller, 1995). Program accessibility can also mean that instructors and other personnel understand the needs of golfers with disabilities and that they are skilled in modifying existing golf activities to meet these needs.

Accommodations Required by the ADA

As mentioned in chapter 1, the Americans with Disabilities Act of 1990 was implemented to remove barriers that have prevented society from promoting the participation and contributions of individuals with disabilities. Basically, the ADA requires public facilities, including golf courses, to provide goods and services to people with disabilities on an equivalent basis with the rest of the general public. The fundamental tenet of the ADA as it relates to golf facilities is to guarantee accessibility and accommodations for golfers with disabilities and to ensure they are not subject to discrimination.

Accessibility Guidelines for Design and Construction

Courtesy of the ADA Accessibility Guidelines, http://www.access-board.gov/recreation/guides/pdfs/golf.pdf.

The U.S. Access Board is responsible for the development of minimum-accessibility guidelines for recreation areas, including golf courses. These guidelines will serve as the foundation for standards to be implemented by the Department of Justice for new construction and alteration of recreational facilities covered by the Americans with Disabilities Act. The Access Board is an independent federal agency consisting of public and government members selected by the president. In 1993, the Recreation Access Advisory Committee was assembled to supply the Access Board with information and recommendations for the development of accessibility guidelines for recreation facilities and developed outdoor areas. Subcommittees, including a Golf Subcommittee, of the Recreation Access Advisory Committee were formed. The Golf Subcommittee was composed of representatives from the PGA of America,

the Golf Course Superintendents Association of America, others from the golf industry, and representatives from organizations that promote golf for people with disabilities.

The Golf Subcommittee met for one year and developed suggested accessibility guidelines for construction of new golf courses and alterations to existing golf courses. Areas around the golf courses such as the clubhouse, other buildings, and parking lots were covered under the original ADA when the act was passed in 1990. The goal of the subcommittee was to identify architectural guidelines that would ease the assimilation of people with disabilities into golf while preserving the tradition and integrity of the game. Their first draft of the proposed guidelines was published for public comment, along with other guidelines for recreational facilities, in an advance notice of proposed rulemaking (ANPRM) in the September 21, 1994, Federal Register. The Access Board staff evaluated the comments and redrafted a proposed rule, which was published for comment in July 1999. A summary draft of the final guidelines was issued in July 2000. On September 3, 2002, the guidelines became final and were published in the Federal Register.

The guidelines apply to any public course as well as private courses that host corporate outings or nonmember functions. Basically, if a course accepts any kind of play or offers any services to nonmembers, it must abide by the guidelines of the Access Board. The guidelines apply to new construction and any major alterations to existing courses. A major alteration is the renovation of an element on the golf course such as new greens or addition of a tee box. The standards are fairly simple to comply with and are intended to make golf accessible for people with disabilities, particularly those with mobility impairments. The following sections summarize the guidelines of the Access Board for particular aspects of the golf course and provide specifications for compliance (U.S. Access Board, n.d.). Note that these are the minimum guidelines and, whenever possible, proprietors and staff of courses should go beyond the minimum to provide more options and integration potential for all golfers.

Accessible Routes

Accessible routes are continuous, unhindered paths linking all accessible components and spaces of a building or facility on a golf course. The accessible route must comply with all Americans with Disabilities Act Accessibility Guidelines (ADAAG) specifications regarding location, width (minimum of 36 inches or 92 centimeters), head room, passing space, surface, slope (maximum of 1:12 or 8.33 percent), level changes, doors, egress, and areas of rescue assistance, unless modified and noted in the following guidelines.

Providing an accessible route that complies with ADAAG specifications may be impractical throughout a golf course. The route of play for a golfer is unpredictable and dependent on where the ball lands. Requiring an accessible route throughout a course could also alter slopes within some courses and alter the nature of the game by eliminating some of the challenge. Therefore, a golf car passage may be substituted for an accessible route inside the boundaries of the golf course (see figure 2.1). A golf car passage is an uninterrupted passage on which a motorized golf car can operate. A golf car passage must be usable by golf cars; however, it does not necessarily have to be a prepared surface and may be part of a golf car path. The golf car passage can be located anywhere on the course such as fairways, greens, and teeing surfaces (see figure 2.2). A golf car passage must be at least 48 inches (122 centimeters) wide and can be substituted for all or part of the accessible route connecting elements within the boundary of the course (see figure 2.3). While handrails are not required on the golf course, where they are provided along the golf car passage the guidelines expand the minimum width of the route to 60 inches (153 centimeters) to allow the passage of a golf car. A golf car passage may also be substituted for an accessible route outside the boundary of the golf course, but only when connecting the golf car rental area, bag drop, practice putting greens, accessible practice teeing stations, toilet areas on the course, and on-course weather shelters (see figure 2.4).

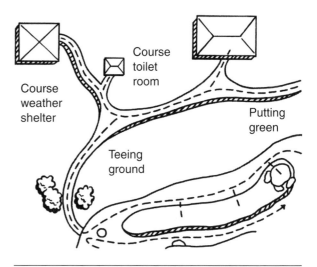

Figure 2.1 An accessible route links all accessible components and spaces of a golf course (a golf car passage may be substituted for an accessible route inside the boundaries of the golf course).

Courtesy of the ADA Accessibility Guidelines, www.access-board.gov/recreation/guides/pdfs/golf.pdf.

Curbs or other manmade barriers line many golf car paths to restrict golf cars from getting on certain portions of the course or to diminish erosion. When barriers prevent a golf car from entering the course, gaps at least 60 inches (153 centimeters) wide at intervals not exceeding 75 yards (69 meters) must be provided (see figure 2.5). These dispersed openings will allow access to the course at reasonable distances, permitting a golfer using a golf car to play the game without extensive travel distances and time requirements.

Teeing Grounds

The teeing ground is the starting place for each hole of golf. According to the rules of golf, the teeing ground is a rectangular area two club lengths in depth; the borders are defined by the outside limits of two tee markers (see figure 2.6). Golf cars must be able to enter and exit all newly constructed teeing grounds as well as existing teeing grounds that have been altered.

For newly constructed golf courses, the forward teeing ground on each hole must be accessible. The forward teeing ground does not have to be accessible on existing

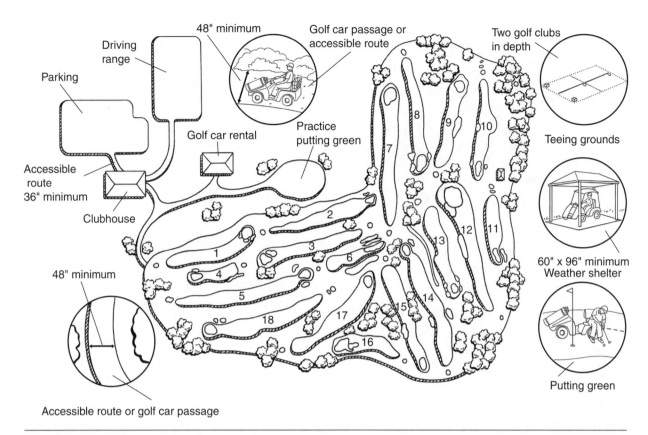

Figure 2.2 Accessible route or golf car passage connecting elements. The golf car passage can be located anywhere on the course such as fairways, greens, and teeing surfaces.

Courtesy of the ADA Accessibility Guidelines, www.access-board.gov/recreation/guides/pdfs/golf.pdf.

Figure 2.3 Golf car passage or accessible route. A golf car passage must be at least 48 inches (122 centimeters) wide and can be substituted for all or part of the accessible route connecting elements within the boundary of the course.

Courtesy of the ADA Accessibility Guidelines, www.access-board.gov/recreation/guides/pdfs/golf.pdf.

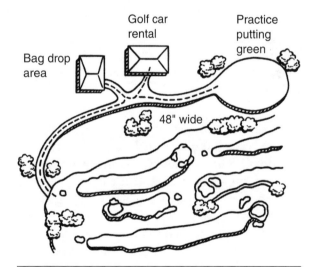

Figure 2.4 Accessible route or golf car passage outside the boundary of the golf course.

Courtesy of the ADA Accessibility Guidelines, www.access-board.gov/recreation/guides/pdfs/golf.pdf.

Figure 2.5   Course barrier with gap.

Courtesy of the ADA Accessibility Guidelines, www.access-board.gov/recreation/guides/pdfs/golf.pdf.

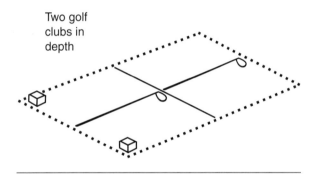

Figure 2.6   Teeing ground.

Courtesy of the ADA Accessibility Guidelines, www.access-board.gov/recreation/guides/pdfs/golf.pdf.

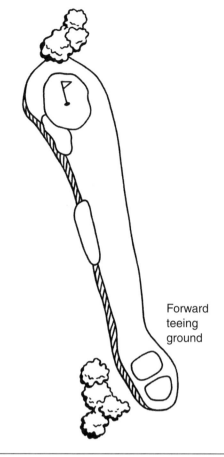

Figure 2.7   Multiple teeing grounds.

Courtesy of the ADA Accessibility Guidelines, www.access-board.gov/recreation/guides/pdfs/golf.pdf.

golf courses that are altering teeing grounds where compliance is not feasible because of terrain. If only one or two teeing grounds are present on a hole, just the forward teeing ground must be accessible (see figure 2.7). To allow persons with disabilities to play from different tees suitable to their skill levels and provide flexibility to course designers, at least two teeing grounds must be accessible when three or more are present on a hole.

Putting Greens

Putting greens must be connected to the rest of the golf course by a golf car passage that enables a golf car to reach the green (see figure 2.8). All putting greens must be designed and constructed in a manner that allows a golf car to enter and exit the green.

Weather Shelters

Weather shelters on the golf course must be constructed to allow a golf car to enter and exit. They must also have a minimum ground space of 60 inches by 96 inches (153 centimeters by 244 centimeters).

Practice Facilities

Practice facilities associated with a golf course and stand-alone practice facilities or learning centers are all covered by the Access Board guidelines. These facilities must have an accessible route or golf car passage that connects accessible teeing stations with accessible parking spaces. The accessible route

Accessible route
or golf car
passage

Figure 2.8 Golf car passage to a putting green.

Courtesy of the ADA Accessibility Guidelines, www.access-board.gov/recreation/guides/pdfs/golf.pdf.

must be at least 48 inches (122 centimeters) wide unless handrails are present, in which case the route must be at least 60 inches (153 centimeters) wide. Adequate room must be allowed for a person who plays golf from a seated position in a golf car (see figure 2.9). At least 5 percent, but no fewer than one, of the practice teeing stations must be accessible and provide enough room for a golf car to enter and exit.

Figure 2.9 Accessible teeing station.

Single-Rider Golf Cars

Single-rider golf cars have had many technological advances in recent years and have provided a means of increasing access and participation for golfers with disabilities that include mobility challenges. The topic of the use of these golf cars on the course invites many questions. The Access Board only develops and maintains guidelines for the physical environment; it is out of their jurisdiction to make policies concerning use of the cars. Questions regarding single-rider cars should be directed to the Department of Justice at 800-514-0301 or 800-514-0383 (TTY). However, at this time the Department of Justice has made no official decision about providing single-rider golf cars to players at golf courses.

Temporary Facilities

The ADAAG requires accessible temporary facilities such as bleachers for tournaments, portable toilet facilities, assembly seating areas, and concessions. Access to temporary facilities on a golf course can be achieved with either an accessible route or golf car passage. Golf facilities hosting tournaments or competitions are required to comply with all the other requirements of the ADA, including the general responsibility to provide an equal opportunity for those with disabilities to benefit from the services provided.

Accommodations Not Required by the ADA

Bunkers and other hazards on the golf course are not addressed in the Access Board guidelines. The Access Board determined that these elements are meant to penalize all golfers, and the Access Board did not want to alter the principle of the game. However, the USGA's *A Modification of the Rules of Golf for Golfers With Disabilities* does address this issue to some extent (see appendix A). Golf courses should consider access to bunkers where feasible; this would give golfers a choice. An accessible bunker on the practice range would also allow golfers playing from single-rider cars to practice the shot.

Accessibility in Other Areas

As mentioned previously, the ADA is a federal civil rights law that prohibits the exclusion of people with disabilities from daily activities, such as buying items at the store, going to the theater to watch a movie, having the car serviced at a neighborhood garage, or playing a round of golf. To meet the objectives of the ADA, the law created requirements for private businesses of every size. These obligations went into effect on January 26, 1992, and continue for both for-profit and nonprofit establishments.

For small businesses, observance of the ADA is not complicated. However, to help businesses with their compliance efforts, Congress launched a technical assistance program to answer questions regarding the ADA. The Department of Justice manages a toll-free ADA information line (800-514-0301 for voice and 800-514-0383 TTY), so help is only a phone call away. In addition, many costs of providing access to people with disabilities qualify for tax credits and deductions on an annual basis.

In recognition that many small businesses cannot afford to make considerable physical changes to their places of business in order to provide accessibility, the ADA has requirements for facilities built before 1993 that are less stringent than for facilities built after early 1993 or modified after early 1992. The ADA requires that recently constructed facilities, first occupied on or after January 26, 1993, meet or exceed the requirements of the ADA Standards for Accessible Design. Alterations to facilities (including renovations such as repaving the parking lot, replacing fixtures, or renovating the pro shop) on or after January 26, 1992, must also comply with the regulations. Renovations or changes are considered to be alterations when they affect the usability of the element or space. However, simple maintenance, such as cleaning the carpets or repainting a wall, is not considered by the ADA to be an alteration. Although not required by law, facilities in existence before this time should also try to take measures to become more accessible. Many communities also have separate accessibility codes enforced by local building inspectors. When a local or state accessibility code exists, you must adhere to both that code and the ADA requirements.

ADA Accessibility Guidelines for New Construction and Alterations

All newly constructed commercial facilities must be accessible to individuals with disabilities to the extent that it is not structurally infeasible. Only when unique characteristics of terrain prevent full compliance of accessibility features will this be considered acceptable (e.g., marshland that requires construction on stilts). Alterations after January 26, 1992, to existing commercial facilities must be accessible to the utmost extent feasible. When alterations are made to a primary function area, such as the lobby or pro shop, a path of travel to the modified area, including bathrooms, telephones, and drinking fountains serving that area, must be made accessible if the additional accessibility costs do not exceed 20 percent of the original alteration. See appendix D for tips on making your facility accessible.

Chapter 3

Meeting the Needs in Your Community

Every Tuesday for about 25 years, Andy went with his father and two neighbors to the lunch meeting of the local Lions Club to find out how they could help out in the community. Lions clubs are recognized worldwide for their service to people who are blind or visually impaired.

A few years after Andy had become a head golf professional, he decided that he wanted his course to become more involved with the community. Not knowing where to start, Andy called his father, who suggested that he contact the local Lions Club. Andy called the Lions Club and talked to the current president. The president asked Andy if he would be interested in being a guest speaker for the next lunch meeting. Andy agreed.

Once there and after formally meeting the current president, Andy was introduced to many people, all of whom were active in serving the community and in operating area businesses. Andy was treated to a nice lunch and then asked to address the group. He thanked the group for the invitation and the opportunity to express his intentions.

Andy's speech—if it were to be called that—was simply a request for help. He informed the group about his facility and the golf course, where many of the Lions Club members had played. Andy told them that his organization would like to become more involved in the community and encourage people with disabilities to play. Within 15 minutes, Andy had explained the extent of the facility's limited resources and information on how to get started. He simply asked if they could provide direction in this pursuit. By the end of the hour,

(continued)

(continued)

the group had come up with at least 10 possible activities, including methods of delivery and people who would be able to operate the program. All they needed from Andy was a schedule of when new programs could operate so that their ideas would not interfere with normal operations.

A year later, there are six golfers with visual impairments (and their coaches) who use the facility on a regular basis. The Lions Club sponsors and operates a youth program for children with severe vision loss, and a local recreation therapist offers a golf class two days a month. All that the staff at Andy's course had to do was provide some space on a range and reserve a few specific, nonpeak tee times for the programs. It has become a good opportunity for the people at the golf facility to become more involved in the community, and they are helping to promote the game.

Although the number of community-based sport programs for persons with disabilities has grown, these programs are inadequate for meeting current needs of the population, much less those of potential participants (DePauw & Gavron, 2005). This could be true for several reasons, including ignorance, prejudice, and fear. However, the most logical explanation is the belief that sport programs for persons with disabilities should be the purview of rehabilitation professionals. Project GAIN, a program of the National Alliance for Accessible Golf, has begun a nationwide initiative that hopes to meet participants' needs by establishing several inclusive golf programs (see Web site www.accessgolf.org).

Contacting Associations for People With Disabilities

There are several ways to get involved if you or the staff at your golf facility would like to start a program for golfers with disabilities. Involvement can be as simple as informing the public that your facility encourages people with disabilities to play at your course. Or you can be more involved by developing and operating specialized instructional and training programs for specific populations. You can begin the process by contacting local associations that are currently providing assistance to people with disabilities.

At the Local Level

If you want your involvement to begin at the local level, contact your local park and recreation department to determine what activities and support they provide to programs designed for people with disabilities. In addition to the park department, every county school system is required to provide assistance to students with disabilities and will therefore maintain a list of local service specialists. Most chambers of commerce (county and city) maintain a list of active organizations and professional contacts that are currently providing assistance to people with disabilities, and the local hospital should have a list of certified professionals who provide services as well as rehabilitation programs. Finally, established community organizations that include the Lions Club, Rotary Club, Masons, Boy Scouts, Girl Scouts, and faith-based organizations may have information on active programs and services.

At the State Level

Every state Department of Health and Human Services maintains a list of active organizations that are providing services to their residents. Many of these organizations provide assistance to local community programs as well as state programs. The Department of Health and Human Services will give you this list if you call them. These lists are also available on the Internet at www.hhs.gov. (Also see appendix B.)

At the National Level

At the national level, the National Recreation and Park Association's National Therapeutic Recreation Society (NTRS; www.nrpa.org/content/default.aspx?documentId = 530) and the American Therapeutic Recreation Association (ATRA; www.atra-tr.org) will provide assistance in contacting local registered professionals. The NTRS promotes public awareness and support for recreation and park and leisure services that provide social stability to a community and the physical and mental health of individuals. There are a few organizations, some even specific to golf, designed to enhance recreation opportunities for individuals with disabilities. They are the National Alliance for Accessible Golf (NAAG; www.accessgolf.org), the National Center on Accessibility (NCA; www.ncaonline.org), the National Center on Physical Activity and Disability (NCPAD; www. ncpad.org), the USGA Resource Center for Golfers with Disabilities (www.resourcecenter.usga.org), and the National Council for Therapeutic Recreation Certification (NCTRC; www.nctrc.org).

Surveying Local Associations

To determine how involved your organization can become, you will need to find out how existing professionals and programs can utilize what you have to offer. You will need to obtain a list of professionals and organizations that you would consider teaming with or soliciting for ideas. By contacting the associations listed previously, you can easily organize a moderate list of representatives. Be sure to obtain a specific contact person, mailing address, phone number, and if possible, an Internet address.

Once you've developed a list of potential team members, you are ready to draft a letter of intent to each individual or organization's representative. Golf facilities can meet the needs within their community in the following three ways:

1. Promote general use of the course by letting golfers with disabilities know that their participation is encouraged and welcome.

2. Ensure that your facility is available for specific development programs and activities.

3. Provide staff who are available to operate programs and assist in instruction and promoting the game.

In the letter of intent, express your interest to assist in providing opportunities to meet the needs of people with disabilities within the community. Explain *how* your organization would like to assist. Be specific in what your organization would like to accomplish. Your initial objective might be to determine how your facility and organization fit into the overall community plan for providing opportunities to people with disabilities and how your location may be better used in the future. It is prudent to determine which organizations are available for direction, consultation, and support. Furthermore, specific programs may already be operating, and your location could begin its involvement simply by becoming an extension of an existing program. Project GAIN of the National Alliance for Accessible Golf is currently operating in many locations throughout the country and is looking to expand into new communities.

Finally, directly state what your objectives are, and ask for assistance. The result of the survey process should allow you to inform professionals and organizations working with people with disabilities that your golf facility wants to become involved in community efforts. Once this information is obtained, speaking engagements and planning meetings can be organized.

The following is a summary of the surveying process:

- Determine what you have to offer.
- Develop a list of potential organizations and professionals to contact.
  - Contact person
  - Mailing address
  - Phone number
  - Internet address

- Write a letter of intent.
- Express your intent to assist the community in providing opportunities.
- Be specific in what your organization would like to accomplish.
- Send out the letter and follow up with phone calls.

Speaking at Local Association Meetings

Many local organizations operating within your community provide or sponsor activities and programs for people with disabilities. An excellent method of demonstrating your commitment and interest to be involved in providing golf opportunities to these populations is to be the guest speaker for weekly, monthly, or development meetings for these organizations. A guest-speaking engagement provides the golf professional with an opportunity to voice the intent to become more involved with the cause that is being addressed as well as extend an invitation to the individuals of that organization.

Offering Programs for People With Disabilities

Proprietors of a golf facility who want to offer a program for golfers with disabilities need to have a good team in place to operate the entire program before they move forward. Chapter 16 goes into more depth on creating teams to organize and operate an accessible golf program. The two main issues to be addressed before the program begins are the accessibility of the course and practice areas and the development of partnerships and collaboration with organizations that can provide assistance. (Refer to chapter 2 for addressing facility needs.)

It is impossible to operate a successful accessible golf program without assistance from specialists accustomed to working with people with disabilities. A partnership needs to be developed in which all parties benefit from working with each other. The model of collaboration that is developed will vary from place to place depending on the needs and resources of the community. See figure 3.1 for an example of one such partnership.

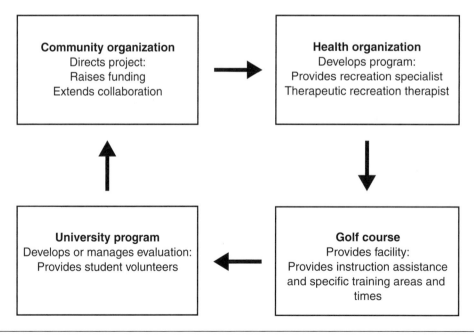

Figure 3.1 Collaborative flowchart.

Using Your Golf Course for Tournaments

There are three ways that your facility can use tournaments to foster golf for people with disabilities. Your course can host fundraising events, host events for golfers with disabilities, and host combined tournaments.

A good way to generate interest and create resources for an accessible golf program is to host a fundraising golf tournament. These events typically follow the standard charity tournament format with members of the community participating and providing sponsorships. Most golf professionals are familiar with the operation of these events and can put one on with ease.

Hosting golf tournaments for people with disabilities requires some more effort and support. These tournaments can be rewarding for everyone involved; however, they require special planning. The needs of participants, both on and off the golf course, must be met. Because golf facilities are typically not accustomed to hosting these events, the assistance of therapeutic recreation professionals and physical therapists is invaluable. The most important point for the golf staff to remember is that they should put in just as much effort to make the competition a success as they would for any other tournament. It is also a good idea to contact other organizations that have held tournaments for golfers with disabilities. Their suggestions and experience can be valuable to you. The USGA Web site (www.usga.org) has a list of golf tournaments for golfers with disabilities that might help you with gathering this information. Also keep in mind that the USGA has developed a document titled *A Modification of the Rules of Golf for Golfers With Disabilities* (see appendix A); you should use this resource for governing play. Golf professionals need to become familiar with these rules in order to answer any questions that may come up.

Perhaps the most important tournament a golf facility can host is a combined tournament for individuals with disabilities as well as nondisabled golfers. The long-term objective of developing opportunities for golfers with disabilities is to provide more possibilities for interaction in mainstream society. A combined tournament is an excellent opportunity for golfers to interact and benefit from one another. A disability does not diminish a person's competitive nature or desire for success, and all golfers can appreciate others' love for playing the game.

Planning Fundraisers for Golfers With Disabilities

There are a variety of methods for raising funds to support any community program. All of these activities can be beneficial in providing financial support to offset operating costs of a program for golfers with disabilities. However, you must remain aware of how specific activities fit into an organization's mission. Any activity an organization decides to become involved with should be directly related to its area of expertise. Golf professionals should remain active with golf course activities, while community organizations can use their volunteer resources for sales and novelty activities. The National Golf Foundation has an excellent book titled *Fund Raising with Golf* by Sally Ling (1997) that may prove beneficial when planning golf-related fundraisers.

A simple search on the Internet will provide a great deal of additional information on fundraising efforts and ideas (use the key word *fundraising*). In addition, there are numerous companies and organizations that specialize in operating fundraising activities. Ideas to raise funds are only limited by your imagination.

The following are some golf-related fundraising activities:

- Tournaments (scramble, best ball, individual, glow ball, one club)
- Putting contest
- Long-drive contest
- Closest to the pin
- Fantasy golf competitions

Here are ideas for other fundraising activities:

- Casino night
- Raffles
- Sales
- Dinner nights and banquets
- Concerts
- Festivals
- Auctions

All golf courses, whether public or private, have a responsibility to be a good community citizen. This can be accomplished by meeting the needs of individuals in the community, including those with disabilities. Meeting these needs can be as simple as hosting a fundraising golf tournament to support accessible golf programs or as extensive as developing an accessible golf program at the facility.

Chapter 4

Understanding the Value of Golf for People With Disabilities

Before an accident left him paralyzed from the waist down, Emil was a typical active teenager. He was an honor roll student and very involved in school activities. He enjoyed playing sports and ran cross country for the high school team. But all of that changed after his accident. He lost interest in school and his grades progressively worsened. He always seemed to be in a bad mood and only wanted to sit in front of the television all day. Due to his inactivity, his health also began to deteriorate. Emil's mother was very worried about him. She read about an accessible golf program at the local golf course in the newspaper and asked Emil if he would like to give it a try. He refused at first but finally gave in after she kept asking him to do it.

Emil had only played golf a few times and was not very excited about participating in the program. However, after meeting the friendly staff and seeing others with disabilities enjoying themselves, he thought it might be fun. He began to look forward to the weekly sessions and even asked his mother to take him to the golf course other times so he could practice. It did not take long for Emil to begin realizing some of the benefits of participating in the accessible golf program. His attitude toward life is much better now and he is back on the honor roll. He is active in school activities again and was even elected vice-president of the Student Government Association. In addition to playing golf, Emil also participates in wheelchair road races. He has as much strength and stamina now as he did before the accident.

Participation in recreation activities such as golf is an important aspect of society. Active, vital, and socially connected people take part in a variety of activities in a variety of settings during their lifetime. This dynamic leisure lifestyle includes participating in individual and team games, athletic programs in schools, recreational sports on college campuses, and team and individual activities in recreational settings. Many people acknowledge the immense value of recreation programs and facilities. Intramural recreation sport programs, for example, are the most commonly attended activities, with the exception of academic classes, by students on college campuses (Bohlig, 1991). Recreation activities that meet the needs of individuals in community and social settings encourage physical health and conditioning and afford participants opportunities for developing social relationships and new skills. They also help people find a balance between leisure and work. Studies have also shown that families that participate in recreation activities together typically are happier and more cohesive as a unit than those who do not (Mactavish, 1995).

Unfortunately, recreation programming for people with disabilities has had a relatively low status in society. This negligence is regrettable because participating in recreation activities has been found to be a vital factor in successful community adjustment (Hayden, Lakin, Hill, Bruininks, & Copher, 1992; Schleien, Meyer, Heyne, & Brandt, 1995).

Psychological Benefits of Golf

The benefits of exercise are not restricted to physical health. The significance of regular exercise in promoting both a healthy body and a healthy mind has been acknowledged from the time of the ancient Greeks. Participation in recreation activities such as golf has been shown to lead to behavior change, improved visual memory, and enhanced learning skills (Roggenbuck, Loomis, & Dagostino, 1991). According to Roggenbuck, Loomis, and Dagostino, the following are other noted psychological benefits of participation in golf activities:

- Professed sense of freedom, independence, and autonomy
- Enhanced self-competence through enriched sense of self-worth, self-reliance, and self-confidence
- Improved ability to socialize with others, including greater tolerance and understanding
- Enriched capacity for team membership
- Sharpened creative ability
- Improved expressions of and rumination of personal spiritual ideals
- Enhanced adaptability and resiliency
- Improved sense of humor
- Increased perceived quality of life

- Balanced competitiveness and a positive outlook on life
- Stress and tension release

Participation in sport activities for people with disabilities has many psychological benefits. According to Bullock and Mahon (2001), studies have indicated an increased level of perceived competence, mood, self-esteem, and confidence in people with disabilities participating in sport programs. People with disabilities face difficult issues in psychosocial adjustment. Accessible golf programs can provide people with disabilities the same opportunity for enjoyment and social interaction as nondisabled persons, and these programs may elevate feelings of normality. Apart from any specific effects of golf-related activity on mental health, accessible golf programs simply help people with disabilities feel good about themselves; exercise and participation in sports such as golf often produce a general sense of well-being. The process is unclear but may entail biochemical changes in levels of neuro-transmitters such as beta-endorphins. Beta-endorphins, released from the brain's pituitary gland, are neurohormones that increase after exercise. An increase in concentration of beta-endorphins provides increased pain tolerance, greater appetite control, reduced anxiety, and feelings of euphoria. In addition to biochemical changes, mastery of golf skills may lead to enhancement of self-concept, self-esteem, and self-confidence, along with a sense of competence and achievement.

A major emphasis of the Project GAIN program of the National Alliance for Accessible Golf is to develop and enhance people's self-efficacy. Self-efficacy is people's belief about their capability to produce desired levels of performance that exercise influence over events in their lives. Beliefs about self-efficacy influence how people feel, what they believe, how they motivate themselves, and how they conduct themselves. People with confidence in their capabilities tackle difficult tasks as challenges to be mastered rather than as situations to be avoided. People with high self-efficacy set demanding goals and maintain a robust commitment to the goals. They sustain their efforts and rapidly recover their sense of efficacy after failures or setbacks. An efficacious attitude generates personal accomplishments, lowers stress, and reduces vulnerability to depression (Bandura, 1994).

The justification for developing accessible golf programs and opportunities in community settings for people with disabilities is well grounded from both theoretical and practical viewpoints. Golf participation in community settings offers the person with a disability the chance to develop a positive self-concept through gratifying experiences and rewarding relationships with peers. Outlets for self-expression, opportunities to interact with the environment, and establishment of a more satisfying way of life are other positive results of participating in an accessible golf program.

More similarity than discrepancy regarding psychological factors has been reported in studies comparing athletes with disabilities and nondisabled athletes. For example, research has shown the iceberg profile (below-average tension, depression, anger, fatigue, and confusion; above-average vigor) to be reported with athletes in wheelchairs or with visual impairments. In athletic endeavors, people with disabilities have also demonstrated responses similar to those of their nondisabled peers regarding motivation in failure and success and measures of anxiety (DePauw & Gavron, 2005).

Physiological Benefits of Golf

Engaging in golf activities (playing, training, and practicing) provides participants with many physiological benefits, including the following:

- Increased flexibility
- Greater aerobic capacity
- Enhanced anaerobic endurance
- Increased eye–hand coordination
- Greater capacity for balance
- Improved metabolic control
- Muscle development and strength
- Enhanced overall physical fitness

- Assistance with weight control
- Increased cardiopulmonary endurance and strength
- Decrease of sedentary lifestyle
- Reduced effects and risks of dementia, especially in older adults
- Increased lung capacity

The benefits of exercise from participation in sports such as golf by people with disabilities are similar to those of people without disabilities. Some people with disabilities will realize even greater benefits from golf than people without disabilities because they tend to lack rigor in their daily activities. People with disabilities are less likely than those without disabilities to engage in regular physical activity. A golf program is an excellent way to encourage people with disabilities to realize the benefits of exercise. Golf engages the mind as well as the body. It holds people's interest and makes people more likely to continue their regular physical activity routines.

Social Benefits of Golf

Golf is fundamentally a social game. It emphasizes development of player etiquette, social responsibility (it is the only sport in which participants call penalties on themselves), and respect for normative value patterns. The game often extends beyond the playing field into social settings after the match has ended. Golf requires participants to demonstrate respect for other players by adhering to the prescribed rules of the game. Golf is also one of the few sports in which players of differing skill levels can enjoy a game together. Usually each player is competing against the course, trying to shoot as low a score as possible. However, players of differing abilities can compete against one another by using the USGA Handicap System and the USGA Modified Rules of Golf. The following are typical social benefits of golf:

- Social acceptance
- Development of friendships
- Enhanced respect for the game and for others

- Opportunity to play with others of different skill levels
- Development and enhancement of business acquaintances
- Camaraderie with peers

People with disabilities have an even greater chance of reaping the social benefits of golf than do golfers without disabilities. People with disabilities spend significantly less time outside the home socializing than do people without disabilities (The Harris Poll, 2000). They tend to feel more isolated and participate in fewer community activities. Participation in a golf program can provide people with opportunities to interact with others in a social setting, to experience group roles, and to take on leadership responsibilities.

A golf program allows participants to develop a support network within the program. Golfers can socially support one another and also receive support in return. A golf program allows participants with diverse levels of ability to develop their games, and at the same time they can share in accomplishments and support each other through learning difficulties. This process can be carried over into other activities and relationships outside the golf environment.

Participation in golf provides benefits to *all* people regardless of their physical abilities. The literature regarding psychological and social benefits of participation in golf by people with disabilities contains convincing verification of the value of the sport. When combined with the evidence related to gains in physical fitness, health, and skill enhancement, it is very clear that golf is indeed an important leisure and recreation pursuit for people with disabilities.

Part II

Learning and Playing With a Disability

Chapter 5

Teaching Golf Using the LPGA Student-Centered Model

Teaching athletes with disabilities requires many of the same skills as teaching athletes without disabilities. Instructors should treat golfers as individuals and should understand their unique differences and capabilities. Instructors should then help golfers develop these qualities to the fullest so that they can realize their potential (Goodman, 1993).

Sometimes people with disabilities are limited in their exposure to physical activity, coordination experiences, and fitness levels. However, the main problem facing most people with disabilities has been limited opportunity at a young age to obtain instruction in and master basic movement patterns, which may affect their confidence levels and interest in physical activity (DePauw & Gavron, 2005).

Certain concepts of coaching and instruction can be used when working with golfers with disabilities. Some of these concepts are similar for golfers without disabilities, while others call attention to special needs or concerns. Throughout this book, strategies for instructing golfers with specific disabilities are discussed. The purpose of this chapter is to present a general model of golf instruction—the LPGA Student-Centered Model—that is appropriate for teaching all golfers.

Adapted, by permission, from the Ladies Professional Golf Association, 2004, *National education program series instruction manual* (Daytona Beach, FL: Ladies Professional Golf Association).

Advantages of a Student-Centered Teaching Model

Golf is a sport that lends itself to participation by all segments of the population. Neither age nor gender dictates whether you can become a golfer. Because of the nature of the game, it may be played both socially, where the emphasis is on friendly recreation and not necessarily on shooting a particular score, and competitively, where there may be intrinsic or extrinsic motivation to shoot the best score. Individuals or a group of up to four may play the game. Within a group, individuals may be participating for a variety of personal reasons.

What is it about the game that provides people with satisfaction and a desire to play again?

For all individuals, golf is an exceptional activity for participation within their capabilities and limitations. The "golf model" allows for the game to be played on a short course or a championship-length course with a few pieces of equipment or a full complement. The "golf model" led to the development of miniature golf, played only with a putter on a specially designed course. The progressive skill opportunities based on the individual needs of the learner foster success and challenges with minimal frustration. Once the individual has expressed an interest and desire to learn golf and all its swings and skills, it is up to the instructor to find and establish a means of communicating the complexities of the game in their simplest terms.

What are the needs of individual learners? Why do they play golf? Who will they play with?

A young businessperson learning to play the game so that she may participate with colleagues will require a different approach from the person who wishes to play with his spouse during their retirement years. A *model* for learning and teaching allows the teacher to develop a simplified approach that will accommodate all students, whereas a *method* of teaching will have limited success. A method is a procedure—a prescribed set of actions for a prescribed set of circumstances; by its nature a method has limitations. A model, defined as a preliminary pattern, takes into account preferences, individual differences, and a need for adaptation. It is the teacher's responsibility to find out what student preferences are before effective learning can take place.

What role will golf play in this person's life?

Wiren's Laws, Principles, and Preferences Model

During the mid-1970s, formal golf education experienced a growth phase led by a group of instructors working together within the National Golf Foundation (NGF). These well-respected teachers of the game were discussing individual styles of teaching and the pros and cons of each style. This prompted Dr. Gary Wiren, who was a member of the group, to create a model and a language that coincided with each of the teachers' styles.

In 1976 Wiren introduced a model for teaching the full golf swing that has become known as Laws, Principles, and Preferences. This model has been used extensively throughout the industry as the framework for teaching and learning the full swing. The model was formulated from the basic laws of physics that affect the flight of a golf ball and the mechanical principles used in swinging a golf club. The laws refer only to the club and the ball; that which is attached to the club has no relevance. The principles and preferences, on the other hand, have everything to do with the person holding the golf club. The model provides a logical approach to golf skills through the application of mechanical principles that may be modified to accommodate the individual. The model does not dictate the manner (preferences) in which the principles must be applied, thereby allowing for individualized instructional approaches.

Each aspect of the model can be defined as the following:

- Laws are statements of an order or relation of phenomena that are invariable under given conditions. Laws are dynamic in that there is a range within them that produces direction (including curvature), distance, and trajectory due to the various types of spin created when a club strikes a golf ball.

- Principles are a first cause, or force. They are a fundamental of high order that must be dealt with. They are directly related to and influence laws.

- Preference is the act of choosing how and why one is going to swing a club based on one's physical, social, emotional, and psychological makeup. Preferences must relate to principles.

Throughout the history of golf there has been a constant search for the perfect combination of preferences within the principles that will produce repeatable perfect swings. The search will go on, for just as there is no one body build, set of talents, or mind for all people, there is no one swing that will be perfect for everyone. Individuals will have to combine the principles with their own personal preferences to produce the most effective and efficient swings for the game.

PGA Teaching Manual: The Art and Science of Golf Instruction, G. Wiren, 1990 (Chapter 3, pp. 43-66). Excerpts reprinted with permission from The PGA of America.

LPGA Student-Centered Swing Model

The LPGA Student-Centered Swing Model is an adaptation of Wiren's model. It emphasizes the importance of understanding the student first. The swing principles are then selected and adhered to according to the individual's goals and physical and psychological characteristics, with the understanding that the principles of the swing relate to the laws and the laws influence the movement of the ball. The LPGA Student-Centered Swing Model recognizes the importance of equipment fit and clubhead speed for learning all the swings of the game (putting, chipping, pitching, sand shots, and full swings). The LPGA Student-Centered Swing Model is not a method but rather a framework or paradigm for learning that can be applied and adapted to all people.

The instructor must assess each student's physical, social, emotional, and psychological needs and adapt the swing mechanics to meet the individual's needs. In order to do this, it is necessary for the instructor to

1. have an understanding of the learner and how people learn,
2. have an understanding of swing mechanics,
3. be able to interpret the observed swing style relative to compatible and efficient motion based on the individual's needs and abilities, and
4. communicate and facilitate learning of motor patterns that will foster individual skill development.

The principles and preferences of the swings (putting, chipping, pitching, sand shots, and full swings) that are emphasized in the LPGA Student-Centered Swing Model can be divided into the following categories:

- Preswing (the components of the address routine or preparation of the swing)
- In-swing (swing motion)
- Postswing (finish position and the outcome of the ball)

Keys to the LPGA Student-Centered Swing Model

- It is a model for teaching all swings of the game with an emphasis on the student.
- It is a change in the paradigm of Wiren's model, which does not take into consideration equipment fit or clubhead speed as they relate to shorter, slower swings; the original model was designed for use of the full swing alone. It interprets the original Wiren model for all skill applications.
- The student-centered model identifies student characteristics before applying Wiren's laws, principles, and preferences.

The underlying tenet of the LPGA Student-Centered Swing Model is creating efficient, effective, and compatible motion based on individual student characteristics and priorities for learning.

Note. Adapted from *Teaching Golf to Special Populations* (pp. 18-21), D.D. Owens, Champaign, IL: Leisure Press. Copyright 1984 by Leisure Press. Reprinted by permission of Human Kinetics, Inc.

Laws, Principles, and Preferences

Contrary to what some believe, there is no one perfect golf swing. However, all efficient golf swings make proper use of the laws, principles, and preferences previously mentioned.

Laws

The laws refer to the physical forces that occur when a golf club strikes a golf ball, that is, the moment of impact. These laws are absolute (absolute in this relative universe, anyway) and a necessary foundation when assessing the motion of the golf ball. The following five factors are the laws of the model.

- Clubhead path—The direction of the arc described by the clubhead in its travel toward the target
- Clubface position—The degree to which the leading edge of the clubface is at a right angle (perpendicular) to the swing path

- Clubhead speed—The velocity with which the clubhead is traveling

- Angle of approach—The angle formed by the descending or ascending arc of the clubhead on the forward swing relative to the slope of the ground

- Centeredness of contact—The exactness with which the ball makes contact on the face of the club relative to the percussion point, or sweet spot

These aspects of the clubhead's movement have different effects on the motion of the ball. They all affect the spin of the ball, which affects the direction (shape of the shot), distance, and trajectory of the golf ball.

- The path of the clubhead during the forward motion and relative to the target line (inside to out, outside to in, or straight) will affect the direction the ball travels. It has commonly been interpreted as affecting the initial direction of the ball; however, the speed of the clubhead along with the clubface position will directly influence the degree to which the path affects the direction of the ball.

- The clubface position as it relates to the path of the clubhead (and to the target) will determine the accuracy of the ball's motion (direction) along that line. The clubface position will affect the sidespin of the ball and ultimately may create a curving ball flight.

- The speed of the clubhead at impact will influence the distance the ball is propelled; slower speeds produce less distance and higher speeds produce more distance. Speed will affect the trajectory and can affect the curvature of the shot.

- The angle of approach influences the spin rate (backspin) of the ball. This in turn affects the trajectory and the distance of the ball. As a rule, a descending angle of approach (sometimes referred to as steep) creates more backspin and therefore creates a higher trajectory and less distance. An ascending angle of approach (some-

times referred to as shallow) will generate a lower trajectory and less backspin that results in more distance. The trajectory of the ball is determined by the golf club being used, the angle at which the club hits the ball, whether the clubface is in a more lofted position or delofted position at impact, and the speed of the clubhead. The design features of the golf ball will also have an effect.

- The degree of centeredness with which the ball is hit by the clubhead relative to the sweet spot will affect the direction, distance, and when applicable, the trajectory of the ball. Contact could either be on the center, toe, heel, and above or below that place. Toe and heel contact will result in a loss of distance and high and low contact will affect the trajectory.

Note that the sweet spot is actually located between two areas on the clubface: the center of percussion and the vibratory node (see figure 5.1). The center of percussion is

© Sport the Library

Figure 5.1 The sweet spot, which is the circle in the middle of this clubhead, is located in the center of the clubhead between the center of percussion and the vibratory node.

the area on the clubface that can be tapped without transmitting any force to the fingers. The vibratory node is the zone on the clubface where the least energy is lost during impact. The area between the center of percussion and the vibratory node is considered the sweet spot. Clubheads are designed so that the center of percussion is located away from the vibratory node, providing an enlarged sweet spot.

In full swings, these influences can cause a ball's flight to take on many shapes. We have chosen to use the term *playable ball flight* for golf shots that arrive at or close to the intended target; that is, effective golf shots. Playable ball flight has more meaning in reference to full swing golf shots versus a putt, chip, or pitch. However, the Laws, Principles, and Preferences Model can apply to these golf shots as well (see figure 5.2).

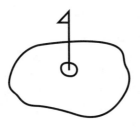

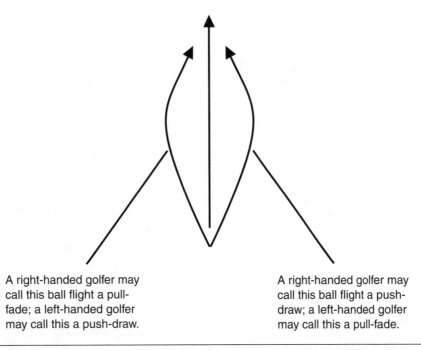

A right-handed golfer may call this ball flight a pull-fade; a left-handed golfer may call this a push-draw.

A right-handed golfer may call this ball flight a push-draw; a left-handed golfer may call this a pull-fade.

Figure 5.2 A ball can fly on a relatively straight path to the target with a small amount of curvature, it can curve from right to left, or it can curve from left to right.

Adapted, by permission, from the Ladies Professional Golf Association, 2004, *National education program series instruction manual* (Daytona Beach, FL: Ladies Professional Golf Association).

When a significant amount of clubhead speed is produced during the full swing, the path of the club will create a push or pull and the clubface position will create the curvature of the shot. For a right-handed golfer, a push-draw occurs when the path of the club is moving away from the player (in to out) and the clubface position is closed to the path (aimed relatively at the target) at impact, thus creating curvature back toward the target. Conversely, a pull-fade occurs when the path of the club is moving toward the player (out to in) and the clubface position is open to the path (aimed relatively at the target) at impact, thus creating curvature back toward the target.

The degree to which this movement is visible is related to clubhead speed and the degree of difference between the path and clubface position. The angle of approach and the centeredness of contact will also influence the shape. The laws are interrelated when it comes to creating ball flight. The principle of plane is also often considered (see the following section) since it directly influences the laws of path, angle of approach, and centeredness of contact.

Principles

Certain fundamental considerations in the full swing and short game have a direct bearing on application of the laws. In Wiren's model they are labeled *principles* of the swing. Whereas the laws are irrefutable and absolute, principles reflect subjective judgment on the mechanics of the skills.

The preswing principles of the model include the following:

1. The hold
2. Aim and alignment
3. Setup

The in-swing principles of the model include the following:

4. Swing plane
5. Width of arc
6. Length of arc
7. Position of target arm and wrist

8. Lever system
9. Timing
10. Release
11. Dynamic balance
12. Swing center (rotational)
13. Connection
14. Impact

The preswing principles greatly influence the in-swing principles. These preswing principles are what golfers know as the fundamentals of golf skills. The goal of the Student-Centered Swing Model is for the teacher to assist the golfer in discovering effective and efficient principles that are compatible with the student's goals and physical and psychological characteristics.

Preferences

The Student-Centered Swing Model includes freedom for the student and teacher to discover the many ways the principles can be used to create player-compatible, effective, and efficient motion (see figure 5.3). The model was created with the idea that all players of the game are unique; therefore, the idea of preferences is the essence of the model.

Following are steps to using the LPGA Student-Centered Swing Model.

1. Identify and understand student characteristics (physical, social, emotional, and psychological characteristics, how they process information, how they sense their world).
2. Apply principles and preferences to student characteristics and priorities for learning golf.
3. Relate laws to compatible preswing principles and in-swing principles.

Preswing Principles

Preswing principles refer to all the principles that golfers incorporate into their routine prior to swinging a club and include the hold, aim and alignment, and the setup.

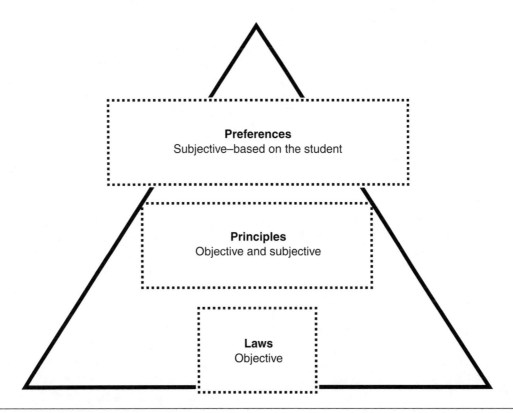

Figure 5.3 LPGA Student-Centered Swing Model.

Adapted, by permission, from the Ladies Professional Golf Association, 2004, *National education program series instruction manual* (Daytona Beach, FL: Ladies Professional Golf Association).

The use of the preswing principles will vary depending on

- the characteristics of the golfer,
- the club being used and the golf shot the golfer wishes to create, and
- the desired ball flight or shape of the shot (in the case of the full swing).

1. The hold—Primary influence is on the direction of the ball because its greatest effect is on clubface position.

How a golfer chooses to hold the club will depend on many factors. The teacher and student must consider the size and shape of the hand and fingers and the anatomical position of the arm, wrist, and hand in a relaxed state. A more inwardly rotated palm on the target side often suggests a hold position of the target hand that displays more than two knuckles. When the palm of the hand hangs naturally facing the leg, a hold position displaying two knuckles will often be appropriate. If the arm hangs in such a way that the palm faces outward, the hold position will likely display no more than two knuckles. Choosing the position for the rear hand is a similar process. Generally speaking, the palms will face each other; however, variations will occur, especially for putting, chipping, and other specialty shots. The key is that the position of each hand on the club should be efficient, effective, and compatible with the player.

Considerations of the hold include the following:

- Placement—Are the hands located near the top of the handle, or are they placed down the handle toward the shaft?
- Position—How many knuckles are displayed by the target hand, and what is the position of the rear hand relative to the palm of the target hand? Is the hold overlap, 10-finger, or interlock? Is the handle of the club more in the fingers

or the palm? Is the golfer using a short thumb position or a long thumb position?

- Pressure—Is the hold light, tight, or somewhere in between (rated on a scale from 1-10)?

- Precision—Can the golfer consistently place the hands on the club in the same position?

2. Aim and alignment—Primary influence is on direction because the clubface aim and the alignment of the body have a strong effect on the clubface position and the path.

A golfer aims the clubface to the target and aligns the body to the ball. An imaginary line through the ball toward the target is referred to as the target line. A square clubface position means that the leading edge of the club is perpendicular (forms a T) to the target line and therefore is aimed at the target. A left-handed golfer will rotate the handle counterclockwise to create an open clubface and clockwise to create a closed clubface. A right-handed golfer will rotate the handle clockwise to create an open clubface and counterclockwise to create a closed clubface.

Alignment of the body refers to the alignment of the eyes, shoulders, hips, and feet. Generally it is preferable that, for example, the shoulders and hips be aligned the same; however, not all bodies will necessarily be in perfect alignment. When the body (eyes, shoulders, hips, and feet) directly faces (perpendicular to) the target line, the alignment is said to be square. When the alignment is square, imaginary lines (or a golf club as an indicator) from the golfer's heels, hips, and shoulders will be parallel to the target line. Since many golfers turn their toes out somewhat at address, an indicator of feet alignment at the heels can be more accurate. When the target foot, hips, and shoulders are pulled back from the line, the alignment is said to be open. When the rear foot, hips, and shoulders are pulled back from that line, the alignment is said to be closed (see figure 5.4).

When observing alignment from a position looking down the target line, notice the alignment of the feet, hips, shoulders, and eyes.

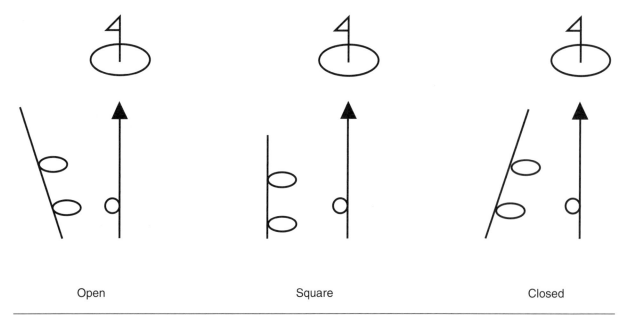

Open   Square   Closed

Figure 5.4 Open, square, and closed stances.

Adapted, by permission, from the Ladies Professional Golf Association, 2004, *National education program series instruction manual* (Daytona Beach, FL: Ladies Professional Golf Association).

3. Setup—Influences the direction, distance, and trajectory because the factors of the setup affect all five laws (speed, clubface, path, angle of approach, and centeredness of contact).

The factors of the setup include posture (forward spine angle), stance (width and weight distribution), torso tilt, and ball position. Each of these factors affects the subsequent motion. The posture of a golfer in the address position is often described as athletic. This position requires a forward movement of the spine from vertical to a position that will allow the arms to fall away from the body. This position is most effective when the body, though not vertical, feels balanced on the feet and legs. The weight distribution may be sensed as more toward the balls of the feet or more toward the heels. The amount of forward spine angle varies from 22 to 44 degrees depending on the golfer's stature and the length of the club. The torso tilt of a golfer (as viewed from either facing the golfer or from behind the golfer) may be slightly forward toward the target, slightly back away from the target, or not evident at all (centered). A golfer's width of stance may be referred to as equal to, wider than, or less than the shoulders. Observe the space between the heels relative to the outside edge of the shoulders. The ball position is noted as relative to the sternum—equal to, forward of, or back of the sternum.

In-Swing Principles

In-swing principles refer to all the principles that golfers incorporate into the motion of swinging the golf club as they attempt to strike the ball. Everyone has a swing that is best for them. It will depend upon their size, natural talent, and deficiencies. In order to produce the best golf swing possible, one must optimize the following in-swing principles: swing plane, width of arc, length of arc, position of target arm and wrist, lever system, timing, release, dynamic balance, rotational swing center, connection, and impact.

4. Swing plane—Primary influence is on direction because it has a strong effect on the path.

The swing plane is determined by the angle of the clubshaft relative to the ground at address. The tilt of the inclined plane can be observed by standing behind the golfer. While the golfer is at address, the plane can be observed by holding a golf club so that its shaft covers the shaft of the golfer's club (use the dominant eye). The swing is on plane when, during the forward swing, the butt end of the club intersects the target line. If the butt end is pointing outside the line, the club is said to be below plane and the path of the clubhead will likely be in to out; if the butt end is pointing inside

Table 5.1 Compatible Positions for Playable Ball Flights

Preswing	Pull-fade	Straight or with slight curve	Push-draw
Hold	Neutral or less knuckles	Neutral	Neutral or more knuckles
Posture	Less	Approx. 36	More
Clubface aim	Open to path	Square to path	Closed to path
Alignment	Open	Square	Closed
Ball position	Forward	Center/forward	Back
Weight distribution (relative to target)	Forward	Center	Rear
Torso tilt	Forward	Center/rear	Rear

Adapted, by permission, from the Ladies Professional Golf Association, 2004, *National education program series instruction manual* (Daytona Beach, FL: Ladies Professional Golf Association).

the target line, the club is said to be above plane and the path of the clubhead will likely be out to in. Plane also influences trajectory. The clubhead can be on an even, ascending, or descending angle of approach and still be on plane.

5. Width of arc—Primary influence is on distance because it has a strong effect on clubhead speed.

The width of the arc refers to the degree to which the arms and hands (especially the target arm) extend away from the body (center of rotation). At impact, the speed of the clubhead will be maximized when the arms are fully extended rather than collapsed.

6. Length of arc—Primary influence is on distance because it is a contributing factor to clubhead speed.

The length of the arc refers to the distance the clubhead travels on the backswing and on the forward swing. A shorter distance will often mean less speed, as in a pitch shot. The length of the arc on the forward swing is a good indicator of the expenditure of energy through the impact.

7. Position—Primary influence is on direction because it has strong effect on clubface position.

The position of the target-side arm and wrist is most often observed at the finish, or top, of the backswing. The wrist may appear to be aligned with the arm or in a cupped or bowed (hyperextended) position. These positions will have a direct correlation to the golfer's hold.

8. Lever system—Primary influence is on distance because the lever system has a strong effect on clubhead speed.

When the arms and golf club are fully extended from the body, one lever exists. When the wrists are hinged, two levers exist, the arms and the golf club. The use of two levers increases potential speed.

9. Timing—Influence is on direction and distance because timing will affect clubhead path and speed.

Timing refers to the sequence of body and club motion away from the target and forward to the finish. As an example, the sequence of the forward swing can be observed as the hands and arms initiating the motion or the hips initiating the motion with the hands and arms following. The sequence of the body and club away from and toward the target will influence the effectiveness and efficiency of the desired ball flight.

10. Release—Primary influence is on direction because the release affects clubface position at impact.

Release refers to the club, hands, arms, and body returning to and moving through impact while expending the energy stored during the backswing. A "natural" release can take place when there is an absence of muscular tension. The release can be observed as a timed release, an early release, or a late release.

11. Dynamic balance—Influence is on direction and distance because dynamic balance will affect clubhead path and speed.

Dynamic balance refers to balance in motion; that is, the transfer of weight during the swing while maintaining control of the body. Balance can be noted at the finish of the forward swing as balanced, falling forward toward the target, falling back away from the target, or a general sense of imbalance.

12. Swing center (rotational)—Influence is on direction and distance because swing center affects centeredness of contact.

The swing center is a point near the top of the spine around which the upper torso rotates and the arms swing (the movement of the clubhead creates an arc). When the center of the arc remains relatively still, centeredness of contact with the ball will improve. Some lateral movement of the swing center often accompanies increased clubhead speed; with shorter shots (less speed required), movement of the swing center may have a greater effect on the contact and therefore the accuracy of the shot. Movements up and down and away from and toward the ball will have a strong effect on the centeredness of contact.

13. Connection—Influence is on direction and distance because connection affects centeredness of contact and speed.

Connection refers to the relationship among body parts during the swing. At address the arms and torso establish a relationship—they are connected or disconnected. The effectiveness of connection or disconnection (separation) during the forward swing will be influenced by the desired speed. Disconnection in a chip shot will have less effect than disconnection during the full swing.

Table 5.2   Primary Influence of Ball Height Principles

Principle	Primary influence
Preswing	
Hold	Direction
Aim and alignment	Direction
Setup	Direction, distance, trajectory
In-swing	
Plane	Direction (trajectory)
Width of arc	Distance
Length of arc	Distance
Position (at top)	Direction
Lever system	Distance
Timing	Distance, direction
Release	Direction
Dynamic balance	Distance, direction
Swing center	Distance, direction
Connection	Distance, direction
Impact	Distance, direction, trajectory

Adapted, by permission, from the Ladies Professional Golf Association, 2004, *National education program series instruction manual* (Daytona Beach, FL: Ladies Professional Golf Association).

14. Impact—Influences direction, distance, and trajectory because the impact position of the club and body will affect path, clubface position, speed, angle of approach, and centeredness of contact.

A golfer's basic intention is to create a motion that will impact the ball with the golf club and create a specific outcome. Observing the motion and the subsequent impact must go hand in hand with understanding the student's perceptions and intentions.

Table 5.3   Relationship and Influence of Ball Flight Laws and Principles

Principle	Law
Preswing	
Hold	Clubface position
Aim and alignment	Clubface position, path
Setup	All five laws
Plane	Path (angle of approach)
Width of arc	Clubhead speed
Length of arc	Clubhead speed
Position (at top)	Clubface position
Lever system	Clubhead speed
Timing	Clubhead speed, path
Release	Clubface position
Dynamic balance	Clubhead speed, path
Swing center	Centeredness of contact
Connection	Speed, centeredness of contact
Impact	All five laws

Adapted, by permission, from the Ladies Professional Golf Association, 2004, *National education program series instruction manual* (Daytona Beach, FL: Ladies Professional Golf Association).

Observation Systems

A teacher who tries to observe and analyze skills without any preparation complicates an already difficult task. Preparation for observation should include a review of the critical checkpoints of the skill being learned. The preswing checkpoints serve as a focal point for a teacher's observation system.

Directed observations or guidelines for skill observations help direct communication. The two basic observation positions include the following:

1. The "down the line" view (from behind the player looking down the target line) to observe club aim, hold position and placement, body alignment, weight distribution (toes or heels), posture (muscular readiness and knee flex), swing plane and path, position, connection, impact, and ball flight

2. The front view (facing the player) for hold position, ball position, stance width (muscular readiness), weight distribution (forward or rear), length of arc, width of arc, lever system, timing, release, dynamic balance, swing center, and impact.

These two observation positions should be used for viewing all the swings of the game. Occasionally, the view from the backside of the golfer can be effective for noting torso tilt and dynamic balance.

What to Observe

1. Preswing fundamentals and address routine for all swings
2. Complete swing motion
3. In-swing principles
4. Balance

5. Fit of clubs and compensations for improper fit

The teacher must be able to observe all parts of the swing and recognize individual differences and preferences. Instructors have an obligation to observe and consider all aspects of the preparation and motion and to note muscular and psychological readiness.

Observation skills are used to take in information about the swings (behavior). Observe skills systematically. Then ask the following questions:

1. What is the student's intention?
2. What are the student's perceptions?
3. What is the resulting motion and what happens to the ball in relation to the motion?
4. Ask open-ended questions that will lead students to discover how they perform well.

Using the LPGA Student-Centered Swing Model allows the instructor to individualize a golf program based on the student's needs and abilities. Understanding how people learn, understanding the basic mechanics of golf skills through Wiren's Laws, Principles, and Preferences model, and being able to observe skills and interpret the observations relative to compatible and efficient motion based on the individual's abilities are critical to successful learning and the basis for this unique approach to teaching.

Chapter 6

Playing the Game of Golf

Alice loves to play golf. She particularly likes playing with her 14-year-old granddaughter, who is just learning the game. Alice had been playing golf for 20 years before she was diagnosed with osteoporosis and severe arthritis in one of her hips. This condition now requires her to use a cane in order to get around the golf course. When Alice plays golf, she normally rides in a golf car, but she needs her cane to walk to her ball, especially on uneven terrain.

During a recent round of golf, quite a few circumstances arose that called for a modification of the rules, and Alice conscientiously explained each one to her granddaughter. For instance, Alice's ball ended up in a fairway bunker and she needed to use her cane to get to the ball. The standard rule states that no club or device may touch the sand prior to striking the ball. However, in this case it was permissible for Alice to use her cane for support as long as she did not intentionally try to test the surface of the sand, which would breach the rules of golf.

Another case in point occurred each time Alice putted. Once Alice approached the ball and took her

stance, she laid her cane on the green and proceeded to putt. As long as she did not use her cane as an alignment aid or lay it across the line of the putt in front of or behind the ball, it was acceptable for her to place it on the putting surface.

Alice recognizes the importance of understanding the rules of the game, and she has expressed that importance to her granddaughter. In fact, Alice typically carries a copy of the official rules of golf when she plays. She has also studied alterations to the rules that have

(continued)

(continued)

been officially approved by the USGA and published in *A Modification of the Rules of Golf for Golfers With Disabilities* (2001). The full text of those guidelines can be found on the USGA Web site at www.usga.org/playing/rules/golfers_with_disabilities.html and in appendix A at the end of this book.

This chapter contains an overview of the basic rules of golf for those who are not familiar with them. In addition, modifications to the rules for golfers with disabilities are discussed for competitive and casual golf. Because most amateur golfers play golf and count their scores by strokes (as opposed to match play), the rules for stroke play are emphasized. Basic golf safety and etiquette are also addressed with an emphasis on situations that could affect golfers with disabilities.

Rules of the Game

Golf is a simple game in concept. The object is to get the golf ball from the teeing ground (also known as the tee box) into a small hole in as few swings of the golf club as possible. One of the major obstacles to learning the game is its unique terminology. For a list of basic terms used in golf, see table 6.1. The playing field in golf is known as the golf course. A standard golf course is divided into 18 separate fields of play known as holes. Note that the word *hole* also refers to the actual cavity in the ground that is the end point for each of these fields of play. The basic short-term objective of golf is to get the ball into the hole in the fewest possible strokes. The basic long-term objective is to complete the 18 holes in the fewest possible total strokes.

Scoring

Keeping score in golf is relatively simple. For each individual hole, the golfer counts the number of swings it takes to get the ball into the hole from the tee box. If any penalty strokes are incurred when playing the hole, they must also be added to this total (penalty strokes are explained throughout the chapter).

For example, if a golfer hit the ball four times before it ended up in the hole and was also assessed one penalty stroke, the golfer would score a 5 for that hole.

Each hole has a standard called par, which is the number of shots it would take an expert player to get the ball from the tee box to the green and into the hole. For instance, a par-3 hole, usually 85 to 230 yards (78 to 210 meters) long, allows for the tee shot (the initial shot from the tee box) to be hit directly onto the green, where two more shots are allotted to get the ball in the hole. The hole, which is sometimes referred to as the cup, is located somewhere on the green and marked by a flagstick. On a par-4 hole, usually 230 to 460 yards (210 to 421 meters) long, an expert player is allowed two shots to get the ball on the green and then two putts to get the ball into the hole. On a par-5 hole, usually more than 460 yards (421 meters) long, an expert player is allowed three shots to get the ball on the green and two putts to get the ball in the hole.

Some golfers refer to their score in relation to par with specific terms. Finishing a hole in one stroke under par is called a birdie. Two strokes under par is referred to as an eagle. Birdies and eagles are both desirable and very hard to accomplish. When a golfer finishes a hole in more strokes than the allotted par, it is referred to as a bogey. One stroke over par is called a bogey, two strokes over par is called a double bogey, three strokes over par is called a triple bogey, and so forth.

Basic Rules

The United States Golf Association (USGA), in conjunction with the Royal and Ancient Golf Club of St. Andrews (the R&A), publishes an

Table 6.1   Basic Golf Terms

Ace	Completing the hole in one stroke, or a hole-in-one.
Address	The position or stance of the body taken in preparation of hitting the ball.
Away	The ball that is the greatest distance from the hole; it should be the next ball played.
Birdie	A hole played in one stroke less than par.
Bogey	A hole played in one stroke more than par.
Bunker	A depression in the ground that is usually filled with sand.
Casual water	A temporary accumulation of water that is not located in a hazard.
Clubhead	The area of the club used to hit the ball.
Double bogey	A hole played in two strokes more than par.
Draw	A shot that curves slightly from right to left, for a right-handed golfer.
Drive	The first shot on a hole hit from the teeing ground.
Eagle	A hole played in two strokes less than par.
Fade	A shot that curves slightly from left to right, for a right-handed golfer.
Fairway	The closely mowed area between the teeing ground and the green.
Fore	A warning cry given to anyone in danger of being hit by a golf ball.
Green	The putting surface at the end of the hole.
Handicap	The numerical representation of a golfer's playing ability.
Hazard	Any bunker or water on the course designed to provide difficulty to the golfer.
Hook	A shot that curves dramatically from right to left, for a right-handed golfer.
Lie	The position of the ball as it rests on the ground.
Out of bounds	The area outside of the course where play is prohibited.
Par	The number of strokes an expert golfer should take on a hole.
Putt	A shot played from the green.
Putter	A straight-faced club designed for putting.
Rough	The longer grass surrounding the fairway.
Slice	A shot that curves dramatically from left to right, for a right-handed golfer.
Stance	The position of the feet when preparing to strike the ball.
Stroke	An attempt to hit the ball, whether successful or not.
Teeing ground	The area where play begins on each hole.

official *Rules of Golf* book each year. It provides a thorough interpretation of each of the 34 rules that make up the game of golf. It is a complex document that is often misunderstood, even by PGA and LPGA touring professionals. The complete rules can be found at www.usga.org/playing/rules/rules_of_golf.html.

Although anyone desiring to play golf should become familiar with the entire rule book, there are a few rules that even beginning golfers should be aware of and understand. Basic rules that define the game are explained in the following material.

General Points

Before commencing your round you should read the local rules, which are special rules that apply only to that golf course and have been deemed necessary by the golf committee. Many golfers use the same brand of golf ball so you should put an identifying mark on your ball before beginning play. If you are asked to identify your ball and there are no special markings, it is considered lost. It is also a good idea to count your clubs before starting a round of golf; the maximum allowed is 14. During the round, it is not permissible to ask for advice from anyone other than your partner, and it is also against the rules to give advice to anyone except your partner. During a hole you may not play a practice shot.

Teeing Off

Tee off between and not in front of the tee-markers. You may tee off up to two club-lengths behind the front line of the tee-markers. In match play there is no penalty for teeing off outside the boundaries of the tee markers, but your opponent may ask you to replay the shot. In stroke play you would incur a two-stroke penalty and be required to the play the shot from within the proper area.

Playing the Ball

Play the ball as it lies. Don't improve your lie, or the area of your intended swing or your line of play, by moving, bending, or breaking anything fixed or growing except in fairly taking your stance or making your swing. Don't press anything down or build a stance. If your ball lies in a bunker or a water hazard, don't touch the ground in the bunker or the ground or water in the water hazard before your downswing. The ball must be fairly struck, not pushed or spooned. You get a two-stroke penalty for playing the wrong ball, and you must then play the correct ball. (Playing the wrong ball refers to a ball belonging to another player. Everyone should put an identifying mark on the ball they are playing with to prevent confusion.)

On the Putting Green

You may repair ball marks and old hole plugs on the line of your putt but not any other damage, including spike marks. You may mark, lift, and clean your ball on the putting green. Always replace it on the exact spot where it was before you picked it up. Don't test the putting surface by scraping it or rolling a ball over it. If a ball played from the putting green strikes the flagstick, you incur a two-stroke penalty.

Ball at Rest Moved

If your ball is at rest and you, your partner, or your caddie move it, except as permitted by the rules, or if it moves after you have addressed it, add a penalty stroke and replace your ball. If your ball is at rest and is moved by someone else or another ball, replace it without penalty.

Ball in Motion Deflected or Stopped

If you, your partner, or your caddie deflect or stop your ball, you incur a two-stroke penalty and play the ball as it lies. If someone else deflects or stops your ball, you may play it as it lies without penalty, or you must replay the stroke if it originated from the putting green. If your ball is deflected or stopped by another ball that was at rest, play it as it lies with no penalty, unless both balls were on the putting green when you played the stroke. In that case you would incur a two-stroke penalty.

Lifting, Dropping, and Placing the Ball

If a lifted ball is to be replaced, you must mark its position. If you are dropping a ball or placing it in any other position (e.g., taking relief from ground under repair, which is discussed on page 49), it is recommended that you mark the ball's original position. When dropping, stand erect, hold the ball at shoulder height and arm's length, and drop it. If a dropped ball strikes you or your partner, caddie, or equipment, it is redropped without penalty. You may lift your ball if doing so might assist any other player. You may have any ball lifted if it might interfere with your play or assist any other player.

Loose Impediments

You may move a loose impediment unless it and your ball are in a hazard. However, if you touch a loose impediment within one club-length of your ball and your ball moves, the ball must be replaced and, unless your ball was on the putting green, you incur a penalty stroke.

Obstructions

Movable obstructions (e.g., rakes, tin cans) anywhere on the course may be moved. If the ball moves when removing such obstructions, replace it without penalty. If an immovable obstruction (e.g., water fountain) interferes with your stance or swing, you may drop the ball within one club-length of the nearest point of relief not nearer the hole. There is no relief from an immovable obstruction based on line of play.

Casual Water, Ground Under Repair, Abnormal Conditions

If your ball is in casual water, ground under repair, or a hole or cast made by a burrowing animal, you may drop without penalty within one club-length of the nearest point of relief not nearer the hole.

Water Hazard

When your ball is in a water hazard, you may play the ball as it lies or, under penalty of one stroke, you may drop any distance behind the water hazard, keeping a straight line between the hole, the point where the ball crossed the margin of the water hazard, and the spot where the ball is dropped; or you may play again from the place where you hit the ball into the hazard. If your ball is in a lateral water hazard (see figure 6.1), in addition to the options for a ball in a water hazard, under penalty of one stroke you may drop within two club-lengths of the point where the ball crossed the margin of the hazard or at a point on the opposite side of the hazard equidistant from the hole.

Ball Lost or Out of Bounds

Check the local rules on the scorecard to identify the boundaries of the course. If your ball is lost outside a water hazard or out of

Figure 6.1   Lateral water hazard.

bounds, under penalty of one stroke you must play another ball from the spot where the last shot was played (i.e., stroke and distance). You are allowed five minutes to search for a ball, after which if you do not find or identify it, it is lost. You do not have to wait the entire five minutes before declaring your ball lost. If you think your ball may be lost outside a water hazard or out of bounds, you may play a provisional ball. You must state that it is a provisional ball and play it before going forward to search for the original ball. If the original ball is lost or out of bounds you must continue with the provisional ball under penalty of one stroke. If the original ball is not lost or out of bounds, you must continue play with it and abandon the provisional ball.

Ball Unplayable

If you believe your ball is unplayable outside a water hazard (and you are the sole judge), you may, under penalty of one stroke, drop within two club-lengths of where the ball lay not nearer the hole; drop any distance behind the point where the ball lay, keeping a straight line between the hole, the point where the ball lay, and the spot where the ball is dropped; or replay the shot. If your ball is in a bunker you may proceed using any of these three options. However, if you elect to proceed under the first two options, you must drop in the bunker.

A good score may be spoiled or a match lost due to a penalty incurred through ignorance or confusion concerning the rules. A sound knowledge of the previous summary should aid golfers in most rules situations. Nevertheless, the complete *Rules of Golf* should be consulted where any doubt arises.

Modifying Rules to Accommodate Golfers With Disabilities

In 2001, the United States Golf Association developed an official set of rules for golfers with disabilities. As mentioned previously, it is called *A Modification of the Rules of Golf for Golfers With Disabilities* and is available on the USGA Web site and in appendix A of this book.

Informal Modifications

Although the USGA has developed modifications to the *Rules of Golf* for individuals with disabilities, many golfers with and without disabilities modify the rules in their own way to make the game more enjoyable **when not playing in competition.** The following informal modifications are neither encouraged nor discouraged in recreational golf. **However, they should be agreed upon by all players before beginning play.**

The rule most often broken is the fundamental principle of playing the ball as it lies. This precept can sometimes present important logistical, speed of play, and safety challenges to golfers with disabilities. Due to positioning, balance, and mobility limitations, this most often is true with golfers who play from a seated position. Moving the ball, also called bumping, is a practice golfers use. Golfers with disabilities should always try to play the ball from a position that most resembles the original lie of the ball, as long as it is safe to

attempt the shot. If there is a need to dramatically move the ball for safety reasons, the ball should be placed in a position that does not improve the condition of the lie or shorten the distance to the hole. Another modification to this rule is to only take a penalty for an unplayable lie if a nondisabled golfer would have to do the same. Although it is against the rules to ground your club in a hazard, most golfers with a disability do not assess a penalty stroke when bumping the ball for speed of play or safety purposes in such conditions.

When a bunker or normally playable hazard is inaccessible to golfers with disabilities, the original procedure does not allow the ball to be dropped outside the hazard. However, many golfers with disabilities drop a ball near the hazard, no closer to the hole, with a one-stroke penalty.

Another common informal modification to the rules during noncompetitive play occurs on the putting green in the form of taking "gimmies." Instead of putting the ball into the hole, a gimmie allows the golfer to pick up the ball when it is near the hole. A gimmie counts as one stroke. This practice is especially prevalent for golfers requiring the use of a single-rider car. Not only does it avoid bringing the car too close to the hole, it also speeds up play.

Options for Formal Competition

Because the USGA has developed official modifications to the rules of golf for golfers with disabilities, anyone should be able to follow the rules and play in any competition they desire. However, many events designed for golfers with disabilities follow an alternative format.

Scrambles and alternate-shot formats are popular with all golfers and are appropriate competition formats for golfers with disabilities. In the scramble format, each player on a team hits a shot. The best one is chosen, and everyone on the team hits from that position until the ball is holed. Alternate-shot competitions usually consist of teams with two players who take turns hitting shots until the ball is holed.

Special Olympics athletes compete in golf as one of the official events. The Special Olympics have altered the *Rules of Golf* to allow athletes to compete in one of five levels of competition. Official events include an individual skills contest (level 1), an alternate-shot team play competition (level 2), Unified Sports team play (level 3), an individual stroke play competition of 9 holes (level 4), and an individual stroke play competition of 18 holes (level 5). Individual skills contests are intended to train athletes to compete in basic golf skills. Competition is held in short putting, long putting, chipping, and the pitch shot, iron shot, and wood shot. The alternate-shot team play competition pairs one Special Olympics athlete with one golfer without cognitive impairment who acts as a coach and mentor. The format is a 9-hole tournament that is played as a modified four-person scramble. Level 3 allows athletes to play in regulation 9-hole golf competition, while level 4 is designed for play in 18-hole competitions. Level 5 or Unified Sports team play is designed to provide the Special Olympics athlete a chance to play in a team format with a partner without cognitive impairment but with comparable ability.

Golf Safety and Etiquette

Golf is different from most other sports because it is self-governing and a certain level of conduct is expected. Golf is one of the few sports where competitors call penalties on themselves. It is a game of honesty and integrity. If a golfer breaks a rule, whether it is on purpose or by accident, he is expected to call a penalty on himself. You will never see an NFL football player go to the referee to declare that he dropped a pass that was ruled complete or a batter in baseball complain that a pitch the umpire called a ball was really a strike and the call should be changed. Golfers are also expected to conduct themselves based on a code of conduct known as etiquette. The game has many nuances that go far beyond the concrete rules of play, but understanding these nuances can be as important as understanding the rules themselves. Golf etiquette can be overwhelming to some golfers, espe-

cially beginners. However, no one expects casual golfers to know everything about golf etiquette, and even experienced professionals continually learn new aspects of proper behavior on the course. Learning more about golf etiquette comes with experience in the game; however, here are some basic tips to remember that will make you welcome on the course and help keep the game safe:

• Be quiet (don't talk or move) when someone else is attempting to play a shot. Golf requires a lot of concentration, and it is considered rude to speak when a playing partner is trying to hit. Once the player has addressed the ball, it is time to be quiet and let the player attempt the shot.

• Make sure the players in the group in front of you are well out of the way before hitting your shot. Hitting into another group is not only rude, but a golf ball could seriously injure someone. Lawsuits have even been brought against golfers who have injured others by hitting when they were still in the way.

• If you do happen to hit an errant shot that may strike other people, yell "Fore!" as loudly as possible. This is a warning that they could be in danger and should try to protect themselves.

• Keep up with the group in front of you. The best way to determine if you are playing at an acceptable rate is not to keep the group behind you from waiting, but to keep pace with the group in front of you. Your pace of play is acceptable if there is no more than one open hole between you and the group you are following. Of course, this only applies when another group is beginning play on the tee time preceding yours.

• If you have problems keeping up with the group in front of you, let the golfers behind you play through. This is particularly important if the players have to wait for you before they can play their shots. It is best to wave the next group up, move to the side (preferably under some type of protection), and allow them to play their shots and move ahead of your group.

• Leave the course in better shape than when you played it. This requires you to smooth all bunkers as best as possible after playing a shot from the sand, replace divots in the fairway, and fix ball marks you make on the green. Although it is not your responsibility, you should also take care of these tasks for other golfers who did not do their part as long as it does not slow down play too much.

• Let the person farthest away from the hole hit first. Sometimes this is not practical and can slow up play. However, if the person farthest from the hole is ready to play, it is considered good etiquette to let her hit her shot first. You should always be "ready to play" when it is your turn.

• Don't move ahead of members in your group before they have a chance to hit their shot. Not only is this dangerous, you could distract them from playing their best shot.

• Don't walk or move across someone's line of putt on the green. If you do, it could cause small indentations on the green that may affect the ball's distance or direction. You should particularly follow this tip during competitive rounds. It is also considered bad manners to stand directly behind players as they are putting, as this can be very distracting.

• Watch where your shot ends up. It helps your group keep up a good pace of play if you do not have to continually look for wayward shots. If you must look for your ball, remember that the *Rules of Golf* only allow five minutes for the search.

• Know the rules and be respectful of the course and playing partners.

The National Center on Accessibility (NCA) (2003) has also published etiquette tips for golfers with disabilities and golf course operators on their Web site at www.indiana.edu/~nca/. They are also listed in appendix C at the end of this book.

Golf is a game that can be enjoyed in some form or another by all people. Formal and informal modifications to the rules and formats can enhance the enjoyment of the game for people with disabilities. Golf can be challenging, but the most important thing for all golfers to remember is to be safe and to adhere to proper rules and etiquette.

Chapter 7

Creating Safe Learning Environments

Richard is an accomplished teacher, evidenced by the fact that he has been selected as his PGA section's Teacher of the Year on two different occasions. However, when Richard was asked to provide golf instruction for the community recreation department's program for golfers with disabilities, he was apprehensive and had many concerns. He had been a successful golf professional for over 15 years but had never really been around people with disabilities, and he questioned his ability to effectively help them learn the game. He didn't have any medical training and was scared that he might do something to hurt one of the participants. Richard decided to get in touch with one of his old college buddies, a certified therapeutic recreation specialist, to ask for help.

His friend reassured Richard that he would be fine and sent him a book on therapeutic recreation so he could learn more about assisting people with disabilities. Richard eagerly read the book and learned a great deal about working with people with disabilities in a recreation setting. He especially learned from the chapter about communication techniques for instructing people with disabilities. From reading the book, Richard also realized that it would be easy to make some minor modifications at his golf course that would make the facility more accessible to golfers with disabilities. Richard widened the hitting stations on an entire section of the practice facility so golfers in single-rider golf cars could maneuver and hit from a seated position. He also installed an automatic teeing device in two of the stations so golfers would not have to bend down to put golf balls on a tee.

Richard was beginning to feel more comfortable and excited about the upcoming program. However, he was still uneasy about his lack of medical knowledge. Richard decided to meet with a rehabilitation specialist at a local hospital. She gave Richard some background information on specific disabilities along with a copy of a presentation she had done on golf-related injuries. He learned about precautions that need to be taken with golfers with disabilities to decrease their chances of getting injured. They were basically the same precautions that need to be taken for golfers without disabilities.

The golf program has flourished under Richard's guidance. Richard says that the work he does with golfers with disabilities is the most rewarding teaching he has ever done. He now feels lucky to have been asked to provide instruction for the program.

Designing Practice Spaces to Accommodate Golfers With Disabilities

As discussed in chapter 2, practice facilities associated with a golf course and stand-alone learning centers and practice facilities are all covered by the U.S. Access Board guidelines. There must be an accessible route or golf car passage that connects accessible practice stations with accessible parking spaces. Refer to chapter 2 for specific requirements regarding practice facilities.

For golf course proprietors who would like to cater to golfers with disabilities, other measures can be taken to make the practice area more accessible, including the following:

- Designing practice putting greens to be easily accessible by golfers who use single-rider golf cars

- Designing practice chipping greens to be easily accessible by golfers who use single-rider golf cars

- Designing at least one practice bunker that is easily entered and exited by golfers using single-rider golf cars.

- Providing single-rider golf cars for use on the practice range

- Providing a static hitting chair at one of the hitting stations

- Providing automatic ball feeders and teeing devices

- Providing assistive devices that help pick up golf balls at the practice putting and chipping greens

- Having adapted clubs available for use by people with disabilities

- Providing golf instruction geared toward golfers with disabilities

- Providing guides or coaches for golfers with visual disabilities

- Making the ball dispenser accessible

Providing Psychologically Safe Learning Opportunities

Golf can be exceedingly challenging physically, mentally, and psychologically. Even tour professionals get "first-tee jitters" and hit poor shots under stressful situations. Providing psychologically safe environments and increasing the comfort level for golfers with disabilities are especially important for instructors. Some people with disabilities already have low self-esteem. Their participation in golf activities should be designed to enhance self-esteem and socialization skills rather than add to their anxiety.

Dattilo (1999) identifies four guidelines that should be considered when designing and implementing accessible golf programs: Concentrate on the person first, promote participant autonomy, engage participants in the adaptation process, and evaluate adaptations. The first three guidelines concentrate on the person first and can be very helpful to instructors as they strive to provide psychologically safe learning opportunities for golfers with disabilities.

To use a "focus on the person" model, golf instructors need to consider the unique characteristics of each participant in an accessible golf program. One key to this tactic is to individualize adaptations for each student. A cookie-cutter approach will not work for every golfer with a disability. Another strategy is to concentrate on individual abilities. Too often, golf programs ascertain what a person cannot do and focus on ways to accommodate these limitations. A more useful formula is to concentrate on the abilities of participants and make adaptations to foster these skills. When the participants' abilities become the primary focus, they will develop additional independence and the instructor will not make unnecessary adaptations that can stifle their progress. It is also important to design instruction that balances the challenge of golf activities and the ability of the student. If an activity is too easy, it often results in boredom for the student. If an activity is too complicated, the student may become frustrated. Either way, the student may not wish to continue participating in golf activities. By accurately assessing each student, a proficient golf instructor will be able to plan instruction that creates an acceptable balance between the challenge level of the activity and the ability of the student. This is important when working with all golfers, but it is critical when working with golfers with disabilities.

People with disabilities will feel better about their golf pursuits when the instructor encourages autonomy. Golf instructors need to design instruction that facilitates student independence. Modifications should be designed to decrease the need for golfers with disabilities to rely on others and increase their independence in golf activities as much as possible. Golfers with disabilities would like to play the game with as few modifications as possible, so consider the necessity of all adaptations before implementation. Most experienced golf instructors are highly skilled at making modifications to meet the needs of golfers with disabilities. Sometimes these modifications are based on general characteristics of golfers with disabilities rather than the characteristics of a specific individual. However, as mentioned, what works for some students will not necessarily work for others. For example, some golfers with physical disabilities may be flexible while others may have a limited range of motion. Another important consideration is to view each adaptation as transitional. As a golfer acquires skill and knowledge, previous modifications to the swing and game may no longer be required. Other participants may have degenerative or progressive conditions that require repeated modifications for their continued participation.

Each student has individual needs that the instruction program must address. Independence should be a chief goal of the program. However, the real key to providing psychologically safe learning opportunities is for the instruction to be student-centered and for the instructor to understand the unique abilities of each student. Instructors should create programs that are simple, successful, and fun.

Minimizing Injuries

Golf is generally viewed as a safe sport with significant health benefits. Testimonials from golfers who productively rehabilitated themselves through participation in golf are commonplace. Dr. Alistar MacKenzie, the renowned Scottish golf architect and physician, has observed that patients he once saw frequently for minor complaints were rarely back in his office once they had been introduced to golf (Milton, 2001).

However, there are some drawbacks associated with playing golf. The injury rate, 40 to 57 percent of participants, is disturbingly high (Batt, 1992; McCarroll & Gioe, 1982; McCarroll, Rettig, & Shelbourne, 1990; McNicholas, Neilsen, & Knill-Jones, 1998). Golf injuries are rarely serious, but the effects of a golf-related injury on a person who already has a disability could be devastating.

Most golf injuries occur in the back, shoulder, elbow, and hand (Batt, 1992). The golf swing is a contrived movement, taking place in about a second and supplying nearly a ton of force to a stationary golf ball (Milton, 2001). Even the slightest flaw in the swing results in extensive forces and torques that are passed on through the hands, arms, and shoulders into the back. These forces, along with the golfer's eagerness to duplicate the same movements repeatedly, lead to many golf injuries, such as tendonitis in the elbow, lower back strains, sprained wrists, and torn rotator cuffs.

Three main factors trigger golf-related injuries: overuse, improper swing technique including the use of ill-fitted equipment, and absence of a sufficient warm-up routine (Raskin & Rebecca, 1983). Taking lessons from a golf professional, using properly fitted equipment, and minimizing time spent hitting practice balls from mats placed on a cement slab help reduce these risks of injury.

When working with people with disabilities, there must always be a balance between the benefits of golf and the potential hazards that could cause an injury. For example, a person who only has the use of one arm could develop tendonitis in that arm from overuse while participating in golf if precautions are not taken. Because of their conditions, people with disabilities sometimes require unique health and safety considerations when participating in golf activities. For instance, many golfers with disabilities lack endurance and strength, particularly when first taking part in a new activity, and must be protected from overexertion.

All possible precautions should be taken to protect golfers with disabilities from injury during a golf program. Primary issues to consider include strength, balance, flexibility, fine and gross motor coordination, heart conditions, stamina, and endurance. Make sure a first aid kit, sunscreen, hats, and drinking water are available at the golf instruction site. As with any program, a risk-management plan should be in place and should be constantly evaluated. All staff and volunteers should be trained in CPR, emergency procedures,

and safety issues. During volunteer orientation, potential hazards to participants in the golf program should be addressed. It is also important that golf instructors be aware of each participant's strengths, weaknesses, and medical issues before the program begins in order to help protect them from injury.

When creating safe learning environments, it is important to consider both psychological and physical factors. When working with golfers with disabilities, it is critical to design learning methods that will enhance self-esteem rather than add to the student's level of apprehension and anxiety. Most golfers with disabilities will get maximum benefit if you emphasize having fun. As far as physical factors are concerned, it is most important that the minimization of injuries be the paramount objective. Understanding each individual's condition, abilities, and limitations will serve as a guide in this endeavor.

Chapter 8

Assessing Golfers With Disabilities

Becky has always enjoyed athletics. While enjoying athletics is not a big deal for girls in this day and age, it is a little bit surprising for Becky. Becky has hemiplegic cerebral palsy. This condition affects her ability to move the left side of her body, causing her to walk with a limp and to not use her left hand. Becky's cerebral palsy also has affected her speech. She can make sounds, but she primarily uses signs, gestures, and pictures to communicate. Becky also has mild cognitive impairment, which makes it difficult for her to read.

Yet Becky always has a smile on her face, and she has always loved to move and play. When she was in elementary school she loved to run and gallop and especially play tag. She also was on the tee-ball and soccer teams for a few years in first and second grade. In middle school, Becky enjoyed shooting baskets in her driveway with her dad, taking her dog on walks around the neighborhood with her mom, and going to the local college to watch women's basketball and soccer games. Now a high school student, Becky participates in physical education classes and continues to shoot baskets and walk at home. But Becky and her parents would like to see Becky learn some new sport skills that she can use when she becomes an adult. After some careful con-sideration and discussion with Becky's special education and physical education teachers, it was decided that golf might be a good sport for Becky to learn.

Becky's physical education teacher con-tacted a friend of his who worked at a local golf course. The plan was for a teacher assis-tant to take Becky once a week to the golf course during her physical education class and for her parents to take her on Saturdays. The goal for the first six weeks was for Becky to learn the basic swing and putting stroke and some of the rules of golf. Becky was eager to learn a new sport, and she was excited when a teacher assistant from her school drove her to the golf course for the first series of les-sons. Becky smiled when she was introduced to the golf instructor, and she tried her best to do exactly what the instructor said. But it was clear to Becky and to the instructor that Becky was not going to be able to hold the golf club in the typical way. In addition, com-municating with Becky was difficult for the instructor. He was never quite sure if Becky understood what he was telling her, and he had a hard time understanding Becky's point-ing and gesturing. Before her next lesson the golf instructor knew he needed to learn a lot more about Becky.

Golf professionals, therapists, and teachers need to know as much as possible about the individuals with disabilities they will be teaching in order to create and implement the safest and most appropriate golf program. While ongoing assessment is important, the initial assessment of each golfer is particularly important. Initial assessment allows the instructor to develop an individualized golf program and includes preparing for safety issues, determining present skill level and realistic goals for the golfer, determining the need for unique teaching strategies, and identifying necessary skill modifications and adapted equipment. The purpose of this chapter is to present an outline of the initial golf assessment for golf instructors and therapists preparing to teach golfers with disabilities. Three main themes in the assessment process will be covered:

1. Understanding the golfer's disability and abilities

2. Determining what golf skills to teach

3. Identifying how to teach the selected golf skills and include adapted equipment

Understanding the Golfer's Disability and Abilities

The first and perhaps most important step in the assessment process is learning as much as you can about the golfer's disability and abilities. Some golfers may have health issues that could lead to medical emergencies on the practice range or golf course. Some golfers may need to perform golf skills differently than others or need adapted equipment to be successful. And some golfers may need to be instructed differently than other golfers. The more information the instructor can gain before the golfer starts the program, the better the instructor will be able to individualize the program and ensure the safest and most conducive learning environment. The Golfer Medical Information Form (see page 65)

provides a checklist that can be sent home and filled out by the golfer or the golfer's parents or caregivers prior to the start of the program. The following material describes each component of this checklist.

Type of Disability

The first thing the golf instructor will want to learn about is the golfer's disability. Simply identifying that a golfer has cognitive impairments or cerebral palsy will not help the golf instructor create an appropriate program. Additionally, it is important to treat each golfer as an individual to avoid stereotypes (Owens, 1984). Nevertheless, learning about the type of disability and then reading about the general characteristics associated with that disability (see chapters 9-13) will help you anticipate safety concerns and modifications that might be necessary. For example, by learning about Down syndrome, you will know that you will most likely have to modify instruction but probably not how the skill is performed for a golfer who has Down syndrome. People with Down syndrome typically do not have any physical disabilities that would affect their ability to learn the skills of golf. However, people with Down syndrome have cognitive impairments that make it difficult for them to understand spoken and written language, so you should be prepared to slow the instruction and use more demonstrations and physical assistance. Similarly, knowing that a golfer has one arm will cue you that this golfer needs to learn how to hold the club and swing a little differently than golfers with two functioning hands and arms.

Specific Health Problems

Some golfers with disabilities will have medical issues that might affect their ability to play golf or require extra safety precautions. It is imperative that the instructor learn as much as possible about the golfer's medical condition in order to create a safe program and to be prepared for possible medical emergencies. For example, some golfers with a spinal cord injury have trouble regulating their body heat, some golfers with cognitive impairment or cerebral palsy have seizure disorders, and some golfers with muscular dystrophy have breathing problems. In addition, any golfer may have asthma, allergies, or other health problems that the instructor should be aware of. If a golfer does have a medical condition, the instructor or therapist should create an emergency plan in case the golfer suffers a medical emergency. The list of emergency procedures on this page provides some key points to consider when creating an emergency plan.

Some golfers with disabilities may not be able to perform the golf swing and other golf skills the same way as golfers without disabilities. For example, golfers who play from a wheeled device clearly need an alternative way to address the golf ball and swing the club. Similarly, some golfers with cerebral palsy will have balance problems that may require the use of a crutch, chair, or other balance aid, and golfers with limited grip strength such as those with muscular dystrophy may need a grip modification. It is important for the golf instructor to determine early on each golfer's capabilities and

Emergency Procedures

Prepare

1. Identify kinds of injuries, emergencies, and health incidents that might occur.
2. Learn emergency care for each of these incidents.
3. Create an incident surveillance system to track all incidents for a particular golfer, for the facility, or for the program.
4. Examine medical information and talk to the golfer or golfer's parents and other professionals for clues to possible medical situations for individual golfers with disabilities.

Plan

1. Create a written emergency action plan.
2. The plan should include, but not be limited to, identification of the injured person, recognition of injury or medical need, initiation of first aid, and when and how to obtain professional help.
3. Post in appropriate places detailed protocols for seeking assistance and talking with medical personnel.
4. Create the system with input from community emergency medical crews.

Learn and Rehearse

1. All instructors and employees should know their role in the emergency plan.

2. First aid, rescue, and emergency equipment should be adequate, routinely checked, and ready for use.
3. Staff members should know how to use all equipment.
4. Rehearse the plan with the staff and with the community emergency medical crews. Each of these agencies determines approximate times required to reach a facility.
5. Conduct rehearsals periodically and whenever new staff members are employed.
6. Prepare and retain records of all practices and those involved.

Follow Up

1. Follow-up procedures for seriously injured persons exist and are used.
2. Parents or guardians are notified in a uniform fashion.
3. A means of working with the media exists and is used.
4. The entire system is known by all, rehearsed often, and periodically monitored for flaws.
5. Legal counsel and insurance representatives are invited to review the entire system.

Taken, in part, from the "Emergency Action Plan," in Clement, A. (2004) *Law in Sport and Physical Activity,* pp. 227-229. Sport and Law Press, P.O. Box 625, Dania, Florida.

Questions to Determine if Golfers Need Alternative Ways to Perform Skills

1. Does the golfer have a physical disability that appears to preclude typical performance?
2. Is the golfer having extreme difficulty performing the skill using the typical form or equipment?
3. Is the golfer making little or no progress over several sessions using the typical form or equipment despite consistent instruction and many practice opportunities?
4. Does the golfer seem more comfortable and

motivated using a different pattern or equipment?
5. Will an alternative pattern or equipment still be useful (i.e., allowed) on the driving range and on the course?
6. Will the alternative pattern increase the golfer's success and enjoyment in golf?
7. Will the instructor have access to technical expertise to design, construct, adjust, and repair the adapted equipment?

potential to play golf and whether or not the golfer will need an alternative way to perform various skills. The list of questions at the top of this page can be used to guide the decision process regarding the need for an alternative way to perform golf skills and the need for adapted equipment.

Medications

The golf instructor should find out as much as possible about each golfer's medications they may be taking before the golf program is started. Again, the Golfer Medical Information Form (page 65) provides a place for such information to be documented by the golfer or the golfer's parents or guardian.

Determining What Skills to Teach

With basic background information collected, the next step in the assessment process is to determine what specific skills to teach a particular golfer. Decisions regarding what specific skills and concepts to teach will be based on the golfer's motivation to take up golf, the golfer's previous experience with golf, realistic expectations for the golfer, and assessment of the golf skills selected. Each of these components will be discussed in the following sections.

Motivation

Why has the golfer decided to take up the game? Golfers with disabilities who have chosen on their own to learn the game will most likely be more motivated to try harder, focus on instruction, and practice on their own. On the other hand, golfers who have had golf chosen for them by a caregiver or therapist might be less motivated to learn the skills and attend to instruction (Owens, 1984). Simply asking the golfers at the beginning of the program why they have taken up golf will provide some insight as to each golfer's motivation.

Similarly, golfers with disabilities may have specific goals in mind. Some may just want the exercise of going to the range and hitting balls or walking the course without particular concern about skill level. Others may want to become skilled and knowledgeable enough so they can play recreationally with their friends. And still others may want to get to a level where they can compete in events designed for golfers with disabilities or in events open to all golfers. The important thing is to ask all golfers what their ultimate goal is. Knowing each golfer's goals will help determine what skills to teach (e.g., just hitting a 5-iron off the tee at the range versus using all the clubs) as well as the depth of knowledge each golfer will need (e.g., basic etiquette versus detailed rules and strategies). The golf instructor must understand each golfer's motivation and goals in order to make the program successful and enjoyable (Owens, 1984).

Previous Experience

As is the case with other golfers, golfers with disabilities who have previous golf experience will be at a different level both mentally and physically than novice golfers. As part of the preassessment process, ask golfers to share their previous golf experience. This will be particularly important for golfers who have acquired their disability later in life (Owens, 1984). For example, a person may have been an avid golfer for years before gradually losing his vision to macular degeneration. This golfer already knows the rules, etiquette, and strategies of golf, and he already knows the golf swing and which clubs to use in various situations. What this golfer needs is to learn how to play golf without vision. Similarly, a skilled golfer may have an acquired spinal cord injury due to a car accident and now must learn how to play golf from a wheeled device. In both cases, these golfers have an established history and love of the game, and the instructor's job is to get them back into the game with a modified swing, adapted equipment, or extra assistance.

One note of caution—golfers who played the game without disabilities and now have to play it differently may become easily frustrated with their limitations. For example, it is simply impossible to generate the same clubhead speed when swinging from a single-rider golf car, so the former "big hitter" might be frustrated with a 150-yard (137-meter) drive. In such cases part of your job as an instructor is to counsel the golfer and offer advice such as changing to a finesse game that focuses more on the short game.

Realistic Expectations

Many golfers with disabilities will be able to learn all the skills, rules, and strategies of golf. However, some individuals with disabilities, particularly those with cognitive disabilities such as mental retardation and autism, will take longer to learn and master even a few golf skills. Therefore, an important part of the assessment process is to make a realistic appraisal of which golf skills you should focus on for each golfer. Early in the process, make an educated guess based on general observations of the golfer along with feedback from the golfer and the golfer's parents or caregivers. For example, you may be introduced to two teenage golfers, a novice golfer with autism, and an experienced golfer with a leg amputation (she played for many years and was a 15 handicapper before her accident). Based on discussion with both golfers and with each golfers' parents, you make an educated guess that you will focus on the basic golf swing with the novice golfer (teach the golfer to hit a ball off a tee consistently with a 5-iron), while your focus with the experienced golfer will be to prepare her for competition in a local golf league (teach all the basic golf skills and strategies).

The individual's particular abilities or disabilities are not the focus at this point in the assessment process. Only after specific activities and skills are defined do you begin to ask how well the individual can perform the skills and what modifications are needed for the individual to be successful. Also, you may add to or subtract from the program plan as you learn more about the golfer. For example, the golfer with autism may learn how to hit a ball off a tee much more quickly than you thought, so you might decide to add hitting with a driver and putting to the program. On the other hand, the golfer with an amputation may have trouble learning how to hit a driver, so you might scale back the program to just hitting irons off the tee.

Assessing Golf-Related Skills and Abilities

At this point the golf instructor has a reference of what to teach a particular golfer. That is, rather than assessing all aspects of golf for the golfer with autism, you know that you only have to assess the golfer's ability to hit a ball off a tee. There is no need to assess other golf skills such as putting and chipping since at this point in the program these skills are not part of his individual golf program. This skill can be measured in two ways: how well the person performs the skill (qualitative assessment of the pattern the individual uses; see Qualitative Assessment: Addressing the Ball With 5-Iron and Qualitative Assessment: Golf Swing With 5-Iron on page 67), and how much of the skill the person can do (quantitative assessment such as how far the ball travels, how often the ball goes up in the air, and how many times the person actually hits the ball; see Quantitative Assessment: Hitting a Ball on page 68). The qualitative assessment is particularly important because it breaks the skill into components. By using this qualitative breakdown as an assessment tool, the golf instructor will know exactly what to teach the golfer. Note that the instructor or therapist will need to create unique qualitative assessments for golfers who use an alternative swing such as golfers who play from a wheelchair.

In addition to the golf swing, it is important to measure other factors necessary for a skilled swing and the ability to play the game such as physical fitness, general motor abilities, and perceptual skills. However, these factors are measured only as they relate to the golf swing. For example, cardiovascular endurance is usually measured by having an individual run or walk a certain distance for time. While this measure may be useful to determine overall cardiovascular integrity, it does not indicate if the person has adequate cardiovascular endurance to hit a ball off a tee or walk 9 or 18 holes of a golf course. A better measure of cardiovascular endurance for our golfer with autism is his ability to hit a bucket of golf balls without stopping and without getting overly tired. If he needs to stop and rest after just a few swings, then he is functionally deficient in cardiovascular endurance as it relates to hitting golf balls off a tee at the range (see Assessing Physical Fitness Skills Related to Golf on page 69 for a sample functional fitness assessment form for golf).

Determining How to Teach Skills

The instructor now has a better understanding of the golfer's background and interests, goals, and basic level of ability. The next step in the assessment process is to determine unique characteristics of the golfer that might require unique instruction. Two aspects of unique instruction need to be considered: how to present information to the golfer and modifications that might be necessary to accommodate the golfer's disability.

Instructional Modifications

Many golfers with disabilities will need instruction modified to meet their needs. For example, Deaf golfers will not be able to pick up auditory cues, while golfers who are blind will not be able to pick up visual cues. Golfers with cognitive impairment will need simpler language, and golfers with autism often do best with demonstrations and pictures to copy. The point is to determine how you will present golf instructions and important concepts to your golfers with disabilities. The Checklist to Determine Instructional Modifications to Accommodate Golfers With Disabilities (see page 70) will guide you in implementing instructional modifications. Factors to consider include teaching style, class format, levels of motivation, and how to present information. For example, you will want to determine if a golfer understands and prefers verbal cues (telling the golfer what to do), visual cues (demonstrations), or physical assistance (physically guiding the golfer). Some golfers with autism do not like to be touched, for example, so it is important to determine the best way to work with each golfer. This checklist should be viewed as a tool for determining general guidelines for instructional modifications. Not all golfers with disabilities can be taught in the same way, and instructors have to be able to use a variety of instructional techniques.

Perhaps the most important idea of instructional modification is to develop an appropriate interactional or psychological approach to teaching. All new golfers but especially golfers with disabilities need constant encouragement, praise, and feedback. Teaching golfers with disabilities the principles of self-efficacy is critical, maybe even more so than teaching the proper mechanics of the swing. People with disabilities tend to respond better to the person-centered approach to feedback. For example, "You hit a good shot" or "You are making good progress" would be more effective than breaking down faults in their swing. Building self-confidence from the beginning is important when working with golfers with disabilities.

Skill Modifications

For some individuals, changing instruction or even breaking a skill into smaller components may not be enough. For example, people with physical disabilities such as spinal cord injuries or cerebral palsy may not be able to perform skills the way people without physical disabilities do. Forcing them to perform the skill the way others do can lead to frustration and maybe even dropping out of the program. In such cases the individuals should be given an alternative way to perform the skill that meets their unique abilities. Again, this decision should be driven by assessment data. As discussed earlier in this chapter, Questions to Determine if Golfers Need Alternative Ways to Perform Skills (page 60) can help guide this decision. Generally speaking, if an alternative way to play golf makes the golfer more successful and the entire experience more enjoyable, then the alternative pattern should be used. However, caution should be taken when deciding if an alternative pattern should be introduced. If the alternative pattern does not give the individual any advantage and even creates a disadvantage versus the regular pattern, then it may not be appropriate.

Modifying Rules and Using Adapted Equipment

In addition to alternative ways to play the game, simple modifications to the rules or the use of adapted equipment can make golf-ers with disabilities more successful. These modifications can be used to accommodate golfers with disabilities who have problems such as limited strength, limited endurance, or limited coordination. For example, golfers with limited strength such as some golfers with cognitive impairments or certain types of physical disabilities can use a lighter, shorter golf club with a built-up grip. In addition, they can play from the forward tees when playing with friends. They might even determine it is best for them to tee off from somewhere down the fairway. Similarly, golfers with limited endurance can hit 10 balls on the range and then take a two-minute rest, or they can play every other hole when playing with a friend or sit on the ground while waiting their turn to play. The Checklist to Determine Adaptations for Golfers With Specific Limitations (see page 71) is a simple assessment tool that can be used to help determine what rule and equipment modifications might be useful for individual golfers with disabilities.

As noted earlier, golfers with disabilities should be given every opportunity to learn skills without modifications or special equipment because such adaptations can be costly and difficult to transport, and they could heighten the difference between golfers with and golfers without disabilities. However, if a golfer is having difficulty with a particular skill or aspect of the game, then rule modifications and adapted equipment should certainly be considered. Also note that you can use some rule modifications and adapted equipment temporarily to motivate or assist an individual in learning a particular skill. If modifications or equipment are to be used temporarily, develop a plan to quickly and easily wean the individual away from these adaptations. For example, a golfer who is recovering from a stroke may need to swing a lighter, shorter club from a wheelchair until she regains some of her lost strength and balance. As the golfer begins to recover her previous abilities, these modifications can be slowly removed.

Understanding as much as possible about the golfer with disabilities is critical if the golf instructor or therapist is going to provide a safe and successful program that is enjoyable and motivating for the golfer. No two golfers with disabilities are alike, so it is important to assess each person in order to create an individualized, appropriate program. From a safety standpoint it is imperative that the instructor learn about the nature of the golfer's disability, including any medical conditions that may require an emergency plan. It also is important to understand the golfer's motivation to take up the sport in the first place, the golfer's previous experience with the sport, and what the golfer can realistically learn. Finally, it is necessary to understand what skills particular golfers should learn, which golfers might need alternative ways to perform skills, and when rule modifications and adapted equipment might be needed. The purpose of this chapter was to provide an outline for assessing golfers with disabilities as well as to present easy-to-use assessment tools that can be used as a starting point. The information in this chapter is just a start—the golf instructor and therapist should use their unique skills and knowledge to assess each golfer with disabilities in order to create the best golf program possible.

Golfer Medical Information Form

I. General Information (to be filled out by golfer or parent or guardian)

Name: _____ Date of birth: _____

Parent or guardian:_____ Telephone: _____

II. Medical Information (to be filled out by golfer, parent or guardian, or doctor)

Part A: Type of disability

1. What type of disability or disabilities does the golfer have?

    _____

    _____

2. Please describe in more detail the characteristics of the golfer's disabilities.

    _____

    _____

3. Is there anything I should be aware of as it relates to golf?

    _____

    _____

Part B: Specific health problems (if the golfer does not have any health problems, skip to part C)

Asthma _____ yes _____ no

   1. If yes, does the golfer use an inhaler? _____ yes _____ no

   2. If yes, will the golfer bring the inhaler to golf? _____ yes _____ no

Bee-sting allergies _____ yes _____ no

   1. If yes, does the golfer have a bee-sting kit? _____ yes _____ no

   2. If yes, will the golfer bring the kit to golf? _____ yes _____ no

Diabetes _____ yes _____ no

   1. If yes, does the golfer take insulin? _____ yes _____ no

   2. If yes, will the golfer bring insulin to golf? _____ yes _____ no

From *Accessible Golf: Making It a Game Fore All* by LPGA, 2006, Champaign, IL: Human Kinetics. Adapted, by permission, from M.E. Block, 2000, *A teacher's guide to including students with disabilities in general physical education,* 2nd ed. (Baltimore, MD: Paul H. Brookes Publishing Co., Inc.), 293-295.

(continued)

Heart problems _____ yes _____ no

  1. If yes, please explain in more detail.

  _____

  _____

  Are there any other health problems, limitations, or allergies I should be aware of?

  _____

  _____

Part C: Medications

  1. Does the golfer take any medications? _____ yes _____ no

  2. If yes, what is the name of the medication, and what is it used for?

  _____

  _____

  3. When is it administered? _____

  _____

  4. Does it have any effects on physical or motor performance (please explain)?

  _____

  _____

  5. Are there any specific concerns regarding medications that I should be aware of?

  _____

  _____

Your name: _____ Relationship to golfer: _____

Date: _____ Daytime phone: _____

From *Accessible Golf: Making It a Game Fore All* by LPGA, 2006, Champaign, IL: Human Kinetics. Adapted, by permission, from M.E. Block, 2000, *A teacher's guide to including students with disabilities in general physical education,* 2nd ed. (Baltimore, MD: Paul H. Brookes Publishing Co., Inc.), 293-295.

Qualitative Assessment: Addressing the Ball With 5-Iron

_____ Grips club appropriately.

_____ Stands facing ball with feet shoulder-width apart.

_____ Slightly bends legs.

_____ Keeps arms straight with right arm slightly bent.

_____ Places head of club behind ball.

Qualitative Assessment: Golf Swing With 5-Iron

_____ Addresses ball appropriately (see previous list); always keeps eye on ball.

_____ Draws club back with shoulder movement.

_____ Keeping left arm straight, slowly twists body as club is brought back.

_____ Bends right arm so elbow of right arm is close to body.

_____ Stops at comfortable point in backswing and then begins to untwist and swing down.

_____ Contacts ball with arms fairly straight.

_____ Continues swing motion, twisting and wrapping club around the body.

From _Accessible Golf: Making It a Game Fore All_ by LPGA, 2006, Champaign, IL: Human Kinetics.

Quantitative Assessment: Hitting a Ball

How many times does golfer contact ball with 5-iron hit off a tee?

____/10 ____/10 ____/10 ____/10 ____/10 ____/10 ____/10 ____/10 ____/10 ____/10

How far does ball travel with 5-iron hit off a tee?

_____ yards/meters   _____ yards/meters   _____ yards/meters

_____ yards/meters   _____ yards/meters   _____ yards/meters

How many times does ball get up in air with 5-iron off a tee?

____/10 ____/10 ____/10 ____/10 ____/10 ____/10 ____/10 ____/10 ____/10 ____/10

From *Accessible Golf: Making It a Game Fore All* by LPGA, 2006, Champaign, IL: Human Kinetics.

Assessing Physical Fitness Skills Related to Golf

Cardiovascular Endurance

_____ Tires almost immediately after hitting only a few balls at the range.

_____ Hits golf balls at range without stopping for (circle one).

3 minutes   5 minutes   10 minutes   15 minutes

_____ Walks or plays how many holes on the golf course before needing to rest (circle one)?

1   2   3   4   5   6   7   8   9

Strength

_____ Cannot grip club without assistance or an assistive device.

_____ Has enough strength to hold club with very short swing.

_____ Has enough strength to hit ball off a tee with 5-iron (circle estimated distance):

10 yards (9 meters)   20 yards (18 meters)   30 yards (27 meters)

40 yards (37 meters)   50 yards (46 meters)   75 yards (69 meters)

Flexibility

_____ Does not have flexibility to twist at all when swinging club.

_____ Can slightly twist when swinging club.

_____ Has moderate ability to twist when swinging club.

_____ Has full range of motion available to swing club.

Balance

_____ Needs support from an adult to sit or stand and swing club.

_____ Can sit or stand with a balance device and swing club.

_____ Can independently sit or stand and swing club.

From _Accessible Golf: Making It a Game Fore All_ by LPGA, 2006, Champaign, IL: Human Kinetics.

Checklist to Determine Instructional Modifications to Accommodate Golfers With Disabilities

Golfer's name: _____

Golf instructor's name: _____

Instructional component	Suggestions (circle most appropriate—you can circle more than one)
Teaching style	Command (direct), problem solving (leading questions), exploration (let golfer figure it out on own)
Group size	1-on-1, 2-5 in group, 6-10 in group, 10 or more in group
Class format	Instruct everyone together, pair golfers with partners, have stations where 3-4 golfers rotate
Methodology level	Verbal cues, pictures, demonstrations, physical prompting, physical assistance
Starting and stopping signals	Whistles, hand signals, physical assistance
Time of day	Early a.m., late a.m., early p.m., late p.m.
Duration of instruction	How long individual will listen to instruction (1 minute, 2 minutes, 3 minutes, 4 minutes or more)
Duration of expected participation	How long individual will stay on task (1 minute, 2 minutes, 3 minutes, 4 minutes or more)
Distractors	Does golfer have problems dealing with new people, extra equipment, noises?
Structure	Set organization of instruction each day, have written or picture schedule
Level of difficulty	Keep instructions simple, limit number of verbal cues, do not give multiple cues at one time
Level of motivation	Needs extra motivation such as verbal praise, high-fives, stickers, drinks, money

From *Accessible Golf: Making It a Game Fore All* by LPGA, 2006, Champaign, IL: Human Kinetics. Adapted, by permission, from M.E. Block, 2000, *A teacher's guide to including students with disabilities in general physical education,* 2nd ed. (Baltimore, MD: Paul H. Brookes Publishing Co., Inc.), 136.

Checklist to Determine Adaptations
for Golfers With Specific Limitations

Does the Individual Have Limited Strength?

Selected modifications (if any) and comments:

Shorten distance to hit ball _____

Use lighter equipment (e.g., balls, clubs) _____

Use shorter clubs _____

Allow individual to sit down _____

Does the Individual Have Limited Endurance?

Selected modifications (if any) and comments:

Shorten distance golfer has to walk _____

Allow golfer to ride in golf car _____

Decrease practice time _____

Allow more rest periods (play every other hole) _____

Allow player to sit while waiting turn _____

Does the Individual Have Limited Balance?

Selected modifications (if any) and comments:

Provide chair to lean against _____

Teach balance techniques (widen base) _____

Use carpet square on slick surfaces _____

Allow individual to sit during activity _____

Does the Individual Have Limited Coordination?

Selected modifications (if any) and comments:

Use larger ball or club with larger head _____

Shorten backswing _____

Make targets larger _____

From *Accessible Golf: Making It a Game Fore All* by LPGA, 2006, Champaign, IL: Human Kinetics. Adapted, by permission, from M.E. Block, 2000, *A teacher's guide to including students with disabilities in general physical education,* 2nd ed. (Baltimore, MD: Paul H. Brookes Publishing Co., Inc.), 141-142.

Part III

Understanding the Needs of Golfers With Disabilities

Chapter 9

Cognitive Impairments

Jeremy loves to play golf. He would play every day if he didn't have to go to school and do homework at night. But you can bet that Jeremy and his father are out on the golf course every weekend, and often they sneak out once or twice a week to hit a bucket of balls. It certainly helps that Jeremy's father loves golf as much as Jeremy, and it also helps that Jeremy and his parents live in a house backing up to the eighth tee at the North River Golf and Country Club. Jeremy's family moved to the house at North River before Jeremy was born, and Jeremy's father would tell his friends he couldn't wait until he had some children to share his love for golf. It wasn't long before Jeremy was born, and he received his first golf hat from his father right after he was born.

But the doctors immediately noticed that Jeremy had some unique features that indicated he might have Down syndrome, a genetic disorder that causes cognitive impairment. It did not take long for a blood test to verify what the doctors suspected: Jeremy had Down syndrome. Not surprisingly, Jeremy's father was devastated, and he thought his dream of playing golf with his son was over. As Jeremy grew, his father played a lot of games with Jeremy, but never golf. The idea that his son would never learn the game that brought him so much joy was overwhelming for Jeremy's father.

Then one summer when Jeremy was 10 years old, his mother signed him up for a golf camp at the club. She also signed him up for private

lessons with the club's teaching professional. Jeremy's father didn't know about the camp or the private lessons, and Jeremy's mother was careful to keep it a secret from Jeremy's father. Then, at the end of the summer she told Jeremy's father that Jeremy had a surprise for him. Jeremy took his father out to the backyard, took a plastic golf ball, picked up a junior 5-iron from the set his mother had bought him, addressed the ball just as he had been taught, and took a swing. It was not a perfect swing by any means, but it wasn't bad, either, and Jeremy managed to get the ball up in the air a

(continued)

(continued)

little. Jeremy looked at his father, said, "Wait, I can do better," and proceeded to hit another ball. This second effort was about the same as the first, prompting Jeremy again to say, "Wait, I can do better." This time his father stopped Jeremy before he could get another ball out of the bucket. Jeremy's father, noticeably moved, smiled and noted how well Jeremy was doing. He then gave a quick pointer to correct a slight flaw he saw in Jeremy's arm position. Jeremy listened intently and tried his best to make the changes his father suggested. While the ball flight was no better than his first two efforts, Jeremy's swing was a little better.

Jeremy and his father spent the next hour hitting plastic golf balls, analyzing each other's swing, laughing, and talking golf. The next day Jeremy and his father went to the practice range to practice with some real golf balls. They also went to the practice green to practice putting. They both joked about each other's putting game, and they even had a little putting contest before they finished for the day. From that day on, Jeremy and his father were regulars at the practice range and putting green, and it was not long before Jeremy and his father were out on the golf course. They played just a few holes at first, gradually building up to 9 and then 18 holes. Jeremy slowly got better, still a long way from his father's level, but good enough to keep the ball and play and have fun. Now Jeremy and his father are well known at the club, often entering father–son tournaments. Despite his cognitive impairment, Jeremy turned out to be the golfing partner and son of his father's dream.

Approximately 2.5 percent or 2 or 3 out of 100 people in the United States have cognitive impairment (The Arc, 1998). For many parents, cognitive impairment can be a devastating diagnosis. Learning is often slower and academic achievement is less than that of children without cognitive impairment. However, with proper education and support, the vast majority of children with cognitive impairment can learn and grow into adults who can live and work independently and have productive, happy lives. The purpose of this chapter is to introduce cognitive impairment. The chapter begins with a simple definition of cognitive impairment along with common causes and types. This is followed by two common classification systems used to distinguish between different levels of cognitive impairment. The chapter concludes with teaching strategies for golf teachers when working with individuals with cognitive impairment.

Cognitive Impairment

The American Association for Mental Retardation (AAMR) has created the following authoritative definition of cognitive impairment:

Cognitive impairment refers to substantial limitations in present functioning. It is characterized by significantly subaverage intellectual functioning, existing concurrently with related limitations in two or more of the following applicable adaptive skill areas: communication, self-care, home living, social skills, community use, self-direction, health and safety, functional academics, leisure, and work. Cognitive impairment manifests before age 18 (Luckasson et al., 1992).

There are two main criteria to the definition. In practical terms, people with cognitive impairment have difficulty with academic skills such as reading, writing, arithmetic, memory, and attention as well as dealing with abstracts and problem solving. Some individuals with cognitive impairment may do fairly well with academics, developing academic skills equal to the fourth- or fifth-grade level, while others never develop even the most rudimentary abilities to read and write.

The first criterion, adaptive behavior, refers to "how effectively individuals cope with common life demands and how well they meet the standards of personal independence expected of someone in their particular age group, sociocultural background, and community setting" (APA, 1994). The AAMR feels that a deficit in intellectual functioning alone is not enough for a diagnosis of cognitive impairment. After all, how well a person actually functions in daily life is just as important as a score on an IQ test. However, the vast majority of people with a significantly low IQ have related deficits in adaptive behavior, whether it involves appropriate social skills with peers, communication skills, or being able to live and work independently. For example, a person with cognitive impairment might be able to live relatively independently but still need occasional support with budgeting, cleaning, cooking, and getting up on time. Note that adaptive skills can be taught and general adaptive behavior improved much more readily than general cognitive functioning (IQ scores tend to be fairly stable over time). Thus, many people with cognitive impairment can learn to lead relatively independent lives even though they may continue to have cognitive deficits in areas such as reading, math, abstract thought, and problem solving.

The second criterion has to do with the age of onset. For a person to have the diagnosis of cognitive impairment, the damage to the brain must occur before the 18th birthday. Otherwise, the person would receive another label such as traumatic brain injury. For example, a 30-year-old who was in a motorcycle accident and received a severe blow to his head may exhibit behaviors similar to a person with cognitive impairment (i.e., cognitive and adaptive behavior deficits). However, this person would be labeled as an individual with a traumatic brain injury (TBI) rather than an individual with cognitive impairment. In fact, most doctors and schools use the term *TBI* rather than the term *cognitive impairment* for children who were developing normally but who experienced some type of head trauma that resulted in cognitive and adaptive behavior deficits.

Causes of Cognitive Impairment

Cognitive impairment is the direct result of damage to the brain before birth, during the birth process, or sometime after birth into childhood. There are hundreds of known causes of cognitive impairment (see Luckasson et al., 1992, for a comprehensive list). The most common causes during pregnancy include genetic abnormalities (e.g., Down syndrome, fragile X syndrome), inadvertent exposure to toxins that affect fetal development (e.g., an expectant mother being exposed to radiation or contracting rubella), and purposeful exposure to substances that affect fetal development (e.g., expectant mothers who drink alcohol or take drugs). Problems at birth are often related to the baby not getting enough oxygen during the birth process (e.g., the umbilical cord accidentally getting wrapped around the baby's neck). In addition, premature births are related to an increased incidence in cognitive impairment. Finally, health problems (e.g., meningitis or a very high fever), accidents (e.g., a fall from a high place or a severe blow to the head), and severe environmental deprivation (e.g., severe malnutrition or extreme lack of stimulation) are causes of cognitive impairment during infancy and childhood (NICHCY, 2002). The exact cause of cognitive impairment is unknown in more than one-third of cases. This is particularly true in children and adults with more mild forms of cognitive impairment.

Classification of Cognitive Impairment

There are two major classification systems used to determine different levels of cognitive impairment. A system that was popular in the 1970s and 1980s used IQ as the key distinguishing factor (see table 9.1). Generally speaking, a person with mild cognitive impairment (the school term used to be *educable mentally retarded*) would be able to learn to a fourth- or fifth-grade level (read and do basic math) and work, live, and play relatively independently. A person with moderate cognitive impairment (the school term used to be *trainable mentally retarded*) would be able to learn to about a kindergarten or first-grade level and develop basic self-care and social skills but likely would not be able to read more than a few sight words (Turnbull et al., 2002). Finally, a person with severe or profound cognitive

Table 9.1   Classification of Mental Retardation by Level of Intellectual Functioning

Level of mental retardation	Approximate IQ
Mild	50-55 to approximately 70
Moderate	35-40 to 50-55
Severe	20-25 to 35-40
Profound	Below 20-25

Reprinted with permission from the *Diagnostic and Statistical Manual of Mental Disorders,* Copyright 2000, American Psychiatric Association.

impairment would be able to develop some basic self-care skills but would most likely need assistance for typical daily living skills such as preparing meals, getting dressed, and basic grooming. Individuals at this level most likely would have limited speech and would be unable to recognize the meaning of letters or numbers. The American Psychological Association (APA) (1994) still uses this classification system, and many school systems continue to identify and place students in classes based on this system. Thus, it would not be surprising to see a group of children from the "moderate and severe or profound" or "functional skills" class going on a trip to the local public practice facility to learn how to hit a bucket of golf balls as part of their leisure training.

Unfortunately, labeling children as having mild, moderate, severe, or profound cognitive impairment often leads to stereotypical expectations and special placements in classes (and in some cases special schools) with other children with mild, moderate, severe, or profound cognitive impairment (Turnbull et al., 2002). For example, a teacher might not try to teach reading to a child who was labeled with moderate cognitive impairments since the expectations are that these children will never be able to learn to read. Similarly, a teacher might not try to teach children who are labeled with severe cognitive impairments how to work, how to take care of themselves, or how to learn basic recreation skills (e.g., hitting a bucket of balls at the range) since the expectation for a person with this level of cognitive impairment

is total assistance. The reality is that IQ may not be a fully reliable indicator of what an individual with cognitive impairment can or cannot accomplish. In addition, placement in self-contained classes limits opportunities for children with cognitive impairment to interact with peers without disabilities and be a true member of the school.

In an effort to correct problems associated with the original classification system, the AAMR created a new classification system focusing on the amount of support a person needs to lead a productive life in school and in the community (Luckasson et al., 1992) (see AAMR's Intensities of Supports). The key to this system is the examination of different settings (e.g., work, home, community, play), what is required in each setting, and what support a person needs to be successful in each setting. No one is necessarily excluded from any setting or activity within a setting because he or she happens to have a label of cognitive impairment. For example, all people with cognitive impairment would be able to play golf, but the level of support and modifications needed would vary. One person with cognitive impairment might need intermittent support including golf lessons and someone to teach the basic golf rules and etiquette. Another person might need more extensive support including help getting to the golf course, checking in at the clubhouse, locating the first tee, determining which club to use, finding his ball, finding the next hole, keeping score, and using appropriate behavior and etiquette. This help could be provided by a friend who is the person's golf partner once a week.

Common Characteristics

It should be clear from the classification systems just outlined that identifying common characteristics for people with cognitive impairment can be difficult. Clearly people with mild cognitive impairment or who need intermittent support will have different cognitive, social, and physical characteristics than people with severe cognitive impairment or who need extensive support. Furthermore,

AAMR's Intensities of Supports

Intermittent

Intermittent supports are given on an as-needed basis and are episodic in nature, meaning people don't always need the supports or the supports are short term, such as during life transitions (e.g., job loss or acute medical crisis). Intermittent supports may be high or low in intensity. For example, a person starting a new job might need high intensity intermittent support to adjust to the new setting, learn the bus route to get to work, and learn the job basics. A person at this level can live and work independently in the community with more intermittent visits and support from a counselor.

Limited

Limited supports are consistent over time, time-limited but not intermittent, and may require fewer staff members and less cost than more intense levels of support. Examples include time-limited employment training and transitional support during the school-to-adult provided period. For instance, a person may need limited support to develop some independent job or living skills. Once these skills have been developed, occasional checking up on the person would be needed to make sure the person is maintaining the skills. A person at this level could live in a supervised apartment with regular weekly visits by an independent living counselor.

Extensive

Extensive supports require regular involvement (e.g., daily) in at least some environments (e.g., work or home) and are not time-limited (e.g., long-term support and long-term home living support). For example, a person might need to live in a group home and need regular supervision for safety and to function. The person could participate in cooking and cleaning at the group home, but direct, ongoing support is needed.

Pervasive

Pervasive supports are constant, high in intensity, provided across environments, and may be life sustaining in nature. Pervasive supports typically involve more staff members and intrusiveness than do extensive and time-limited supports. For example, a person at this level would need support for dressing, feeding, and other activities of daily living on an ongoing basis.

Adapted, by permission, from R. Luckasson, D.L. Coulter, E.A. Pollaway, S. Reiss, R.L. Schalock, M.E. Snell, D.M. Spitalnik, and J.A. Stark, 1992, *Mental retardation: Definition, classification, and systems of supports* (Washington, D.C.: American Association on Mental Retardation), 26.

---

people within a single category, such as people with mild cognitive impairment, may differ greatly from one another. The degree to which a particular characteristic is visible and causes problems for a person with cognitive impairment will vary based on IQ, complexity of the situation, quality of training, assistance provided in the situation, and support of family members, friends, and the community. Nevertheless, there are some common characteristics of people with cognitive impairment that golf instructors and course attendants should consider.

Cognitive Characteristics

People with cognitive impairment can learn, but learning is going to be slower compared to people without cognitive impairment. Learning usually follows the same sequence as it does for people without cognitive impairment, it just takes longer to process information, make sense of what is being taught, remember what was learned, and generalize the information to a variety of settings. In addition, people with cognitive impairment often have trouble maintaining their attention as well as attending to relevant aspects of the task (Auxter, Pyfer, & Huettig, 2001). For example, trying to teach people with cognitive impairment something as simple as the correct grip and stance may take several lessons because they may have trouble focusing on key aspects of the grip and understanding exactly what they are supposed to do. In addition, when you leave to work with another person, they may lose their attention and focus on the shape of the clubhead rather than practicing the grip as you requested. Even when they seem to have learned the grip and stance, they may have forgotten by the next lesson.

Problem solving and dealing with the abstract are two other areas that can be particularly difficult for people with cognitive impairment. People with cognitive impairment do best when things are laid out in simple, black-and-white terms with no exceptions. Problems arise when there are gray areas or something goes wrong. For example, on the course a person with cognitive impairment may hit the ball into the woods and then spend too much time trying to find it. You explain that you should only look for a ball for two or three minutes so as not to hold up the group behind you. On the next hole, another player in the group who does not have cognitive impairment hits his ball into the woods. This player looks for the ball when suddenly from across the fairway he hears, "It's been three minutes, stop looking and play another ball!" How long one looks for a lost ball is a judgment call and not set at a strict three-minute time limit, but this concept can be difficult for a person with cognitive impairment to grasp.

Social and Emotional Characteristics

Social and emotional skills vary widely in people with cognitive impairment. Some people may have social skills that make them indistinguishable from their peers without cognitive impairment while others may appear socially inept, overly aggressive, overly affectionate, or overly passive. Regardless of the exact nature, most people with cognitive impairment have some social and emotional problems. Social and emotional characteristics of people with cognitive impairment often determine whether or not they will be integrated into typical classes in school, a typical work setting, and typical community sport settings. Simply stated, regardless of cognitive and golf abilities, a person with cognitive impairment who has good social skills will be welcome at the local golf course whether as a golfer or as an employee. On the other hand, a person with cognitive impairment who displays poor social skills will not be welcome, regardless of cognitive and golf abilities.

Lower cognitive abilities coupled with limited adaptive skills may lead to social and emotional behavior that makes a person stand out even more (Bierne-Smith, Patton, & Ittenbach, 1994). For example, a person with cognitive impairment drops her wallet in the clubhouse while eating lunch. When it comes time to pay for the bill, the person is understandably upset that she cannot find her wallet. However, she doesn't have the problem-solving skills to ask a waiter or manager for assistance, so she proceeds to panic and get very upset, making others in the clubhouse take notice. The person's behaviors are not unlike what one might expect of a young child who loses a valued possession. In essence, the main social and emotional characteristic of people with cognitive impairment is that they tend to display behaviors that make them appear less mature than their actual age, particularly in unexpected, unfamiliar, or stressful situations.

Two other related social and emotional characteristics of people with cognitive impairment are learned helplessness and a mixed-up locus of control. Learned helplessness means the person plans to fail and thus gives up before even trying. Phrases such as "I can't do this" or "I'm not good at this" can make golf instruction and motivation difficult. Locus of control refers to how people perceive they achieved success or failure. Most people with healthy psyches view success and failure as the result of hard work and ability or the lack thereof (internal locus of control, or within their control). In contrast, people with cognitive impairment often view success as the result of luck or some external factor beyond their control (external locus of control), while failures are viewed as the result of lack of ability and effort (Bierne-Smith, Patton, & Ittenbach, 1994). As with learned helplessness, people with cognitive impairment who display an external locus of control will be more difficult to motivate and to convince they are learning and getting better.

While people with more severe cognitive impairment tend to have lower social and emotional skills, this is not always the case. For example, some people with relatively mild cognitive impairment may have poor social skills such as standing too close to a person when talking, interrupting conversations, speaking too loudly, and generally behaving inappropriately for the situation. On the other hand, some people with more severe cognitive impairment who have poor cognitive and academic skills can display appropriate social skills, fitting in quite well with their peers.

Physical and Motor Characteristics

As with cognitive and social skills, motor skills and fitness levels in people with cognitive impairment typically vary from normal levels to severe deficits. Many children with mild cognitive impairment do not have any motor or fitness delays and do quite well in general physical education classes. As adults, they participate in typical community sport programs without any accommodations. They will have motor and eye–hand coordination that allow them to learn a good golf swing and have a relatively low handicap.

However, most people with cognitive impairment will have some motor and fitness delays compared to people without cognitive impairment. Children with mild cognitive impairment tend to be one to three years behind their peers in motor and fitness development, and children with more severe cognitive impairment may have delays of three to four years or more (Sherrill, 1998). Because of limited opportunities and the ever-increasing complexity of sports, these delays tend to grow as the child reaches high school and adulthood. Some people who have mild cognitive delays may have quite noticeable motor and fitness problems, and some people with more severe cognitive impairment may have fairly good motor and fitness skills. But in general, people with more severe cognitive impairment tend to have significant motor and fitness deficits.

People with more severe cognitive impairment may have difficulty with simple locomotor skills such as running, and many will have severe deficits in ball skills such as throwing and catching. Coordination in general is often a problem in people with more severe cognitive impairment, especially eye–hand coordination. Since golf requires fairly complex, coordinated movements, it can be difficult to teach. In terms of fitness, children with more severe cognitive impairment often have very low fitness including endurance, strength, and flexibility, and there is a tendency toward obesity. A person with very low fitness may have trouble swinging a club with any force and walking the golf course.

Health Characteristics

The health of people with cognitive impairment is generally similar to the health of people without cognitive impairment. Some people with cognitive impairment will have asthma, diabetes, heart problems, obesity, and arthritis. But most people with cognitive impairment will not have any special health problems. The exceptions occur when the cause of cognitive impairment has some biological basis. For example, people with Down syndrome often have mild heart conditions such as a hole in their heart, problems with hearing and vision, very elastic ligaments, and very low muscle tone. People with fetal alcohol syndrome have heart and lung problems as well as vision and hearing problems. Some people with cognitive impairment may also have movement problems associated with cerebral palsy. The golf instructor should talk to the person with cognitive impairment and the caregiver to determine what health conditions the person might have and if accommodations are needed.

While people with cognitive impairment are not necessarily predisposed to health problems, research shows that people with cognitive impairment have more chronic health-related problems than people without cognitive impairment (McConaughy & Salzberg, 1988). Adults with cognitive impairment may not be as careful with their diet and often do not exercise or participate in community sport programs as readily as people without cognitive impairment (CDC, 1999). This results in a higher incidence of obesity in people with cognitive impairment, which in turn can lead to health trouble such as heart and lung problems, diabetes, and strokes (Rimmer, 1994).

Teaching Golf to People With Cognitive Impairment

As noted, people with cognitive impairment share some common characteristics, and the following teaching suggestions focus on ways to accommodate these characteristics. Since most people with cognitive impairment do not have any physical disabilities, the teaching suggestions address strategies to accommodate common communication, learning, and attention problems. These strategies have been adapted from Block (2000), Sherrill (1998), and Auxter, Pyfer, & Huettig (2001). You will quickly see that you probably already use some of these teaching strategies with beginning golfers and children. The key to instructing people with cognitive impairment, as is the case with all beginners as well as children, is to make your directions and instructions as clear as possible. It also is important to remember that each person with cognitive impairment is a unique individual with unique strengths and weaknesses, and therefore you will have to determine for each golfer what teaching strategies are most appropriate.

Communication

Understanding verbal directions may be difficult for some golfers with cognitive impairment, particularly those with more severe cognitive impairment. To accommodate communication problems, use the following strategies.

1. Use shorter sentences with a focus on concrete cue words that are easy for the golfer to remember. For example, saying "Swing like a pendulum" may be too abstract for a golfer with cognitive impairment to understand.

Better cue words might be "back and forth" or "up and down." Then encourage the golfer to repeat these cue words as she swings the club.

2. Directions and teaching cues may need to be repeated often to ensure understanding. Again, using simple cue words will make your instruction easier for the golfer to understand. Also, asking the golfer to repeat back to you what you just said is a good way to check for complete understanding. For example, after telling the golfer to follow through so his chest faces the target, you might then ask him to repeat the cue words "Face the target" back to you.

3. When a person with cognitive impairment is having trouble understanding verbal directions, you will need to add extra cues, demonstrations, physical prompts, and even physical assistance to make sure the person understands what to do. In fact, golfers with cognitive impairment will learn best if you give a short verbal direction or cue along with a demonstration highlighting the cue. For example, tell a golfer to bend her knees slightly when addressing the ball. Then demonstrate what a slight knee bend looks like. If the golfer still does not seem to understand what to do, provide physical assistance or use a prop (e.g., a chair with a pillow on it) to make sure the athlete fully understands what the correct knee bend should feel like. Similarly, placing foot markers on the ground (e.g., two pieces of paper or a chalk outline) can clarify the concept of standing with the feet shoulder-width apart.

4. Break skills down into smaller components and help the golfer focus on one component at a time. For example, there are many parts to addressing the golf ball. For most golfers without cognitive impairment, quick demonstrations of the grip, setup, and stance are all that are needed for the golfer to understand how to address the ball. For a golfer with cognitive impairment, each of the components of addressing the golf ball may need to be further broken down into parts. The grip, for example, might include just practicing the left hand position, then the right hand position, and then the

two combined on the shaft. Putting markings on the club can make it even clearer for the golfer to know where to place each hand, thus making the grip easier to understand.

Practice

While most golfers with cognitive impairment can eventually learn how to hold and swing a club about as well as golfers without cognitive impairment, it will take the golfer with cognitive impairment many more practice trials with much more specific feedback. Unfortunately, many golfers with cognitive impairment do not know how to use their practice time wisely, so you will have to structure practice sessions more carefully for these golfers. The following teaching suggestions focus on how to optimize practice sessions for golfers with cognitive impairment.

1. Explain exactly what to focus on when practicing, how to practice, and how many turns to take. For example, after teaching a preaddress routine to a golfer, tell her, "Use your driver to hit 10 golf balls off the tee. Make sure you go through your preaddress routine before every shot, including one practice swing. Don't forget, preaddress before each shot, including one practice swing."

2. Teach golfers how to focus on specific parts of the golf swing. For example, you cannot expect a golfer with cognitive impairment who went through a brief session on chipping in which you focused on a short backswing and follow-through to be able to go and practice a short backswing and follow-through. Chances are the golfer will practice this one or two times and then go back to a full swing or forget the focal point. To teach the person with cognitive impairment how to practice this specific aspect of chipping, repeat the cue words "Short swing" and give the player a clear task to work on, such as "Chip 10 balls using your 7-iron from the fringe where I placed a marker." Then give the person a way to focus on the key component, such as "Say 'short swing' when chipping." Finally, give the person a simple way to self-evaluate each performance, such

as "If you are doing it correctly your club should just barely go past your back foot on the back swing and just past your front foot on the follow-through like this" (be sure to demonstrate).

3. Most golfers with cognitive impairment will need to receive more feedback during practice trials than golfers without cognitive impairment to clearly understand what they are doing correctly and incorrectly. It is also important to develop a concept of self-efficacy and include lots of praise in the feedback. In one-on-one lessons this means giving feedback after every practice stroke or every other practice stroke. In group lessons, the golfer with cognitive impairment should receive about twice as much feedback compared to peers without cognitive impairment. Another strategy is to pair golfers with each other and have them give each other feedback on specific aspects of the swing after every practice trial or every other trial. Regardless of who provides feedback (you or a peer), follow the communication guidelines mentioned earlier (keep feedback simple, use cue words, and provide demonstrations and physical assistance to make sure the person understands what he is doing correctly or incorrectly).

Attention

Many individuals with cognitive impairment have short attention spans compared to people without cognitive impairment. The following are simple strategies to accommodate golfers with cognitive impairment who have trouble with attention.

1. Have more activities but conduct each activity for shorter periods of time. Golfers without cognitive impairment can usually stay with one skill such as chipping or putting for 20 minutes. However, with some golfers with cognitive impairment, you may need to have shorter bouts for each activity. For example, you can have a person with cognitive impairment practice short putting for 5 minutes, then practice chipping for 5 minutes, then mid- to long-range putting for 5 minutes, then lob wedge chipping for 5 minutes.

2. Another strategy to help the golfer with cognitive impairment stay attentive to instruction and practice is to move the practice area around. While this may add some downtime, moving from, say, the practice range to the putting green to the sand bunker area and then back to the range will help the golfer maintain interest and focus.

3. Structure the environment so the golfer knows exactly what to do. While golfers without cognitive impairment can go off and practice on their own for 15 to 20 minutes, many golfers with cognitive impairment will need more structure. Similar to the practice strategies just described, structured instructions might include setting goals (e.g., "Hit 20 balls with your 5-iron so that at least 15 go up in the air and straight at least 100 yards [91 meters]") and clarifying what to focus on (e.g., "Make sure to follow through so your chest faces the target and your club wraps around your back") will help the golfer stay more focused on the task at hand.

4. Limit distractions as much as possible. For example, when speaking to the golfers, make sure you position yourself so that you are the only person they see. When giving instruction, do not position yourself so that your golf students can also see other golfers checking in with the starter or putting on the practice green. Similarly, try to find practice places that do not have a lot of other distractions. Something as simple as going to the end of the practice range away from other golfers or finding a quiet, safe place in the woods not directly on the course to practice chipping will help golfers with cognitive impairment focus on you rather than on other things in the environment.

5. Avoid downtime as much as possible. Waiting more than a few minutes to take a turn may be acceptable for golfers without cognitive impairment because they will likely use their wait time wisely by watching their peers practice. But waiting around is more or less a waste of time for some people with cognitive impairment. To prevent wait time, spread the golfers out so there is one golfer at each station on the range and there is no wait

time. If this is not possible, have shorter waiting periods by pairing golfers up rather than having groups of four share a practice station. Also, help golfers with cognitive impairment use their wait time more wisely. For example, give them a task, such as "Watch Jamie to see if her back is to the target during her backswing."

6. Provide praise and incentives to keep the person focused on practicing golf. Praise can be as simple as giving high-fives and telling them "Good job" for doing what you asked. More tangible rewards might be necessary for some golfers with more severe cognitive impairment. For example, make a simple chart to show the schedule for the next 45 minutes. Show the chart to the golfer, and then place a mark on the chart every time the golfer completes a task, such as hitting each club in the bag five times on the range; chipping the ball from the fringe five times with a 7-iron, 8-iron, and 9-iron; and taking 10 putts from 4 feet (122 centimeters), 8 feet (244 centimeters), and 12 feet (366 centimeters). When all activities have been checked off, the golfer gets a sport drink as a reward. Be sure to personalize praise and incentives to each individual.

Environment

While golf itself can be a rewarding and reinforcing activity, some golfers with cognitive impairment will need extra excitement to make practicing and even playing the game more motivating and fun. The following are some suggestions for making the practice and game settings more stimulating.

1. People with cognitive impairment usually need to perceive they are successful when learning and playing the game more often than people without cognitive impairment. This is particularly true for new golfers, whether with or without cognitive impairment. Accordingly, you should think of ways to make the person feel more successful. Many of the ideas described previously can be used to make the golfer feel more successful. For example, reinforce the successful demonstration of a swing component rather than waiting for the

complete correct swing, define success in a variety of ways such as getting the ball up in the air or hitting it straight, and create rewards for parts of the game such as number of putts, number of fairways hit, and number of irons hit straight.

2. Think of ways to make lessons fun for golfers who may not be internally motivated to learn and play the game. For example, have minicontests such as who can hit the ball the straightest with a driver or who can sink the most putts from a certain distance away. Extra incentives can also make practicing more fun, such as having motivating targets to shoot at (e.g., a picture of a golfer's group-home counselor placed at the 100-yard marker on the range) or having relay races (e.g., divide group into two teams of three players per team. One player from each team starts from 10 feet [3 meters] away and putts a ball. The player continues until the ball goes in the hole. Then the next player on the team takes a turn, then the last player. See which team can sink three putts the fastest.).

3. As noted, extra praise and reinforcement can make practicing and playing the game more fun. For example, using the handicapping system when playing 9 holes of golf, play each hole separately rather than looking at the total score so that each player has nine chances to win rather than just one. Have contests for number of fairways hit off the tee, number of greens hit from inside 100 yards (91 meters), number of putts needed, and so on. Again, this gives everyone more chances to win and makes it more fun for everyone.

Age-Appropriate Interactions

Even though individuals with cognitive impairment might function cognitively like children, they should be treated like people without cognitive impairment of the same age. Patting a 20-year-old golfer without cognitive impairment on the head for a good shot is inappropriate; therefore, it is inappropriate to do the same to a 20-year-old golfer with cognitive impairment. The following are some basic principles regarding age-appropriate interactions.

1. While people with cognitive impairment will have trouble understanding longer sentences and complicated directions, do not belittle them by using immature or baby talk. Similarly, slowing down the tempo of speech or speaking loudly is inappropriate. However, using shorter sentences and simpler words is certainly appropriate. Repeating directions and adding demonstrations are helpful, too. Using age-appropriate communication while still making sure the person understands is somewhat of a gray area, but the key is to not use language that would stigmatize or embarrass the person.

2. Equipment should be age appropriate as well. With adult golfers, use adult equipment. For shorter adults (e.g., golfers with Down syndrome or fetal alcohol syndrome), find shorter versions of adult clubs. Similarly, golf aids used to teach parts of a skill or concepts should be the same as those used for adults without cognitive impairment. For example, in a beginning adult golf class it helps to make the ball larger so the golfers focus more on the swing than on hitting the ball. If some of the balls have cartoon characters painted on them, do not give the balls with cartoon characters only to the golfers with cognitive impairment, as this would make them look even more different than their peers.

3. Rewards should be age appropriate. Similar to equipment, avoid giving rewards that would make the golfer with cognitive impairment look different. For example, giving balloons, stuffed animals, or lollipops would not be appropriate. On the other hand, sport drinks, old golf magazines, and special golf markers, golf balls, or pins with the club's logo on them are more appropriate. Golfers with cognitive impairment may actually want age-inappropriate toys or food, but you should avoid giving them these things. Again, the idea behind age appropriateness is to help the golfer with cognitive impairment look and act like a golfer without cognitive impairment.

4. Help golfers with cognitive impairment understand what the appropriate dress is for practicing and playing golf. This usually involves a collared shirt, nice shorts, and appropriate

shoes (golf shoes, if possible, but athletic shoes can be worn as an alternative). Again, the person with cognitive impairment should look like any other golfer so as not to stand out.

5. Help golfers with cognitive impairment understand proper golf etiquette and behavior. Most people without cognitive impairment can pick up appropriate golf etiquette simply by watching other golfers. On the other hand, some people with cognitive impairment will need someone to explain appropriate golf etiquette and then help them practice etiquette in various situations. For example, simply saying "Nice shot" is more appropriate than yelling "You're the man!" or running up and giving your partner a big bear hug. Explain what is appropriate, set up situations where the golfer can practice appropriate etiquette, and then praise or correct the golfer's behavior.

Golf Programs for People With Cognitive Impairment

Special Olympics is an international organization devoted to providing year-round sport training and athletic competition in 26 Olympic-type summer and winter sports for individuals with cognitive impairment. Through sport training and competition, Special Olympics' goal is to help individuals with cognitive impairment become physically fit, active, and productive and respected members of society. Currently, every state in the United States and over 150 countries offer Special Olympics programs to a total of over 1.7 million athletes. Competition is available at the local, state, national, and international levels (Special Olympics, 2002a).

Special Olympics, which started in 1968, added golf as an official sport in 1992. Among all the Special Olympics sports, golf provides one of the greatest opportunities for people with cognitive impairment to learn, practice, and compete in a game that can be played throughout one's lifetime. In addition, the public setting of a golf course is a great venue for people with and without cognitive impairment to interact and enjoy learning and playing golf together (Special Olympics, 2002b).

Special Olympics golf is played according to the *Rules of Golf* as approved by the USGA and the Royal and Ancient Golf Club of St. Andrews (in fact, the USGA has provided financial and technical support for Special Olympics golf in the United States, and the Royal and Ancient Golf Club has endorsed Special Olympics golf and supported its growth in Europe). Modified golf competitions are also available in the form of skill contests, alternate-shot play, and 9-hole tournaments (Special Olympics, 2002c). For more information about golf or other Special Olympics programs in your area, visit the Special Olympics Web site at www.specialolympics.org.

The Special Olympics golf program is centered on two educational phases designed to encompass all skill levels: learning to swing a golf club and learning to play the game. Athletes may participate in individual skills competition, 9-hole stroke play, or 18-hole stroke play. Following are brief descriptions of those events.

Level 1: Individual Skills Competition

The purpose of the Individual Skills Competition is to allow athletes, especially those with lower skill levels, to train and compete in basic golf skills. Six different skills are tested.

1. *Short putting.* Two circles, with radii of .5 and 1.5 meters (1.6 and 5 feet), respectively, are drawn around a selected target hole. The athlete strikes five balls from 2 meters (7 feet) and scores points based on where the ball eventually stops.

2. *Long putt.* The task is identical to the short putt contest, but the athlete strikes the ball from 8 meters (26 feet) instead of 2 meters (7 feet).

3. *Chip shot.* Two circles with radii of 3 and 6 meters (10 and 20 feet), respectively, are drawn around the designated hole. A 3-by-3-meter (10-by-10-foot) hitting area 14 meters (36 feet) from the hole is selected, and the athlete makes five attempts to chip balls as close to the hole as possible. Points are awarded based on where the ball stops.

4. *Pitch shot.* This contest measures the athlete's ability to hit controlled pitch shots in the air and in the proper direction. A target area 12 meters (39 feet) in diameter is used, with a hitting area placed 10 meters (33 feet) from the target area. A barrier 1 meter (3 feet) high and 5 meters (16 feet) wide is placed at an equal distance from the hitting area and the target area. The athlete makes five attempts to chip a ball over the barrier and into the target area. Points are awarded according to where the ball lands.

5. *Iron shot.* With an iron, the athlete has five shots to hit a ball more than 90 meters (98 yards) within a 35-meter-wide (38-yard-wide) area. Four points are awarded for a shot over 90 meters (98 yards), three points for a 60- to 90-meter (66- to 98-yard) shot, two points for a 30- to 60-meter (33- to 66-yard) shot, and one point for making a stroke at and striking the ball.

6. *Wood shot.* This event is similar to the iron shot contest but with different dimensions. The athlete is given five shots to hit a ball with a wood more than 120 meters (131 yards) within a 50-meter (55-yard) boundary area. Points are awarded on distance.

Level 2: Alternate-Shot Team Play Competition

Level 2 pairs an athlete with cognitive impairment with an athlete without cognitive impairment for the purpose of transitioning from skill play to individual play. Using one ball, the players alternate strokes until the ball is holed.

Level 3: Unified Sports Team Play

In level 3, athletes with and without cognitive impairment are paired as teams. This provides Special Olympics athletes the opportunity to play in a team format with teammates without cognitive impairment but with similar golf ability.

Level 4: Individual Stroke Play Competition (9 holes)

Level 4 competitions are for players who wish to play individually in a tournament but who can only play 9 holes of golf.

Level 5: Individual Stroke Play Competition (18 holes)

Level 5 competitions are for players who wish to play individually in a tournament and can play 18 holes.

®Special Olympics, Inc. 2004-2007. Adapted with permission.

(continued)

makes it extremely difficult for her to read, especially new information in front of a group of people. She said it was not a big deal for her, but she asked the golf pro to not ask her to read out loud any more. The golf pro was stunned that such a bright, articulate high school girl could not read well out loud.

The term *specific learning disability,* or SLD, refers to a group of disabilities that affect an individual's ability to learn, which ultimately affects academic performance. These individuals have normal intelligence (some are even gifted) but nevertheless have a problem in the brain that makes learning difficult. One of the hallmarks of learning disabilities is the gap between intellectual ability and actual academic achievement. In other words, they are bright, attentive people who by all accounts should do well in school but for some reason do not; they do not have cognitive deficits such as mental retardation. In addition, these learning disabilities cannot be explained by hearing or vision problems, health or medical problems, attention deficit disorders, or behavioral disorders. See Definition of Specific Learning Disability for more details.

Specific in SLD refers to the fact that some people may have a learning disability in one specific area of learning such as reading, math, or written expression. Reading disabilities, also known as dyslexia, are the most common SLDs and the ones that most often

Definition of Specific Learning Disability (SLD)

Specific learning disability is a disorder in one or more of the basic psychological processes involved in understanding or using spoken or written language, which may manifest itself in an imperfect ability to listen, think, speak, read, write, spell, or do mathematical calculations. The following criteria are used to determine if a child has an SLD.

1. The child does not achieve commensurately with his or her age and ability levels in one or more of the areas listed in criterion 2 when provided with learning experiences appropriate for the child's age and abilities.

2. The child has a severe discrepancy between achievement and intellectual ability in one or more of the following areas:
   - Oral expression
   - Listening comprehension
   - Written expression
   - Basic reading skills
   - Reading comprehension
   - Mathematics calculation
   - Mathematics reasoning

3. A child cannot be identified as having a specific learning disability if the severe discrepancy between ability and achievement is primarily the result of
   - a visual, hearing, or motor impairment;
   - cognitive impairment;
   - emotional disturbance; or
   - environmental, cultural, or economic disadvantage.

Adapted from the *Individuals with Disabilities Education Act, Amendments of 1997* (Washington, D.C.: U.S. Government Printing Office).

Specific Types of Learning Disabilities

- **Dyslexia.** Perhaps the most commonly known SLD, dyslexia is primarily used to describe difficulty with language processing and its effect on reading, writing, and spelling. Dyslexia may affect basic reading (decoding letters and words) or reading comprehension (understanding what is read).

- **Dysgraphia.** Dysgraphia involves difficulty with writing. Also known as a graphomotor disorder, problems might be seen in the actual motor patterns used in writing as well as speed and precision in writing. Also characteristic are difficulties with spelling and formulating written composition. Difficulty in writing may be due to poor language ability, fine motor dysfunction, or poor organizational abilities. Specific learning disabilities in writing are often associated with specific learning disabilities in reading.

- **Dyscalculia.** This learning disorder involves difficulty with math skills and affects math computation as well as math reasoning. Memory of math facts, concepts of time and money, and musical concepts can also be affected.

- **Dyspraxia (apraxia).** Dyspraxia, also known as apraxia, involves difficulty with motor planning, which affects a person's ability to coordinate appropriate body movements. Children with dyspraxia appear clumsy and often have problems with balance. Another relatively new term used to describe children with dyspraxia is developmental coordination disorder.

- **Auditory discrimination.** This learning disorder involves not being able to perceive the differences between speech sounds and then sequence the sounds into meaningful words, which is a key component of efficient language use and is necessary to "break the code" for the phonetics involved in reading. A person with severe auditory discrimination problems may be unable to understand most verbal language.

- **Visual perception.** Visual perception involves the ability to notice important details and then assign meaning to what is seen. Problems may occur with figure background (differentiating objects from the background), spatial relationships (assessing varying sizes and distances), and size discrimination (differentiating between large and small objects). Visual perception is critical to the reading and writing processes.

---

result in a referral for special education. A reading disability may affect basic reading (decoding) or reading comprehension. Other common SLDs affect writing (dysgraphia) and mathematics (dyscalculia) (Shapiro, 2001). See Specific Types of Learning Disabilities for definitions of specific learning disabilities.

Shapiro, B. (2001). Specific learning disabilities. In M.L. Batshaw (Ed.), *When your child has a disability* (revised) (pp. 373-390). Baltimore: Brookes.

Causes of SLD

It is now widely known that learning disabilities are the result of a brain dysfunction. However, experts do not know precisely what causes learning disabilities. Learning disabilities are presumed to be disorders of the central nervous system, and a variety of factors may contribute to their occurrence. However, the exact cause of the brain dysfunction that leads to a learning disability is often unknown. The following are some factors that have been shown to be related to learning disabilities (NCLD, 2003; Shapiro, 2001):

- **Heredity.** Learning disabilities tend to run in families, so it appears that there is a genetic basis for some learning disabilities. It is not unusual to discover that people with learning disabilities have family members who have similar difficulties.

- **Problems during pregnancy and childbirth.** Learning disabilities may be caused by illness or injury to the mother during or before birth. Anything that affects brain development or brain functioning while the mother is pregnant or giving birth can cause learning disabilities. For example, learning disabilities may be caused by the mother's use of drugs and alcohol during pregnancy, RH incompatibility with the mother (if untreated), premature birth, prolonged labor or lack of oxygen, low weight at birth, or trauma to the head during the birth process.

• **Incidents after birth.** Nutritional deprivation, poisonous substances such as lead, head injuries such as those that occur from an accident, childhood diseases such as meningitis, loss of oxygen from something like a near-drowning incident, and child abuse can lead to specific learning disabilities.

Common Characteristics of People With SLD

The major characteristics associated with learning disabilities are the specific learning problems people face, such as difficulty reading or computing mathematics (see Specific Types of Learning Disabilities on page 91 for more details). However, research suggests that a percentage of individuals with learning disabilities have other deficits, including the following:

• **Motor problems.** Many people with learning disabilities do not have motor problems. In fact, many are gifted athletically and play on high school, college, and even professional sport teams. However, research suggests that a certain percentage of people with learning disabilities display motor problems. For example, Sherrill and Pyfer (1985) found that 13 percent of children with SLD scored two to three years below their peers of the same age on perceptual motor tests. Similarly, Miyahara (1994) found that 25 percent of his subjects with SLD were poorly coordinated or clumsy on a general motor ability test and an additional 7 percent had significant balance problems. Finally, Lazarus (1994) found that children with SLD had greater levels of overflow (an inability to keep one arm or leg still while moving the other arm or leg) compared to children without learning disabilities. These studies taken together suggest that some people with SLD who want to learn how to

play golf may have motor problems including balance and overall clumsiness that may slow down their learning.

• **Other characteristics.** Shapiro (2001) noted that as many as one-fourth to two-thirds of people with specific learning disabilities have other problems. The most common problem associated with SLD is attention-deficit/hyperactivity disorder (ADHD). ADHD is generally associated with a neurological impairment (brain dysfunction) that may or may not be related to the neurological cause of the learning disability. ADHD is usually treated with medication. (See page 94 for more details on ADHD). Some people with SLD also have emotional and behavioral problems. These problems may be due to a neurological impairment such as a chemical imbalance in the brain that leads to anxiety disorders or depression. However, in most cases emotional and behavioral problems associated with learning disabilities are due to the struggles of having a learning disability. For example, a person with dyslexia may become withdrawn or develop anxiety or depression due to continued frustration and failure in learning. Withdrawal as well as anxiety and depression may in turn lead to the child having few close friends, not participating in extracurricular activities, or becoming socially clumsy when trying to interact with peers (Shapiro, 2001). That is why it is so important to identify learning disabilities and implement a treatment program when children are young and before they begin to have problems in school.

Teaching Golf to People With SLD

Since people with learning disabilities are such a diverse group (e.g., some can't read, others can't do math, and others have trouble understanding and following directions), the first step in creating teaching methods is to find out the individual's exact learning disability (see the Golfer Medical Information Form on page 65 in chapter 8). Parents, teachers, and the individuals can provide this information. With this information you can then determine what modifications are most appropriate for a particular individual. The following are some general suggestions, modified from Auxter, Pyfer, and Huettig (2001) and Sherrill (1998), for teaching golf to people with learning disabilities.

1. For people with learning disabilities who also have attention-deficit/hyperactivity disorder, the following suggestions are important.

- Use behavior management programs (the individual's special education teacher or parents probably already have one they use) to help an individual who is impulsive, inattentive, or hyperactive.

- Use a highly structured, consistent approach. For example, have your lesson plan laid out in a clear, organized way. Briefly review the lesson plan with the individual to make sure she knows exactly what is going to happen and when it is going to happen.

- Select activities that emphasize moving slowly with control to decrease hyperactivity and impulsivity. For example, have the student practice the swing in slow motion to get a better feel for the movement and to focus on the swing.

- Teach in a quiet, less stimulating environment to decrease distractibility. If possible, have the student practice at the far end of the range where there are fewer distractions. If necessary, put up a partition (something as simple as a cardboard box) to block the person's view of others.

- Reduce class size to allow extra time to work with the person (use peers or volunteers to further reduce class size and provide extra individualized attention). For example, after presenting information on chipping, have a peer review some of the key points with the individual to make sure he fully understands what to do.

2. Use verbal mediation for individuals who are disorganized and distractible (have participants plan out loud what they will do to focus their attention; also have them repeat directions to enhance motor planning). For example, break the golf swing into four or five parts and give each part a name. Then have the golfer repeat each name of the component as she performs the swing.

3. Provide appropriate learning strategies to help disorganized learners focus on targeted components of skills. Again, break skills into easy-to-understand components and then show the components to the golfer. Also, use extra cues such as footprints or other aids to highlight key parts of a skill.

4. Teach participants how to practice correctly and how to use feedback. Many people with learning disabilities do not know how to practice. Teach them techniques such as hitting five balls with a 5-iron, then five with a 7-iron, and so on. Or, teach them to focus on one aspect of the swing for 10 swings.

5. Use a multisensory approach to teaching (e.g., verbal cues, demonstrations, physical assistance). Some people with learning disabilities may have trouble understanding verbal cues while others may have trouble with visual cues. Therefore, you should be prepared to present information in a variety of ways.

6. Help improve participants' self-esteem by praising small amounts of progress. Also, do not have them demonstrate golf skills publicly unless you know they can do it correctly, and try to avoid comparing participants to each other.

7. Review previously acquired skills before teaching more advanced skills. Be prepared to return to previously acquired skills if participants become frustrated with a new, more advanced skill. For example, the golfer has acquired the correct motion and touch for chipping, so you introduce a lob wedge. This is very difficult for this particular individual, and you can tell she is getting frustrated. Have her go back and practice the chip again to regain her confidence.

Attention-Deficit/Hyperactivity Disorder

George has always been an active boy. His parents thought that he was just being a kid when he would climb on the refrigerator, jump from couch to couch, and generally bounce around when they were trying to read or watch TV. But when George went to school, his teachers felt that his energy and activity level along with his inability to attend to instruction for more than 30 seconds was more than just being a kid. By second grade, children are expected to sit in their seats, attend to the teacher for longer periods of time, and do about 20 minutes of homework at night. At this point it became clear to George's teachers and his parents that he had some attention and hyperactivity issues. George's parents had George tested by a school psychologist and his doctor, and the results confirmed that George had attention-deficit/hyperactivity disorder (ADHD). George's doctor prescribed Ritalin, a stimulant that seems to calm and focus children with ADHD. The results were immediate and dramatic as George was able to sit and focus in class and complete his homework at night. George and his parents were thrilled, and George did very well in school for the next several years.

Now a high school senior, George continues to take his medication every day but not during the weekends when it's OK to be more active. This "weekend holiday" was never a problem until George's father decided to take up golf.

He thought it would be fun to learn the game and to have George learn with him. The first lesson was Saturday morning, and George was looking forward to learning how to play golf. The lesson started with introductions by the golf pro and the other participants in the group. Introductions lasted about five minutes, and then the golf instructor talked for several more minutes about golf, the format of the lessons, some of the perks that go along with the lessons such as reduced rates at the golf course, and some etiquette guidelines. The golf pro noticed that George paced in the back of the group, rarely looking at the golf pro. This bothered her, but George's father did not seem to mind. Then the pro asked the golfers to pull out a 5-iron from their bag. She proceeded to talk about the different parts of the golf club, how different clubs have different lengths, and how different club numbers have different lofts. She noticed again that George was not paying attention. Instead, George was looking at all his different clubs, taking them out one or two at a time and comparing them, and trying different grips on the shaft. At this point the pro had enough and in a nice but firm voice asked George to please focus on the discussion. George looked up, put the clubs back into his bag, and attended to the golf pro. But it wasn't long before George again looked away at golfers at the end of the practice facility hitting golf balls.

Attention-deficit/hyperactivity disorder is a condition that makes it difficult for people to focus, pay attention, sit still, and control their behavior. People with ADHD may seem extremely overactive, energized, and unable to anticipate the consequences of their behaviors (known as the hyperactive-impulsive type of ADHD). Other people with ADHD may be inattentive, seem to lack motivation, and become bored easily (known as the inattentive type of ADHD). And still other people have the characteristics of both the hyperactive-impulsive type and the inattentive type (known as the combined type of ADHD). These behaviors do not exist only in school but at home and other places in the community. The condition can range from mild to severe with milder ADHD being more prevalent. One of the peculiarities of mild ADHD is that these individuals seem to be able to focus when they are involved in a reinforcing activity such as playing a video game, when they are introduced to a novel activity, or when they are working or playing one on one with a parent or teacher (Stein &

A. Either 1 or 2:

1. Six or more of the following symptoms of inattention have persisted for at least six months to a degree that is maladaptive and inconsistent with developmental level.

Inattention

a. Often fails to give close attention to details or makes careless mistakes in schoolwork, work, or other activities.

b. Often has difficulty sustaining attention in tasks or play activities.

c. Often does not seem to listen when spoken to directly.

d. Often does not follow through on instructions and fails to finish schoolwork, chores, or duties in the workplace (not due to oppositional behavior or failure to understand instructions).

e. Often has difficulty organizing tasks and activities.

f. Often avoids, dislikes, or is reluctant to engage in tasks that require sustained mental effort (such as schoolwork or homework).

g. Often loses things necessary for tasks or activities (e.g., toys, school assignments, pencils, books, or tools).

h. Often is easily distracted by extraneous stimuli.

i. Often is forgetful in daily activities.

2. Six or more of the following symptoms of hyperactivity-impulsivity have persisted for at least six months to a degree that is maladaptive and inconsistent with developmental level.

Hyperactivity

a. Often fidgets with hands or feet or squirms in seat.

b. Often leaves seat in classroom or in other situations in which remaining seated is expected.

c. Often runs about or climbs excessively in situations in which such behavior is inappropriate (in adolescents or adults, may be limited to subjective feelings of restlessness).

d. Often has difficulty playing or engaging in leisure activities quietly.

e. Is often on the go or acts as if "driven by a motor."

f. Often talks excessively.

Impulsivity

g. Often blurts out answers before questions have been completed.

h. Often has difficulty awaiting turn.

i. Often interrupts or intrudes on others (e.g., butts into conversations or games).

B. Some hyperactive-impulsive or inattentive symptoms that caused impairment were present before age seven.

C. Some impairment from the symptoms is present in two or more settings (e.g., at school or work and at home).

D. There is clear evidence of clinically significant impairment in social, academic, or occupational functioning.

E. The symptoms do not occur exclusively during the course of a pervasive developmental disorder, schizophrenia, or other psychotic disorder and are not better accounted for by another mental disorder (e.g., mood disorder, anxiety disorder, dissociative disorder, or personality disorder).

Types

Attention-deficit/hyperactivity disorder, combined type (if both criteria A1 and A2 are met for the past six months)

Attention-deficit/hyperactivity disorder, predominantly inattentive type (if criterion A1 is met but criterion A2 is not met for the past six months)

Attention-deficit/hyperactivity disorder, predominantly hyperactive-impulsive type (if criterion A2 is met but criterion A1 is not met for the past six months)

Adapted with permission from the *Diagnostic and Statistical Manual of Mental Disorders,* Copyright 2000, American Psychiatric Association.

Batshaw, 2001) (see Diagnostic Criteria for Attention-Deficit/Hyperactivity Disorder on the previous page for a detailed definition of ADHD).

ADHD is one of the more common developmental disabilities, occurring in approximately 5 out of every 100 individuals. It is three times more prevalent in boys compared to girls (NICHCY, 2001; Stein & Batshaw, 2001). ADHD usually appears in early childhood, but often it is not until the child is faced with the rigors of sitting and paying attention at school when the condition is actually diagnosed. For those with milder ADHD, the condition usually fades away as the child reaches adolescence. For those with more severe ADHD, the condition can continue into adulthood.

Causes of ADHD

The exact causes of ADHD are still unknown. However, researchers believe that people with ADHD do not have enough of a certain chemical neurotransmitter in their brain (many suspect this chemical neurotransmitter to be dopamine) that helps control behavior and attention. The cause of this chemical imbalance is unknown, but there seems to be a strong genetic element. In fact, it has been reported that 10 to 25 percent of individuals with ADHD have parents, grandparents, or siblings with the condition (Stein & Batshaw, 2001). Trauma to the brain before, during, or immediately after birth may also somehow create chemical imbalances that lead to ADHD.

Common Characteristics of People With ADHD

There are many characteristics associated with ADHD. Not surprisingly, most of these characteristics revolve around problems with attention hyperactivity. However, some children with ADHD also have motor and social problems that can be as challenging to the golf professional as the attention problems. The following sections highlight common characteristics associated with ADHD.

Hyperactivity, Impulsivity, and Inattention

Specific behaviors such as hyperactivity, impulsivity, and inattention are the most common characteristics of ADHD. *Hyperactivity* refers to people who seem to be too active or always on the go. For example, a person who frequently gets out of her chair in school, runs almost nonstop and aimlessly on the playground, or constantly squirms and fidgets at the movies shows signs of hyperactivity. *Impulsivity* refers to people who do things without thinking about the consequences. A child who never raises his hand before answering a question in school, butts into games or conversations on the playground, or decides to paint his cat without thinking of the consequences shows signs of impulsivity. *Inattention* refers to people who have difficulty paying attention and getting organized. A child who is easily distracted at school, loses things such as toys or play equipment at recess, and can't seem to get focused and organized to do her homework shows signs of inattention (NICHCY, 2001; Sherrill, 1998) (see Diagnostic Criteria for Attention-Deficit/Hyperactivity Disorder for more details on these characteristics). Note that most children at one time or another may squirm and seem overly active, interrupt an adult or do something without thinking, or not pay attention or have trouble starting a project. However, to be considered ADHD these types of behaviors have to occur over several months and to a degree that significantly affects social and academic success (APA, 2000).

Motor Problems Associated With ADHD

Many people with ADHD do quite well in physical activity and sport. However, recent research suggests that some people with ADHD show signs of gross motor delays compared to their peers without ADHD. For example, both Kadesjo and Gillberg (1998) and Piek, Pitcher, and Hay (1999) found that 50 percent of children with ADHD they sampled also had developmental coordination disorder (DCD), a significant impairment in general coordination. Similarly, Harvey and Reid (1997) found that as a group children with ADHD scored lower in basic fundamental motor skills (such as throwing, catching, running, and jumping) compared to peers without ADHD. This was a preliminary study, and the researchers did suggest that more research was needed. However, Beyer (1999) found that boys with ADHD aged 7 to 12 as a group performed significantly poorer in fine motor and timed tasks requiring motor coordination than boys with learning disabilities. There were no differences in balance and upper-limb coordination. Beyer suggested that boys with ADHD might show delays in fine motor and timed motor coordination tasks because these tests require focused attention and motor planning (thinking through a task), areas that might be expected to be a problem for people with ADHD. Finally, Yan and Thomas (2002) found that children with ADHD took more time than children without ADHD to complete rapid arm movements and in general were less accurate and showed more variability. It is clear from these results that many people with ADHD may have some kind of motor problem that makes learning motor skills such as golf more difficult.

Social and Behavioral Problems Associated With ADHD

Many people with ADHD have problems interacting with peers and developing friendships. Part of the problem is no doubt related to their inattention to peers, hyperactivity, and doing things without thinking how their actions might affect others. For example, fleeting attention may make it difficult for people with ADHD to pick up nuances in conversations, facial expressions, tone of voice, and body language. As a result some of these individuals will not realize they are bothering and even boring or angering their peers. They do not understand why peers tease them or do not want to be with them (Sherrill, 1998). A related by-product of social ineptness and isolation in people with ADHD is low self-esteem. In addition, children with ADHD are more likely to have conduct disorders such as truancy, stealing, fighting, running away, and

drug use. Some studies suggest that as many as 30 to 50 percent of children with ADHD are likely to show antisocial behaviors and conduct disorders. Similarly, reports suggest that as many as 50 percent of children with ADHD have oppositional defiant disorder, a condition in which children display severe temper outbursts, argue with and defy adults, blame others, and respond vindictively (Wodrich, 1994). Whether conduct disorders and juvenile delinquency are part of the ADHD disorder or a by-product of social problems is still unclear (Hallahan & Kauffman, 1997; Moffitt, 1990; Werry, Elkind, & Reeves, 1987; Wodrich, 1994).

Teaching Golf to People With ADHD

As noted earlier, some people with ADHD have motor issues that will make learning golf skills a little more difficult. The bigger issues are dealing with inattention, distractibility, hyperactivity, and impulsivity. The following suggestions, adapted from Fowler (1994) and Sherrill (1998), may be helpful for golf instructors, educators, and therapists who work with people with ADHD.

1. Establish a highly structured program. Have a clear lesson plan, and limit downtime whenever possible.
2. Reduce environmental space. If possible, use clear boundary markers to show each golfer where to stand (e.g., putting clubs around a golfer to show where to stand).
3. Eliminate irrelevant auditory and visual stimuli. If the environment is full of distractions, try to move to a less stimulating place. For example, try taking a golfer to the edge of the driving range where he cannot see other golfers or to a secluded place on the course where there are no distractions.
4. Help the golfer focus on the relevant instructional material. For example, color code the arm to show what part of the arm moves at a particular point,

or use footprints to remind the golfer how to address the ball and align with the target.

5. When multiple golf instructors are available, try to place the participant with instructors who are positive, upbeat, and highly organized problem solvers (instructors who use praise and reinforcers liberally and are willing to go the extra mile to help the individual succeed).

6. Provide the participant with a structured and predictable environment by displaying rules of the range, posting daily schedules and assignments for the lesson, calling attention to schedule changes, setting specific times for specific tasks, and providing regularly scheduled and frequent breaks.

7. Modify lessons by mixing high- and low-interest activities (e.g., hitting drivers off the range along with a review of the rules).

8. Simplify and increase visual presentations rather than using a lot of verbal directions. Also, limit how long instructions are presented. It is best to get the golfer up and practicing the skill and then provide instruction after a few swings rather than have the golfer sit for long periods to receive instruction.

9. Teach organization and practice skills. For example, specify how the golfer is to practice (e.g., five shots with each club, starting with the 9-iron). Write out a specific practice routine to help the person remember how to organize practice.

10. Use learning strategies such as mnemonic devices and links. For example, a simple verbal reminder that the player can repeat might be "Slow back, slow forward."

11. When using verbal cues, try to add a visual reference. For example, when teaching the grip and mentioning the idea of making Vs down the shaft, show the golfer exactly how the Vs look.

12. For participants who are excessively active or who have trouble waiting, channel activity into acceptable avenues. For example, have the golfer help organize the area for the next activity or refill buckets with golf balls instead of sitting and waiting with the others. Also, have the golfer start hitting at the range rather than waiting for all the directions you might be presenting to the other participants.

13. Use activity as a reward. For example, if the golfer takes the time to read over the rules and take a quick test, then allow her to go and hit half of a bucket at the practice facility.

14. Don't get too upset when an inattentive participant daydreams while you give instruction. Some golfers with ADHD who don't seem to be paying attention may actually be taking in what you're saying. For other golfers who are truly not paying attention, either try to give them a gentle reminder to pay attention or plan to have a peer repeat directions to them later when practice begins.

15. When a participant has trouble paying attention to routine tasks and activities, decrease the length of the task or try to make the task interesting. For example, if hitting on the range is getting tiresome, ask the participant to try to hit a specific yard marker or other target.

16. When a participant becomes noncompliant and fails to complete tasks, one solution is to increase the choice and specific interest of tasks for the individual. For example, if the participant refuses to practice putting, give him several choices of things he can do around the green area (short putts, long putts, chipping from the fringe). Pair an activity that the participant does not want to do (putting) with an activity he wants to do (hitting at the practice facility). For example, tell the participant that when he sinks 10 putts

from a certain distance he can go to the practice facility and hit.

17. When a participant has trouble at the beginning of a task, increase the structure of the task and highlight important parts. For example, use the participant to help demonstrate a particular technique to the others to make sure the participant is focused and paying attention.

18. When a participant has trouble remembering and completing assignments, ask her to create and use lists, checking off each task she completes.

19. When a participant is forgetful, establish routines to place and retrieve commonly used objects such as clubs and golf shoes. Also, teach the participant that, upon leaving one place for another, he should always stop and question, "Do I have everything I need?"

20. Some people with ADHD have low self-esteem. Identify the person's strengths and weaknesses and highlight strengths by building opportunities for success in the environment (structure the environment for success). For example, if the golfer is good at putting but has trouble chipping, highlight the golfer's putting skills. Also, intersperse chipping with putting so the golfer does not get too frustrated.

21. Try to provide negative feedback privately and positive feedback publicly. Also, never ask an individual to perform a task publicly that you know is too difficult or if you know the golfer might "choke" when performing in front of the group.

Autism

Bridget is a beautiful 13-year-old girl who comes to school every day in beautiful dresses and two pigtails. She is full of energy and usually has a big smile on her face. This energy and smile hide the fact that Bridget cannot speak, understands only a handful of words, and seems to have no interest in interacting with her peers or teachers. Bridget has autism, and she receives her education in a class for other children with autism. Bridget and her peers can learn, and in fact Bridget has learned to follow a schedule, do many tasks independently, and participate in music and physical education classes. Physical education is one of her favorite activities, especially when the class is free to run and gallop and leap around the gym or when they do an aerobics video. Bridget actually has good motor skills; she just doesn't understand all the rules and intricacies of the games they play in physical education. In addition to general physical education, Bridget has adapted physical education with her classmates two times per week with the school district's adapted physical education specialist.

This specialist recently decided that golf would be a good game to introduce to the class, and his plan was to take the class along with the special education teacher and teacher assistants to the local golf course. The adapted physical education teacher is not very good at golf, so he arranged for the golf pro at the club to teach the children how to play golf once a week for six weeks. But when the golf pro walked to the driving range to meet the class, she began to think that maybe this was not a good idea after all. The kids looked pretty normal from a distance, but things began to look different when she tried to talk to the class. First, none of the kids responded when she said hello to the group, although one child seemed to whisper when prompted by his teacher assistant. Then when she asked the kids to pick up their golf clubs they just stood around looking at anything but the golf clubs. The golf pro thought to herself, "This is going to be an interesting six weeks!"

Autism is a disability that significantly impairs an individual's ability to interact and communicate with others. In addition, people with autism often develop unique movements and behaviors such as flapping their hands in the air or rocking back and forth. Other than their unique behaviors and lack of normal language development, children with autism do not look any different than children without autism (Holmes, 1997; Powers, 1989) (see Diagnostic Criteria for Autism). Autism occurs in about 5 out of every 10,000 children, but some reports suggest as many as 20 out of 10,000 children have autism. Boys are five times more likely to have autism than girls, but girls with autism tend to exhibit more severe cognitive impairment along with autism (APA, 2000).

Autism is considered to be a pervasive developmental disorder (PDD) by the American Psychiatric Association (APA) (2000). PDD is an umbrella term used to describe a spectrum of disorders that are all characterized by severe and pervasive (lasting forever) deficits in several areas of development including social interactions and communication skills, and the presence of unique behaviors, interests, and activities. These deficits and unique

Diagnostic Criteria for Autism

A. A total of six (or more) items from 1, 2, and 3, with at least two from 1 and one each from 2 and 3:

1. Qualitative impairment in social interactions, as manifested by at least two of the following:

   a. Marked impairment in the use of multiple nonverbal behaviors such as eye-to-eye gaze, facial expressions, body postures, and gestures to regulate social interactions

   b. Failure to develop peer relationships appropriate to developmental level

   c. Lack of spontaneous seeking to share enjoyment, interests, or achievements with other people (e.g., lack of showing, bringing, or pointing out objects of interest)

   d. Lack of social or emotional reciprocity

2. Qualitative impairment in communication as manifested by at least one of the following:

   a. Delay in, or total lack of, the development of spoken language (not accompanied by an attempt to compensate through alternative modes of communication such as gestures or mime)

   b. In individuals with adequate speech, marked impairment in the ability to initiate or sustain a conversation with others

   c. Stereotyped and repetitive use of language or idiosyncratic language

   d. Lack of varied, spontaneous, make-believe play or social imitative play appropriate to developmental level

3. Restricted repetitive and stereotyped patterns of behavior, interests, and activities, as manifested by at least one of the following:

   a. Encompassing preoccupation with one or more stereotyped and restricted patterns of interest that is abnormal either in intensity or focus

   b. Apparently inflexible adherence to specific, nonfunctional routines or rituals

   c. Stereotyped and repetitive motor mannerisms (e.g., hand or finger flapping or twisting, or complex whole-body movements)

   d. Persistent preoccupation with parts of objects

B. Delays or abnormal functioning occur in at least one of the following areas, with onset prior to age three: social interaction, language as used in social communication, or symbolic or imaginative play.

C. The disturbance is not better accounted for by Rett's disorder or childhood disintegrative disorder.

Adapted with permission from the *Diagnostic and Statistical Manual of Mental Disorders,* Copyright 2000, American Psychiatric Association.

behaviors are not normal for the child's developmental level. Included under the umbrella of PDD are autistic disorder, Rett's disorder, childhood disintegrative disorder, Asperger's syndrome (discussed later in this chapter), and PDD not otherwise specified. Of these conditions, autism is the most prevalent (APA, 2000).

Autism appears in infancy. Children may not be responsive to sounds in the environment, may not want to cuddle with their mother or father, may cling tightly to just one parent, may avoid eye contact, may seem distant and withdrawn, or may make no effort to speak. In some cases parents may suspect something is wrong with the child soon after birth. In other cases parents report that their child actually developed normally (including normal language development and interaction with parents and siblings) until he or she reached the age of one or two. Then suddenly the child seemed to lose the skills he or she had acquired, became withdrawn and unresponsive, and began to show unique behaviors and interests (APA, 2000).

Causes of Autism

No one knows for sure what causes autism. However, it is becoming clear that autism is a neurological impairment and not something that can be caused by child-rearing practices or maternal stress (Powers, 1989). Recent evidence suggests a genetic link to autism as noted in twin studies as well as extensive family histories. Research has shown that 70 to 90 percent of identical twins (those with virtually identical genetic makeup) both have autism, while only 3 percent of fraternal twins both have autism. Another link to genetics is the fact that a family that has one child with autism is 50 to 100 times more likely to have a second child with autism when compared to families that do not have a child with autism. Also, it has been shown that families that have a child with autism often have a relative who has autism or some features of autism (e.g., language delay, rigid temperament, unique behaviors). Most believe there is some

unknown environmental influence on brain development that contributes to autism, and genetics alone cannot fully explain autism. However, while possible environmental factors such as immunizations, infections, and food allergies have been discussed and studied, to date there has been no support for these claims (Holmes, 1997; Towbin, 2001; Towbin, Mauk, & Batshaw, 2001).

Common Characteristics of People With Autism

There are three main characteristics of autism: lack of interest in social reciprocity, communication impairment, and unique behaviors. In addition, many people with autism have cognitive impairments (mental retardation) and motor delays. The following material highlights these major characteristics.

Social Reciprocity

Perhaps the most distinctive characteristic of autism is the individual's inability to interact appropriately with others. Some people with autism want to interact with others but just do not have the language or skills to do so. Others seem to just want to be alone. They seem to be apathetic about others in their environment and do not know how to read others' social cues such as a smile, a laugh, or arms held out for a hug. These people do not actively seek interactions with others, they often do not look others in the eye, and they often seem to be looking right through others. An interest in being with, interacting with, and enjoying others—the reciprocal nature of social interaction—is underdeveloped or missing. For example, a typically developing three-year-old stops what she is doing to look and see what her mother is excited about when she dropped a plate, but the child with autism may not look at her mother or may look in the direction of her mother but not directly at her. Similarly, a typically developing three-year-old is excited to share what she is doing with her mother, such as asking her to look at a picture she is drawing. The child with autism does not seem to seek her mother's interest or praise (APA, 2000; Powers, 1989; Towbin, Mauk, & Batshaw, 2001).

This does not mean that people with autism always want to be alone or never want to share with or seek the comfort of others. Many children with autism love to cuddle with their mother or father, enjoy rolling a ball back and forth with a peer, or enjoy watching others play. For example, an adult with autism might enjoy watching others at the practice facility hit golf balls. He may also enjoy having an instructor show him how to hold the club and hit the ball better, but he may not look the instructor in the eye. In fact, he may seem to be staring into space, showing no interest in what the instructor has to say even though he might actually be listening intently and enjoying the attention of the golf instructor. People with autism just have a difficult time understanding how to seek and accept social contact.

Communication Impairment

The second most noticeable deficit in people with autism is significant problems with communication. In the most severe cases an individual with autism might have no speech whatsoever. Children with this level of expressive communication impairment often learn to point to things they want, take their parents by the hand and lead them to what they want, or point to pictures. Other people with autism might be able to speak, but the tone, loudness, and general quality of their speech might not be the same as that of people without autism. In addition, they may only speak in one- or two-word sentences. For example, an individual with autism might whisper "I hungry" to signal that she wants to eat dinner. Another individual with autism might say with no emotion that he fell and cut his hand. Still other people with autism enjoy the sound and feeling of certain words or phrases and may repeat them often. For example, an individual with autism might like saying "You're the man!" over and over again after hearing it on TV while watching a golf tournament. Still other people with autism have echolalia, a pattern of repeating back what is said to them. For example, a golf instructor says, "Hi Billy, ready to play golf?", and Billy replies, "Hi Billy, ready to play golf?" (APA, 2000; Powers, 1989; Towbin, Mauk, & Batshaw, 2001).

People with autism also have receptive language impairments. They have a difficult time understanding what others are saying or might not react at all to others' attempts to communicate. In fact, in the most severe cases some parents have reported that at first they thought their child was deaf because of his or her complete unresponsiveness to sounds and speech. In milder cases an individual with autism with receptive language problems might simply not understand abstractions or words with more than one meaning. Saying something like "Hit the stuffing out of the ball" could lead to a frustrating session on the range because the individual with autism truly thinks he should be able to hit the stuffing out of the ball. When he tries and tries without success, he may become agitated. Golf idioms such as "worm burner" or "skying the ball" are abstract concepts that will make no sense to many people with autism.

Unique Behaviors

The final hallmark characteristic of autism is unique behaviors and interests. Individuals with autism seem to enjoy repetitive activities such as rocking back and forth, pacing back and forth, watching spinning objects, shaking their hands or head, or tapping objects. Another common behavior of individuals with autism is lining up objects in a particular way. They do not seem to understand appropriate ways to play with toys or they simply prefer playing with objects in their own unique way. The exact reason for these behaviors and rituals is not known. Individuals with autism rarely initiate appropriate play (i.e., playing with toys or playing with peers or family members in a way that is expected for a child's age) or pretend play. For example, a typical five-year-old would play with dolls by dressing and undressing the dolls, putting them into various places in a dollhouse, and making up and acting out stories about the dolls' family and friends. On the other hand, a child with autism might just take the doll and tap it on the side of a chair over and over again.

A related characteristic is the insistence on sameness in the way they play, the objects they use, and the routines they prefer. When play, objects, or routines change, the individual with autism is likely to get anxious and even upset (APA, 2000; Powers, 1989; Towbin, Mauk, & Batshaw, 2001). For example, a person with autism may like to hold a golf ball in his hand as he walks around the course. Trying to take the golf ball away so he can pick up a club and hit the ball can be stressful for him. Similarly, say a person with autism has learned a routine in which she goes to the practice facility every Wednesday after work. But one Wednesday the practice facility is closed for repair. She does not understand why her routine has been changed and still insists on being driven to the practice facility.

Another unique behavior seen in many people with autism is sensitivity to sights, sounds, smells, and feels or textures. For some unknown reason many people with autism find certain sensory stimuli uncomfortable and even painful. For example, some people with autism do not like being touched by others and will only wear loose-fitting clothes. Others prefer food with certain textures, and still others wear earplugs to muffle sounds in their environment. What is fascinating and contradictory about sensory reactions in people with autism is that at one moment they seem to react strongly to a seemingly innocuous sound (e.g., a person screams and holds his ears at the sound of the announcements over the loudspeaker at school) but then seem to not even hear other sounds (e.g., a parent trying to get his attention or a police siren going by). Some people with autism are fascinated by the sensation provided by certain stimuli. For example, some people may enjoy turning the lights on and off or looking through their fingers at a bright light, others may enjoy swinging or running in a circle, and others may enjoy the feel of certain soft or rough textures (APA, 2000; Powers, 1989; Towbin, Mauk, & Batshaw, 2001).

Other Characteristics

Two other characteristics associated with autism are cognitive and motor delays.

Approximately two-thirds to three-fourths of individuals with autism have cognitive impairments. As a general rule, the more severe the autism the more likely the individual will display cognitive impairments (APA, 2000; Towbin, Mauk, & Batshaw, 2001). It is unclear whether cognitive limitations is a functional label or a true indication of the individual's cognitive skills. People with autism are extremely difficult to test because of their severe communication disorder, lack of interest in others, and lack of interest in using objects appropriately—most tests of cognitive function require communication, attention to others, and a specific use of objects. Thus, people with autism often test at a level similar to people with cognitive impairment even though many who work with these people would argue that they are more intelligent than the tests show. To further complicate the issue, some people with autism display extraordinary cognitive skills in very specific areas (APA, 2000). For example, there have been reports of people with autism who can play classical music on the piano, others who can recall dates and names, and still others who can create wonderful artwork.

Motor delays can also be difficult to measure in people with autism. Some researchers suggest that people with autism do not have any motor delays and in fact can demonstrate unique motor skills (Sigman & Capps, 1997; Smith, 2000). But when formally tested, most research shows that people with autism have motor delays. For example, Berkeley, Zittel, Pitney, and Nichols (2001) found that three-fourths of their sample of children aged 6 to 8 with high functioning autism scored at the "poor" to "very poor" level on the Test of Gross Motor Development (TGMD), a test that measures qualitative patterns in gross motor skills such as throwing, catching, kicking, running, jumping, and hopping. Similarly, Slavoff (1997) found that all of the 13 children with autism she tested scored significantly below their age level on the Peabody Developmental Motor Scales, a test that measures overall motor development by examining skills in balance, coordination, speed, and strength. And Manjiviona and Prior (1995) found that two-thirds of their sample of high functioning children with autism aged 7 to 17 performed at a delayed level on the Test of Motor Impairment-Henderson Revision, a test that examines motor abilities such as speed, coordination, and balance. As with cognitive impairments, it is unclear whether these motor delays are a true reflection of deficits in motor development and coordination or if they are the result of not understanding or not being interested in the specific motor task required on the test. Regardless, golf instructors should expect significant motor delays in participants with autism.

Teaching Golf to People With Autism

Individuals with autism will be challenging for the golf instructor, educator, or therapist. As a general rule these individuals will have significant problems understanding verbal instructions and staying focused. In addition, many will be resistive to physical assistance, have unique behaviors, become agitated when routines are altered, and appear to be unmotivated. You should not try to work alone with an individual with autism. A parent, teacher, or therapist needs to be there to help. The following teaching strategies, modified from TEACCH (2002) and Savel (1993), have been designed to help golf instructors, teachers, and therapists deal with the learning issues of people with autism.

1. The physical layout of the setting is important for people with autism. Whenever possible the environment should provide visual cues on where to go and what to do. The environment should not be too distracting, and specific areas for performing certain skills should be clearly marked, such as color coding the station where the participant with autism goes to practice. Also, clearly mark boundaries to make sure the participant knows where to go and where not to go.

2. Try to provide a quiet area free from distractions and stimulation to allow participants with autism to calm down. Something as simple as going to the end of the range and allowing the participant to sit and compose herself can be effective.

3. Scheduling can help participants with autism focus on the tasks they are supposed to complete. Post the golf schedule, either written or using pictures (the participant's teacher can create schedules), in clear view or allow the participant to have his personal schedule with him during the lesson. Whether posted or personal, review the schedule when the participant arrives and then after each activity. This will help the participant know exactly what is going to happen and when it will happen. Reviewing schedules also helps cue volunteers, parents, and teachers who come to help the participant.

4. Use extra cues or prompts when teaching new golf skills. Present prompts systematically—clearly, consistently, and directed toward the golfer. For example, parents may report that the golfer does best when there is a simple verbal cue ("Look here") followed by a demonstration, followed by another simple verbal cue ("Now you do it").

5. Try to find unique reinforcers for people with autism. Again, parents or teachers can provide information about what is reinforcing for a particular golfer. For example, one golfer might simply like to hold two golf balls as a reinforcer while another golfer may prefer to sit under a tree and look at the clouds in the sky. Whatever the reinforcer, use it to entice the participant to do what you want (e.g., "If you hit golf balls until your bucket is empty, you can sit under the tree for a few minutes.").

6. Communication is an issue with most people with autism. Be prepared to simplify verbal directions and supplement these verbal directions with extra demonstrations and physical assistance (talk to the person's speech therapist, parent, or special education teacher for more ideas). Also, pronouns can be confusing for some people with autism. For example, rather than saying "It is your turn," say "It is Sarah's turn."

7. Minimize golf jargon, as it may confuse people with autism. For example, saying something like "Keep your eye on the target" might

cause the participant with autism to walk up to the flagpole and try to put his eye right on the flagpole.

8. Have the person's complete attention when giving directions, especially when giving demonstrations. Also, use a multisensory approach (extra colors to highlight critical components, footprints for stance), demonstrations, and physical assistance (even though some participants are tactically defensive, they will accept some physical assistance if they know it is coming).

9. Many people with autism may exhibit one or more of the following behaviors: wandering, running away, making loud noises, crying or laughing for no apparent reason, aggressive behavior, and self-abusive behavior. To deal with these behaviors, first consult the person's special education teacher, case manager, or parents to find out what behaviors to expect, what may trigger a behavior, and what methods work to prevent or stop the behavior. Brief participants without disabilities regarding what to expect, when to ignore certain behaviors (such as loud noises), how to help with some behaviors (tell them to not touch people with autism), and when to be careful or ask for help.

10. Regardless of the participant's unique behaviors, the best solution is to have a behavior plan in place. Again, consult with the participant's special education teacher or parent to find out if there is a behavior plan already in place and how to implement the plan. Consistency is important when implementing the plan and preventing behavior problems.

11. Anticipate problems with transitions (new activities, new settings, new people to work with). Try to keep some things the same, such as warm-ups or the first activity of the golf session, to ease transitions.

12. Have participants without disabilities help the participant with autism in select ways, such as finding an empty practice station, cuing the participant to focus on the instructor, helping the participant choose clubs, and so on. Note that peers should not be used if the participant is aggressive.

13. Try to catch people with autism doing something they are supposed to be doing and praise them. Try to avoid negative cues such as "No touching" by saying "Hands down."

14. Find activities that the participant has a strong interest in. Many people with autism particularly enjoy repetitive activities such as putting balls into buckets at the range. A repetitive activity such as this can be used as a reinforcer.

15. Teach appropriate use of equipment. People with autism often use equipment in inappropriate or even dangerous ways. For example, a participant may try to lick the steel shaft of a club or twirl a club. Simply redirect and teach the participant the correct way to use equipment and reinforce such use. Also, prevent inappropriate use of equipment by simply asking the participant to put the equipment away when it is not being used.

16. Make sure the session ends with enough time to allow for transitions. Make the end-of-session routine the same, at least for the participant with autism. For example, a simple ending routine to cue the participant that the golf session is over is to have the player put all the clubs in the bag, change to street shoes, and give the instructor a high-five upon leaving the range.

Asperger's Syndrome

William is a bright, energetic 14-year-old who is obsessed with golf. He loves everything about the game, and he is like a walking encyclopedia of golf trivia. He can quickly tell you who won the last 25 U.S. and British Opens, he can tell you each of the PGA tour locations and dates for this year's tournaments, and he can name the top 50 players on the PGA money list (along with how

(continued)

(continued)

much each has made this year and their current scoring average). He also enjoys playing golf and pretending to be different professional golfers. Unfortunately, his golf skills do not match his love and knowledge of the game. In addition, his obsession with the game, which was cute and interesting when William was younger, is now kind of a pain. Golf and golf statistics are all William wants to talk about at home and at school. His friends tease him because of his obsession and because they know William will get mad, and his teachers are having a difficult time getting him to focus on his schoolwork. His mother, who loves golf herself and has worked with William on his golf game, has other interests that she would like to share with William, but all William wants to talk about and play is golf. When she so much as mentions doing something else such as shooting baskets in the driveway or playing a board game, she has to be prepared for William to start to complain. If his mother continues pushing other activities, she knows that William may escalate to a full-blown tantrum. William has Asperger's syndrome.

Asperger's syndrome (AS), also known as Asperger's disorder, is a neurological disorder that is classified by the APA as a pervasive developmental disorder, also known as an autism spectrum disorder. It is more common in boys than girls. People with AS are characterized by problems with social interactions, communication, and restricted interest. However, unlike people with classic autism, people with AS do not show delays in the appearance of major developmental milestones, have no delays in the onset of speech and language, and have no cognitive impairments (see Diagnostic Criteria for Asperger's Syndrome for more information) (Bashe & Kirby, 2001; Kirby, 2003; Smith Myles & Simpson, 2001). In other words, people with AS can talk, read (many learn to read as preschoolers), and write and do not look different from children without AS. The disorder becomes most apparent in social situations including school and recreation settings. It is critical for teachers, therapists, and golf instructors to understand that the quirky behaviors and obsessions displayed by people with AS are not due to willful misbehavior. Intervention can help people with AS learn to accommodate their behaviors, but they will always have this disorder (Bashe & Kirby, 2001).

Diagnostic Criteria for Asperger's Syndrome

1. Qualitative impairment in social interaction, as manifested by at least two of the following:

    a. Marked impairments in the use of multiple nonverbal behaviors such as eye-to-eye gaze, facial expression, and gestures to regulate social interactions

    b. Failure to develop peer relationships appropriate to developmental level

    c. Lack of spontaneous seeking to share enjoyment, interests, or achievements with other people (e.g., lack of showing, bringing, or pointing out objects of interest to other people)

    d. Lack of social or emotional reciprocity

2. Restricted repetitive and stereotyped patterns of behavior, interests, and activities, as manifested by at least one of the following:

    a. Encompassing preoccupation with one or more stereotyped and restricted patterns of interest that is abnormal either in intensity or focus

    b. Apparently inflexible adherence to specific, nonfunctional routines or rituals

    c. Stereotyped and repetitive motor mannerisms (e.g., hand or finger flapping or twisting, or complex whole-body movements)

    d. Persistent preoccupation with parts of objects

3. The disturbance causes clinically significant impairments in social, occupational, or other important areas of functioning.

4. There is no clinically significant general delay in language (e.g., single words used by age two, communicative phrases used by age three).

5. There is no clinically significant delay in cognitive development of age-appropriate self-help skills, adaptive behavior (other than social interactions), and curiosity about the environment in childhood.

6. Criteria are not met for another specific pervasive developmental disorder or schizophrenia.

Adapted with permission from the *Diagnostic and Statistical Manual of Mental Disorders,* Copyright 2000, American Psychiatric Association.

Causes of AS

There is very little information on the cause of AS. As was the case with autism, AS is the result of an anomaly in the physical brain, and there appears to be a genetic link to AS (Bashe & Kirby, 2001). In other words, a child is more likely to have AS if he has a relative who has AS, autism, or another behavioral disorder. Environmental factors most likely contribute to AS and the severity of the disorder.

Common Characteristics of People With AS

The following section divides the major characteristics associated with AS into five categories: cognitive abilities, social skills, behaviors, communication skills, and motor skills. Keep in mind that each individual with AS is a unique person. Some will only exhibit a few of the behaviors at a relatively mild intensity while others will exhibit all the behaviors at a more extreme intensity.

Cognitive Characteristics

Cognitive abilities associated with AS include a normal IQ, exceptional skill or talent in one or two areas (e.g., a musical ability), excellent rote memory, and strong interest in one or two subjects, often to the exclusion of other topics. People with AS often have the ability to comprehend complex math problems, and many have learned to read by kindergarten (hyperlexia). However, this same bright child might forget to take homework home, have poor concentration, be off task frequently, become easily distracted and disorganized, and have difficulty sustaining attention (Kirby, 2003; Smith Myles & Simpson, 2001; Tucker, 2000). These problems may also present themselves when the child is participating in a golf program. For example, a child with AS may continue to hit balls on the range after he was instructed to stop. He was not necessarily being disrespectful to the instructor; he was simply concentrating on something other than the instructor.

Social and Emotional Characteristics

Lack of social skills is one of the major problems associated with AS. A social impairment in people with AS causes them to be extremely egocentric or self-centered. They will change every conversation into an opportunity to discuss their interests. For example, a conversation about responsibility and sportsmanship could lead to an entirely different discussion: "Finishing my homework is my responsibility and when I finish all homework by 8:00 p.m., my parents let me look at my books on birds. Do you like birds? What kind of birds live in your yard? Can I come over to your house and look for birds?"

It is not that people with AS do not want to have friends and behave appropriately, they just do not know how to do so. They have a difficulty understanding social context and social cues, and they have difficulty adjusting physical proximity (personal space). For example, an individual with AS wants to find a partner and practice putting, but she does not know how to approach a peer. Even if she does approach a peer, the way the individual asks to be a partner (e.g., repeatedly says loudly "John's my partner, John's my partner") will no doubt cause problems for the peer as well as the individual with AS. Socially and emotionally inappropriate responses are a result of neurological differences, not rudeness. For example, it would not be uncommon for an individual with AS to turn away from you while you are greeting him (known as gaze avoidance). Because of these social inadequacies, people with AS are often picked on or bullied. The lack of ability to interact appropriately with peers coupled with repeated failures when attempting to interact with peers leads to isolation. As a result, a lack of desire to interact with peers or form age-appropriate peer relationships occurs (Kirby, 2003; Smith Myles & Simpson, 2001).

Behavioral Characteristics

All of the characteristics just discussed will combine to form many behaviors that seem odd or unusual. People with AS perceive the world differently because they are living in their own world, engrossed in their own agenda. Limited interests lead to unusual preoccupations (e.g., all shirts must be organized in the drawer by size and color), talking at length (sometimes in a peculiar voice) about favorite subjects, and repeating the same words and phrases over and over again, such as repeating a line from the game show, *Who Wants to be a Millionaire,* "Is that your final answer? Is that your final answer?" On a positive note, these preoccupations often lead to a career in which the adult with AS can be very successful, such as a research scientist. For example, a child's intense interest in bugs along with the child's exceptional memory can lead to a career as an entomologist. Preoccupations also create a preference for sameness, which leads to obsessive routines, repetitive rituals, and difficulties with transitions or changes. For example, a simple change in schedule such as going to the putting green first instead of the practice facility can be traumatic for people with AS. Similarly, asking an individual with AS to hit from a different practice station or try a different grip can cause frustration and overwhelming anxiety. It is certainly all right to make changes; however, changes should be presented systematically and carefully (see suggestions on page 109).

People with AS love to receive praise, win in competitive games, and be first. They have trouble handling losing, criticism, and imperfection, which is why they feel the need to finish what they have started. They may have vocal outbursts or shriek, especially when they are having a difficult time (Kirby, 2003; Smith Myles & Simpson, 2001; Tucker, 2000). People with AS also perceive things such as rules in black and white terms. For example, after teaching the rules for order of play, a person with AS sees a peer in his foursome hitting out of turn. This breach of rules, which may be an innocent mistake or an effort to speed up play, could cause the individual with AS to start yelling at the player for not following the rules. Teaching people with AS that sometimes some rules can be bent will help them learn the subtle nuances of the sport.

Communication Characteristics

Difficulty in understanding body language and nonverbal cues not only leads to a lack of social skills but also problems with communication. Children with AS usually speak fluently by five years of age, yet they often have problems with pragmatics (using language in social contexts), semantics (recognizing multiple meanings), and prosody (the pitch, stress, and rhythm of speech) (Attwood, 1998; Bashe & Kirby, 2001). Speech and language peculiarities stem from extremely rich, expressive language but limited receptive language. Lack of nonverbal understanding leads to clumsy body language, inadequate use of gestures, and difficulty using language in a social context. For example, all the players run up and give another player a high-five after she chips one in from the sand trap. Understanding the need to communicate but not exactly knowing how in this setting, the player with AS runs up to the teammate and says, "I love ice cream." Again, direct instruction of appropriate communication, both verbal and nonverbal, is critical because people with AS will not pick up this information incidentally (Kirby, 2003; Smith Myles & Simpson, 2001).

Physical and Motor Characteristics

Many people with AS struggle with fine and gross motor deficits: tossing and catching a ball, dressing and undressing, tying shoes, holding an eating utensil properly, balancing, hopping, or following physical movement directions (e.g., "Reach forward with your right arm") (Bashe & Kirby, 2001; Smith, 2000; Smith Myles & Simpson, 2001). These problems are most obvious in odd mannerisms and clumsiness, such as robotic movements as opposed to smooth, rhythmic movements in running (Attwood, 1998). Many times they have lax joints, an immature grasp, slowed pace of movements, and problems with manual dexterity (Kirby, 2003; Smith, 2000; Smith Myles & Simpson, 2001). People with AS also are often very sensitive to sounds, smells, tastes, and sights. Sights and sounds that do not bother peers, such as a dog barking in the distance, could bother a person with AS. Similarly, people with AS often are sensitive to touch and prefer soft, loose-fitting clothing and certain foods (e.g., food without a lot of texture, like a milk shake). It is also common for people with AS to take powerful antianxiety medications, which can cause them to gain weight and can create further fitness deficits.

Teaching Golf to People With AS

People with AS are very bright, so they will be able to pick up golf instruction and rules quickly. The problems in instruction will be related to obsessions, lack of attention, rigid adherence to rules and routines, and some coordination problems. Many of the suggestions previously discussed under ADHD and autism will apply to participants with AS as well. The following teaching strategies for people with AS have been adapted from Groft and Block (2003).

1. Many people with AS are preoccupied with specific interests. Create a period of two to five minutes for discussion of the specific interests. For example, during a rest break allow the participant with AS to talk about his unique obsession. But make it clear that the conversation about this obsession stops when the class restarts.

2. People with AS often have a high level of intelligence and poor concentration skills, so give them tasks that are simple and make it easy to remain on task. For example, have the participant repeat directions back or mirror when demonstrating rather than simply standing and listening to instructions (see teaching suggestions for golfers with learning disabilities and ADHD for more ideas).

3. People with AS typically have significant social deficits and need direct instruction on appropriate social skills. For example, many people with AS do not understand personal space and stand too close to others when conversing. Remind the participant about personal space and cue her on an appropriate distance to stand when talking to a peer. Use "social stories" to explain and help them understand new situations, and provide reinforcement when they respond appropriately. A social story explains what will happen and what is expected of the individual in a given situation. For example, you might write, "Ethan will go to his golf lesson today at 3:00 p.m. Ethan will first stand and listen to instructions given by Mrs. Dunlap. It is important that Ethan does not talk when Mrs. Dunlap is talking. Then Ethan will go to the range and hit golf balls with different clubs. Mrs. Dunlap will come by and help Ethan when Ethan is practicing. Ethan will stop what Ethan is doing and listen carefully to Mrs. Dunlap. Then Ethan will go the putting green and practice putting. . . . "

4. People with AS often have an extremely rich expressive language but have difficulty using this language in social settings. Be prepared to teach appropriate social communication skills and then create a setting that will provide opportunities to practice and use these skills appropriately. For example, not correcting or criticizing a peer and saying "Good try" instead will have to be taught. Remember, people with AS see things as wrong or right without an ability to discern that even though peers are doing a skill incorrectly they may be trying their best.

5. Fine and gross motor clumsiness can be minimized by working on individual skill

components through one-on-one instruction and small group drills.

6. Competition can be an issue. Winning can be all consuming, and losing is seen as failure (and may promote a tantrum). Try to play cooperative activities rather than having participants compete against each other. For example, scatter 100 golf balls on the putting green and then ask the group to see how long it takes to sink all 100 golf balls. This way the group is a team and there are no winners or losers.

Golf Programs for People With Attentional Impairments

There are no specific golf programs for people with learning disabilities, attention-deficit/hyperactivity disorder, autism, or Asperger's syndrome. Many people with attentional impairments have the motor and cognitive skills to play in regular golf leagues or as an individual or with a group on public and private golf courses. Many can become as good as any golfer. For those individuals with motor problems, the built-in handicap system used in golf is a great equalizer, allowing them to participate equally with family and friends.

People with autism, especially those with more severe autism, may have a more difficult time playing golf on a public or private course without accommodations. Cognitive, behavioral, social, and motor deficits will affect participation. Assistance from a family member or peer may make it possible for them to participate in a golf program. On the other hand, Special Olympics golf is a viable option for participation in a modified golf program. Special Olympics golf offers regulation 18-hole golf, 9-hole golf, and skills contests. In addition, Special Olympics offers more support in the form of modified instruction and a better golfer-to-coach ratio. For more information on Special Olympics golf, see page 87 in chapter 9.

Chapter 11

Visual Impairments

John has been an avid golfer for the past 40 years. He started playing golf in college when one of his friends suggested they play a round at the university golf course. He quickly became hooked, took a golf class through the physical education department at the university, and played twice every weekend and once a week until he graduated. After graduation, John took a good job with an accounting firm, joined the local country club, and played golf at least three times a week for the next 30 years.

A few years back, John noticed that he was having trouble reading at work. He had been wearing glasses for the past 20 years, and he had gone through various strengths of lens prescriptions as he got older. But the problems he was having at work were a little different. He could still see the edges of the paper he was reading clearly, but the center

of the paper was blurry. He also noticed when he played golf that he was able to see the edges of the fairway and rough clearly, but the center of the fairway seemed blurred. He tried new glasses, but the new prescription did not help the blurriness. He finally went to an ophthalmologist, who diagnosed him with macular degeneration. John was gradually losing his vision, and there was nothing he could do about it.

John has worked enough years with his accounting firm to retire comfortably, so he is not worried about work or money. As strange as it may sound, John's biggest concern is his golf game. John still loves to play golf, and he still harbors a dream of retiring to a golf community in south Florida with his wife, also an avid golfer. How can he continue to play golf if he can't see the ball or the golf course?

Visual impairment is a catch-all term used to identify a person who has some level of visual loss, whether slight or total loss, that cannot be adequately corrected by glasses. The threshold to qualify as a person who has a visual impairment is based on two measures of vision. The first measures visual acuity, or how clearly you can see. One of the more common tools used to measure

visual acuity is the Snellen chart, which contains letters of the alphabet arranged by line with each line of letters decreasing in size. The single, large letter on the top represents 20/200 vision (legal blindness), while the characters on the bottom represent 20/20 vision. The chart is used with a person seated 20 feet (6.1 meters) away. A person who has normal visual acuity has 20/20 vision—at 20 feet (6.1 meters) the person can see the lines of letters that people with normal vision can see. In other words, a person with 20/200 vision sees at 20 feet (6.1 meters) what a person with normal vision sees at 200 feet (61 meters). To qualify as a person with a visual impairment, visual acuity must be 20/200 or less in the better eye even with correction (e.g., eyeglasses).

For young children who cannot identify letters, the Lighthouse Flash Card Test is often used. This test is similar to the Snellen chart but substitutes pictures such as an apple, a house, or a square for letters. For people with more severe vision loss, visual acuity can be measured by having the person count fingers (CF) or identify hand movements (HM) from a certain distance or detect light (Holbrook, 1996). Rather than a score of 20/200, a person might have a score of CF 2' (counts fingers from 2 feet, or 61 centimeters, away).

The other type of vision that is measured is visual field, or the total area that can be seen without moving the eyes or head. Visual field is tested by having people keep perfectly still and focus on a spot directly in front. Then objects are slowly brought from behind into their visual field. When the object can be identified, the ophthalmologist records the degree of the field. The test is conducted for each eye. Young children are tested seated in their parent's lap while familiar toys are slowly brought into the visual field. A normal visual field is approximately 160 to 170 degrees. To be considered visually impaired, one must have a visual field of 20 degrees or less in the better eye. Note that some people have both visual acuity and visual field loss while others just have visual acuity loss or visual field loss (Holbrook, 1996).

Causes of Visual Impairment

There are three main causes of visual impairments. First, there may be a structural impairment or damage to one or more parts of the eye itself. This type of damage prevents critical structures in the eye from carrying out their function. For example, when the macula, a small area in the center of the retina that makes sharp, detailed vision possible for the center part of the eye, is damaged as in macular degeneration, people will have visual loss in the central part of their visual field. Second, the eyeball itself may have imperfections or be proportioned incorrectly, making it difficult for the eye to focus images to the back of the retina. Also known as refractive errors, such imperfections can often be corrected with glasses or contact lenses. One common example of refractive error is myopia, or nearsightedness, in which the person can see near objects clearly but has trouble focusing on objects at a distance. Third, the part of the brain that processes visual information may not work properly. Also known as cortical visual impairment, the structure of the eye and its various components may be normal, but the brain is unable to analyze and interpret visual information (see Common Causes of Visual Impairments for a list and explanation of common causes of visual impairments) (Holbrook, 1996).

Classification of Visual Impairment

There are many classification systems used to identify varying levels of visual impairment. In an educational classification system, children qualify as *visually impaired* if their visual disability adversely affects their educational performance. Children are classified as *blind* when education must be carried out through nonvisual methods, and children are classified as *partially sighted* when education can be carried out through vision but often with the support of special aids (print either made larger or magnified) (Auxter, Pyfer, & Huettig, 2001).

In more general terms, a person is considered partially sighted if visual acuity is 20/70 in the better eye after correction. *Legally blind* is visual acuity of 20/200 or greater in the better eye or a visual field of 20 degrees or less. *Travel vision* is the ability to see at 5 to 10 feet (1.5 to 3 meters) what the nonimpaired

Structural Impairments

- **Cataracts.** Cataracts are cloudiness or film that forms on the lens of the eye. Cataracts prevent light from passing through the lens properly, which in turn affects vision. Cataracts can occur at birth or develop later in life, they can occur in one or both eyes, and they can remain stable or become worse. In severe cases, an individual with cataracts might only be able to detect light from dark. Surgery to remove the cataract is often prescribed.

- **Glaucoma.** This is a condition in which pressure from fluid inside the anterior chamber of the eyes is too high. If the condition is not detected early and treated, the excessive pressure can irreversibly damage the optic nerve. Nerve damage results in loss of peripheral vision initially, and damage to the central vision occurs as the disease progresses. Prescription eye drops or oral medications may decrease the pressure, but in some cases surgery is necessary to drain the excess fluid. The degree of visual impairment from glaucoma depends on the age of onset, how soon the condition is diagnosed and treated, and how well the condition responds to treatment.

- **Amblyopia.** Amblyopia usually occurs in children when the child uses one eye more than the other. For some reason the brain ignores visual information from one eye. Over time the nonused or "lazy" eye may experience a permanent loss. Treatment consists of treating any condition that may cause the child to use only one eye (e.g., cataracts or refractive errors), then patching the good eye, forcing the child to use the lazy eye for several months to a year. If amblyopia is detected and treated before the visual system has fully matured (around age nine), the visual loss may be reversible.

- **Retinitis pigmentosis.** This is a progressive condition in which the retina breaks down and no longer works properly. At first, the person has trouble with night vision. The disease often progresses to the point where the person develops tunnel vision with blurriness along the periphery of the visual field. There is no treatment for retinitis pigmentosis other than magnification.

- **Retinal blastoma.** This is a type of cancer that affects the retina. There is no cure for this type of cancer, and the treatment of choice usually involves complete removal of the eye. People who have an eye removed often wear a nonfunctional prosthetic eyeball.

- **Strabismus.** Strabismus is a condition in which one or both eyes are misaligned or crossed. Treatment is based on the cause. If a child is having trouble focusing, then glasses are often prescribed. If the condition is congenital (the child is born with crossed eyes), then surgery is used to correct the misalignment. If untreated, strabismus can lead to the child favoring one eye over the other (amblyopia), which can in turn lead to visual loss.

- **Nystagmus.** In this condition one or both eyes move or oscillate back and forth or up and down seemingly on their own. Visual acuity is reduced, with distance vision ranging from 20/40 to 20/400. Nystagmus may be congenital or may be secondary to cataracts, albinism (see the following condition), or cortical blindness. Children often find a "null point" in which they can position their head to reduce nystagmus and enhance vision. Surgery may be recommended to align this null point with proper head position. There is no other treatment for nystagmus.

- **Albinism.** This is an inherited (from birth) condition that causes a decrease in pigment in the skin, hair, and eyes, though it can occur in the eyes only. The lack of pigment in the front of the eye (iris) is most noticeable and leads to a very blue iris. People with albinism have an incompletely formed macula (the central part of the retina, which provides the sharpest vision), and as a result have reduced visual acuity. Treatment involves corrective lenses that can improve visual acuity to 20/100 to 20/200. People with albinism are also very sensitive to light and must wear tinted glasses at all times.

- **Macular degeneration.** In this condition, the macula, a small area in the center of the retina that makes sharp, detailed vision possible, deteriorates over time either through atrophy, scar tissue formation on the macula, or the formation of yellow deposits that cause the macula to dry out and thin. The result is a blind spot and thus a loss of some or all central vision. There is no treatment other than prescribed aids such as handheld magnifiers, pocket telescopes, and other assistive devices. Macular degeneration is the leading cause of vision loss among older adults.

(continued)

(continued)

Refractive Errors

• **Myopia.** Also known as nearsightedness, in myopia the cornea (the clear dome on the front of the eye) is excessively curved, the lens is too strong, or the eye is elongated. As a result, images of distant objects are not focused precisely on the retina, but in front of the retina. This makes distant objects appear blurry. Near vision is usually unaffected. Myopia is very common, affecting approximately 20 percent of all adults. Glasses are often prescribed to counterbalance the refractive error.

• **Hyperopia.** Also known as farsightedness, in hyperopia the cornea is relatively flat, the eye is not as long as normal, or the focusing power of the eye is too weak. As a result, objects focus at a point behind the retina, causing the individual to have trouble focusing on nearby objects. As with myopia, glasses are often prescribed to counterbalance the refractive error.

• **Astigmatism.** In astigmatism, the cornea is not shaped correctly, causing light rays passing through to be improperly focused. Usually the cornea is curved more vertically than horizontally. The result is that both near and far objects may appear blurry. Astigmatism often appears in conjunction with myopia or hyperopia, but astigmatism and other refractive problems usually can be corrected with glasses.

Cortical Visual Impairment

Cortical visual impairment is due to damage to the optic nerve or the brain rather than any structural or refractive impairment. The damage prevents the individual from receiving or interpreting information from the eyes even though the eyes may function normally. Damage may result in a loss of some visual acuity or even total blindness. Causes of cortical visual impairment range from insufficient oxygen to the brain prior to or during birth or during heart surgery, hydrocephalus (fluid buildup on the brain), stroke, or trauma. In children, cortical visual impairment often is related to brain impairments such as cerebral palsy or mental retardation. There is no medical treatment for cortical visual impairment, but occasionally glasses are prescribed to correct any secondary refractive errors. Cortical visual impairments do not worsen, but in some cases, particularly when the damage to the brain is due to trauma or stroke, vision may improve over time.

Adapted, by permission, from S. Stiles and R. Knox, 1996, Medical issues, treatments, and professionals. In *Children with visual impairments,* edited by M.C. Holbrook (Bethesda, MD: Woodbine House), 21-48.

Adapted, with permission, from L. Lieberman, 2005, Visual impairments. In *Adapted physical education and sport,* 4th ed., edited by J.P. Winnick (Champaign, IL: Human Kinetics), 206-207.

eye can see at 200 feet (61 meters), or visual acuity of 5/200 to 10/200. *Motion perception* is the ability to see movement but not identify what is moving at 5 to 10 feet (1.5 to 3 meters) what a person without visual impairment can see from 200 feet (61 meters). *Total blindness* classifies people who have no residual vision and cannot recognize a strong light shone directly into the eyes (Lieberman, 2005).

One of the more common sight classifications used in sports to distinguish among people with varying levels of vision is the three-pronged classification system used by the International Blind Golf Association (IBGA) and the United States Association for Blind Athletes (USABA). Both systems are used to make competition as equal as possible. In other words, it would not be fair to

have a person who only has light perception compete against a person who has 20/200 vision (see Classification Systems for Visual Impairment) unless the USGA modified rules were in effect. Athletes who have more significant visual losses (e.g., B1 athletes) would be allowed more accommodations (e.g., a coach to walk with the player, line the player up for shots, and give correct distances).

Common Characteristics of People With Visual Impairments

It is difficult to identify a set of characteristics common to all people with visual

Classification Systems for Visual Impairment

International Blind Golf Association Classification System

These categories are accepted and recognized by the International Blind Golf Association (IBGA) and the United States Blind Golf Association (USBGA).

Totally Blind Division

B1: No light perception, or light perception that is not functional, central, or peripheral, with or without light projection, up to the inability to differentiate between a blank sheet of white paper and a sheet of white paper with a black symbol on it. (The black symbol is displayed on the IBGA/USBGA Sight Form and is used as part of the exam.)

Vision Impaired Division

B2: From the ability to recognize the shape of a hand up to visual acuity of 20/600.

B3: From the visual acuity above 20/600 up to visual acuity of less than 20/200.

All classifications are in best eye with best correction.

United States Association for Blind Athletes Classification System

B1: No light perception in either eye up to light perception and unable to recognize the shape of a hand at any distance or in any direction

B2: Able to recognize the shape of a hand up to a visual acuity of 20/600 or a visual field of less than 5 degrees in the best eye with the best practical eye correction

B3: From visual acuity above 20/600 and up to visual acuity of 20/200 or a visual field of less than 20 degrees and more than 5 degrees in the best eye with the best practical eye correction

Courtesy of the United States Blind Golf Association (USBGA). www.blindgolf.com.

---

impairments. Age of onset, cause of visual loss, severity of visual loss, current age, and having other disabilities all affect how a person might act, think, and move. Nevertheless, the following are some common characteristics associated with people who have visual impairments.

Cognitive Ability

Most people with visual impairments have normal cognitive development and abilities. In fact, many people with visual impairments may be very bright because they tend to spend more time on academic pursuits such as listening to audiobooks and using a computer with voice synthesizers rather than motor pursuits. People with visual impairments also tend to have good verbal skills and can communicate quite well. People whose visual impairments are secondary to other cognitive disabilities (e.g., mental retardation) may have cognitive problems.

Motor Development, Skill Level, and Physical Fitness

The inability to see properly does not in itself cause a person to have delayed motor development or limited levels of physical fitness. However, people with visual impairments often have fewer opportunities to practice motor skills or to work on physical fitness compared to people without visual impairments (Lieberman, 2005). For example, it's simple for a child without visual impairments to go out to the driveway and shoot basketballs or walk up the street to join a group of friends in a kickball game. Similarly, a person without visual impairments can easily get up and go for a walk or jog in the neighborhood or drive to the local health club to work out. But for a person with a visual impairment, shooting baskets, finding a group of friends to play games with, and exercising often require some sort of help from others. Spontaneity is just not as available to people with visual impairments, and the effort and the desire to not burden a parent, neighbor, or friend may be enough to prevent the person from playing or exercising. In addition, most children and adults learn a great deal about how to move by observing others, whether watching friends, teachers, and coaches or watching professional athletes on TV. Such observational learning is not available to people with visual impairments. Finally, people with visual impairments may be less skilled because they have fewer opportunities to practice and observe and thus are less successful in sports compared to their peers with normal vision, which often makes them less interested and motivated to participate in physical activity.

The bottom line is that research clearly shows that children who are blind or who have visual impairments are delayed in motor development, children and adults with visual impairments usually do not reach the same skill level as children and adults without visual impairments, and children and adults with visual impairments are less physically fit compared to children and adults without visual impairments. Again, this does not necessarily have to be the case. People who lose their vision later in life have had the opportunity to learn motor skills (including golf) with the aid of vision. Motor skills should be fairly well developed in these individuals, and fitness levels have a great chance of approaching average or better levels. People close to children born with visual impairments should encourage participation in physical activity from an early age to prevent poor skill development, low fitness, and low motivation and interest in sports.

Social Characteristics

People who are blind or who have visual impairments should have normal social skills and behaviors. However, as is the case with motor development and fitness, the inability to see appropriate body language and behavior, the inability to see how others react to conversations and interactions, and fewer opportunities to be in social settings often lead to some social inadequacies in people with visual impairments. For most people with visual impairments, the social inadequacies are minimal and can be improved with some insight and instruction from parents or friends. In other cases, particularly with people who were born with a visual impairment and never had a chance to see appropriate social behaviors, inappropriate behavior can be a problem. For example, some people who are born with a visual impairment exhibit blindisms, or self-stimulatory, repetitive behaviors such as rocking back and forth, shaking their head, and rubbing their eyes. The exact cause of these behaviors is unknown, but such behaviors make the person with a visual impairment stand out more than necessary.

Teaching Golf to People With Visual Impairments

The vast majority of individuals with visual impairments have no cognitive or learning impairments, nor do they have any physical impairments. Therefore, suggested modifications focus on accommodating problems associated with limited vision. One consideration is whether or not the golfer was born with a visual impairment or lost vision later in life. As noted, those who were born without vision or lost their vision at a very young age will have no visual reference for movement and what certain movements such as a golf swing should look like. In addition, understanding movement concepts such as "Slow down your swing" or "Use more rotation" will be more difficult for someone who never had a chance to learn and practice movement with vision. On the other hand, people who have learned how to move, particularly those who played golf before they lost their vision, may have a much better swing and understanding of the game. However, since these individuals will have had less time to adjust to their visual impairment, they will most likely have more difficulty with simpler things such as reading Braille, using a cane, and generally feeling comfortable with their vision loss. The following suggestions for teaching golf to people with visual impairments have been adapted from Auxter, Pyfer, and Huettig (2001), Block (2000), Lieberman and Cowart (1996), and Sherrill (1998).

Communication

How you communicate with golfers who are blind or visually impaired will be one of the greatest challenges. Clearly, demonstrations are not going to be effective, so other techniques will be necessary. The following suggestions focus on how to communicate with golfers with visual impairments.

1. Feel free to speak naturally to the person who is blind. Do not speak louder than normal unless the person also has a hearing impairment, and do not be afraid to use *see,* such as "Good to see you again" or "See you later." State your name and the names of anyone who might be with you when approaching the golfer ("Hey Sally, it's Mark, and I'm here with Jill and Marie. How are you doing with your short putting?"). Similarly, tell the golfer when you are leaving the area ("Sally, Jill and I are going to the range to see how the other golfers are doing."). Finally, speak to the golfer, not to the golfer's coach or friend. For example, if you want to know how many putts Sally made, ask her rather than her coach—her coach will know how many putts she has made and convey this to her as she practices, but it is more considerate to ask Sally directly.

2. Demonstrations will not be effective for most golfers who are blind or who have visual impairments. However, some golfers will have residual vision and benefit from at least some aspect of demonstrations, so ask the golfer if he can see aspects of demonstrations. If so, find out how to make the demonstration more effective. This may be as simple as allowing the person to stand closer to you when you demonstrate, slowing down the demonstration, or wearing contrasting colors (e.g., wearing a red armband against a white shirt)

to highlight a key aspect of the hand or arm position or the swing.

3. Regardless of the amount of residual vision the golfer has, the golfer who is blind or who has visual impairment will rely mostly on verbal and physical cues. However, verbal cues will have to be more specific to compensate for the golfer's inability to see a demonstration. For example, giving verbal cues such as "Swing like this," or "Take your backswing to about here," will obviously make no sense to a person with a visual impairment. Better verbal cues might be, "Swing so that your hands reach a position about 2 o'clock while keeping your left arm almost straight while bending your right arm to about 90 degrees." It will take some practice, but using references that do not require vision, such as the face of a clock for start and stop positions, degrees for proper angles, and inches or feet for distances to move, will be the easiest for people with visual impairments to understand. If a coach is available, she can work with the person with visual impairment to help him get the feel for the path he should follow away from the ball. The coach can turn the head of the club so the toe, the end away from the shaft, is pointed toward the ground. Then she can place a shaft under the club so the golfer could drag his club up the shaft and follow the best line for his take away.

4. Specific verbal cues are also necessary to explain the layout of the hole and to give feedback after the shot. Again, use the clock coupled with specific measurements as a reference such as, "There are trees to the right starting around 2 o'clock, there is a pond straight ahead at 12 o'clock about 10 yards in front of the tee box and running for about 50 yards, and there is a sand trap at 11 o'clock about 200 yards from the tee." Feedback after the shot should include not only telling the player where the ball went but also explaining what the ball flight looked like. Ball flight information (e.g., slice, draw) can help the person compare what the swing feels like to how the ball moved. For example, you might say "Your ball went about 150 yards and ended

up in the right rough about 10 yards from the fairway. It started straight for about the first 20 yards then started to curve a little to the right. It landed in the fairway about 5 yards from the rough but then bounced and rolled into the rough."

5. While specific verbal cues will compensate for the inability to see demonstrations, in many situations physical assistance will be needed to help the person who is blind or who has a visual impairment understand the exact movement. Physical assistance can occur in three ways. First, simply place the golf club in the correct position or move the golf club through the proper swing to help the golfer get a feel for the correct technique. If this does not work, more hands-on physical assistance might be necessary. For example, physically put the golfer's hands on the club in the correct placement to help her understand the correct grip. For more complex movements such as the swing used for a lob wedge, you may need to allow the golfer to actually stand behind you, hold your arms, and feel how you swing the club. Also known as brailling, this technique allows the golfer to feel what the movement is like as modeled from an expert.

6. If a golfer does not have an Internet connection to access the rules of golf online, written material (e.g., rules and etiquette or the scorecard) will need to be converted to large print or Braille or recorded on audiotape depending on the vision of the players and how they read. Ask the golfers where they go to get written material converted, or contact your local association for the blind (e.g., local affiliate of the American Foundation for the Blind or American Council for the Blind) for information on who in your area can convert written material. Also, if a coach is not available, tape-record the yardage, handicap, and layout for each hole on the course so the player can listen to the recording just before each hole.

Equipment and Rule Modifications

Most golfers who are blind or who have visual impairments will use regulation golf equip-

ment and follow the rules of golf without modification other than using a "coach" to help with lining up the shot and getting feedback on the result of the shot. However, the following equipment modifications can help players learn the game during practice.

1. Auditory cues such as a sound placed on the driving range can help the player be more independent when lining up the shot. For example, place a radio 20 yards (18 meters) down the range to line up long shots or at a specific place 80 to 120 yards (73 to 110 meters) down the range as an auditory target for short irons. Feedback will still be required to help the player understand if the shot was successful. For putting, a peer can tap the flagpole against the hole to help the player line up or a radio can be placed just behind the hole.

2. Sighted golfers can practice on their own away from the range, hitting and then retrieving golf balls. This is not possible for golfers with visual impairments unless some adaptations are made. One relatively simple adaptation involves having the golfer hit a ball into a net or suspended blanket. Below the blanket are two boards 8 feet (244 centimeters) long and 2 inches (5 centimeters) wide laid out into a triangle and placed over a 6-by-6-foot (183-by-183-centimeter) piece of 1/2-inch-wide (1.3-centimeter-wide) plywood with the wide part below the blanket and the narrow part near the golfer. Slightly elevate the wide part of the triangle (e.g., place some books under the piece of plywood at the wide end) so that the ball rolls down toward the golfer. This way the golfer can practice on his own.

3. Setting up the golf bag in a specific order can help people who have residual vision. Then they can simply return the club to the spot they retrieved it.

Safety Modifications

Safety is important for all golfers, but having a visual impairment makes safety an even greater concern. The following are some safety considerations for golfers who have visual impairments.

1. Analyze the environment to look for potentially dangerous obstacles and then either remove the obstacles or make them safer for the golfer who is blind. When an obstacle cannot be removed (e.g., practice sand trap next to driving range), consider putting a barrier around it, such as cones, so the player does not fall into it.

2. Provide a detailed explanation of the environment to the golfer. Also known as anchoring, this gives the golfer a better understanding of the layout of the setting, people near the golfer, and potential hazards. This includes explaining unique sounds or smells in the area (e.g., the banging sound of the carpenter working on the roof of the clubhouse). For example, at the range say, "The range has 12 stations to hit from with plastic dividers 3 feet high between each station. There is a sidewalk running parallel to and 4 feet behind the hitting stations. If you are on the sidewalk, you are safe from getting hit by someone's golf club. There is a practice sand trap at the far end of the range about 20 yards past the last hitting station, but you will be positioned at the first station (closest to the clubhouse). Sarah will be positioned next to you, and David will be next to Sarah. In each area is a 4-by-5-inch piece of carpeting that is about 1 inch thick. Be careful stepping up on the carpet. After the carpet you will feel concrete for about 1 foot, and then there is a drop-off of about 5 feet that leads into the range." Let the golfer physically walk or touch as many features as possible as long as it is done in a safe manner.

3. Modify the setting to make it safer. For example, in the driving range example where there is a drop-off at the end of each station, you might put a piece of bright yellow ribbon at the start of the drop-off to help a person with low vision see where it begins. Similarly, putting bright orange ribbons or balloons on the small flags in the holes on the putting green might prevent golfers with low vision from walking into the flagpoles. Highlight obstacles that might be potentially dangerous by adding bright colors (e.g., colored paper, ribbons, or balloons) or adding barriers (e.g., putting cones in front of an area near the range that drops off).

4. Create some simple procedures to ensure safety. Before a golfer who is blind starts his swing, it is vital that the player ask the coach, if available, if he is clear. This is done to be sure the coach has moved away from the golfer, and just to be sure nothing else has moved in the way. For example, sometimes a person may top a ball that doesn't roll very far and decide to walk in front of another player in order to pick that ball up and play it again. But a golfer who is blind should never assume it is safe to swing and should check with the coach to make sure he is clear. Note that golfers with residual vision might want to be more independent on the course; however, they may not have as much vision as they think. In such cases, watch the golfer and see how she moves around the course. If the golfer has no problems, allow her to play independently unless she asks for help. But do not assume the golfer needs or wants help. The worst thing you can do is rush up to the golfer and take her by the arm and say "Let me help you!" If the golfer is having trouble moving around the course, it's fine to warn, and use the words "Watch out" or "Careful" or "Watch out for the hill right in front of you, it's steep."

Golf Programs for People With Visual Impairments

The governing bodies of golf for people with visual impairments are the International Blind Golf Association (IGBA) and the United States Blind Golf Association (USBGA). Like other sports associations for the blind, golfers are divided by visual abilities (see Classification Systems for Visual Impairment on page 115). Golfers who are totally blind (B1) are considered BGA members; golfers who have a visual impairment (B2 and B3) are BGA associate members; and golf professionals, coaches, or family and friends are BGA support members. The USBGA was founded by players who were totally blind, and it is written in the bylaws that only totally blind golfers may become BGA members. The IBGA and USBGA follow the rules of regular golf with only a few modifications. One major modification is allowing golfers who are blind to ground their club in a hazard. Other modifications practiced, but not considered *rule* modifications, are the use of a coach who assists the golfer in setting up the ball and aligning the body and club before playing a stroke and explaining where the coach can stand when the golfer is putting. This modification is considered "in equity," but if you read the rules of golf, it is only mentioned as being equitable, not "allowed."

The USBGA holds local, regional, and national golf tournaments in the United States. For more information about modified rules used by the USBGA, how to join the USBGA, or about tournaments in your area, visit www.blindgolf.com.

Chapter 12

Hearing Impairments

Deafness and *hard of hearing* are basically synonymous terms used to describe a person with a hearing loss in which hearing is inadequate for comprehending auditory information, even with the use of a hearing aid. The term *hard of hearing* refers to a person with a hearing loss that makes it difficult, but not impossible, to understand speech through the ear. Most people with a hearing loss are hard of hearing with some residual hearing, not totally Deaf. People in the Deaf community actually prefer the term *deafness* over *hearing impairment,* because many deaf people do not consider themselves disabled. Additionally, people in the Deaf community prefer to be referred to as a Deaf person rather than a person who is Deaf. Note that the term Deaf is capitalized, indicating that the Deaf community is a culture with a language (sign language) and not just a group of people with hearing issues (Lieberman, 2005).

Hearing loss as well as residual hearing are measured in two ways: intensity and frequency. Intensity refers to the perception of loudness or sound, and the standard that is used to measure intensity of hearing is decibel (dB) levels. Most children can hear sounds as faint as 0 to 25 dB. Everyday conversational speech occurs in the range of 40 to 50 dB, while noise over 125 dB is considered extremely loud and even painful. A person with a slight hearing loss would be able to hear sounds as low as 25 to 40 dB, and a loss of 55 dB or greater qualifies a person to compete in sports sanctioned by the USA Deaf Sports Federation (USADSF) (Paciorek & Jones, 2001).

Frequency refers to perception of high and low pitch, which is measured in terms of hertz (Hz). Most people with average hearing perceive frequencies from about 20 to 20,000 Hz. A low-pitched sound such as the lowest key on the piano is about 30 Hz. Middle C on the piano is about 250 Hz, and a high-pitched sound such as the highest key on the piano is about 4,000 Hz. Frequencies between 125 and 8,000 Hz are most important in everyday conversation, so losses in these areas will have the greatest influence on understanding speech. More typical hearing-loss profiles include a hearing loss above 2,000 Hz (difficulty hearing higher-pitched sounds) or below 500 Hz (difficulty hearing lower-pitched sounds).

Causes of Hearing Impairments

There are three main causes of hearing loss: conductive hearing loss, sensorineural hearing loss, and central auditory processing problems. (There also is a fourth type of loss known as a mixed type in which the person has both conductive and sensorineural hearing loss.) A conductive hearing loss is a condition in which an obstruction or deficit in the outer or middle part of the ear prevents sounds from being carried to the inner part of the ear. Basically, the intensity or loudness of the sound is muffled or reduced before entering the inner ear. There is usually no distortion of the sound, it just sounds faint. Putting your fingers in your ears creates about a 25-dB conductive loss.

Conductive losses usually affect hearing at all frequencies evenly and rarely result in a severe hearing loss (NICHCY, 2001). The most common causes of conductive hearing loss are otitis media, an infection of the middle ear common in young children, mastoiditis, chronic inflammation in the middle ear, rupture of the eardrum from a blow to the head, congenital distortions of the ear canal, and impacted ear wax. Many conductive hearing impairments can be corrected with surgery, and all types of conductive losses can be improved with amplification (hearing aids) (Sherrill, 1998).

Sensorineural loss is a condition in which structures within the inner ear, where sensory receptors convert sound waves to neural impulses that then travel to the brain, are damaged. Damage to the inner ear may occur either in the sensory units (the cochlea) or the neural units (the eighth cranial nerve). The result is not only a loss of the ability to hear loud sounds but sounds may be distorted. Sensorineural losses often affect the ability to make sense of sounds in the higher speech frequencies, making it difficult to understand speech. Amplification only helps the person hear distorted sounds, so many people with sensorineural losses do not wear hearing aids except to hear gross sounds (Auxter, Pyfer, & Huettig, 2001; NICHCY, 2001). Since the vestibular apparatus that assists in balance is located in the inner ear, some people with sensorineural hearing losses also have trouble with activities that require balance (Sherrill, 1998). Causes of sensorineural hearing loss include recessive genetic problems, maternal rubella or venereal disease during pregnancy, lesions or tumors in the inner ear, long-term exposure to loud sounds, deterioration through aging, and infections in childhood such as mumps, inner ear infections, meningitis, and encephalitis (Auxter, Pyfer, & Huettig, 2001).

Central auditory processing problems occur when damage to the nerves of the central nervous system, either in the auditory pathways to the brain or in the brain itself, prevents the translation of sounds to meaning. In other words, sounds may be transmitted faithfully from the outer and middle ear and through the inner ear, but the brain cannot translate these sound waves into anything meaningful. The person may or may not be able to hear sounds, but in either case he or she is unable to make any sense of the sounds that are heard (NICHCY, 2001). Causes of central auditory processing problems are usually congenital, resulting from the brain not forming properly or some type of trauma such as lack of oxygen during fetal development.

Classification of Hearing Impairment

Hearing loss can range from slight to profound depending on the intensity of loss, and categories of loss have been established to distinguish among different levels of loss (see table 12.1). Note that a loss of 70 dB or greater is commonly used as the frequency loss that separates hard of hearing from deafness. Frequency loss is also used when deter-

Table 12.1 Classification of Hearing Loss

Degree of loss	Loss in decibels	Levels of loudness
Slight	25-40 dB	Difficulty hearing faint speech (e.g., whisper)
Mild	41-55 dB	Difficulty hearing normal speech at a distance greater than 3-5 ft (91-153 cm)
Marked	56-70 dB	Difficulty hearing loud speech, even at close range; discussions
Severe	71-90 dB	Difficulty hearing shouted speech, even with amplification
Profound	Greater than 90 dB	Difficulty hearing any speech, even with amplification, including a ringing telephone and musical instruments

Adapted, by permission, from L. Lieberman, 2005, Deafness and deafblindness. In J.P. Winnick (ed.), *Adapted physical education and sport,* 4th ed. (Champaign, IL: Human Kinetics), 222.

mining the extent of a person's hearing loss, but there are no separate criteria as is the case with intensity.

Another common way to distinguish among people with hearing loss is to note when they lost their hearing. Prelingual deafness refers to people who were born with a hearing loss or who lost their hearing before they developed speech and language (usually before age two). Postlingual deafness refers to people who lost their hearing after they already acquired speech and language. If people lose their hearing before learning speech and language, then learning to speak and to read lips can be extremely difficult. Most people who are prelingually deaf use sign language to communicate. On the other hand, people who have lost their hearing after obtaining speech and language can retain their ability to speak and can lip read with a fair amount of proficiency (Lieberman, 2005).

Common Characteristics of People With Hearing Impairments

As is the case with all the disabilities discussed in this book, it is difficult to identify a list of general characteristics that are commonly found in all people with a hearing loss. People with hearing losses can be intelligent or have learning problems; they can be well adjusted and happy or have psychological problems; they can go to college and become doctors and lawyers or they can go to a trade school; they can be gifted athletes or they can be clumsy. The Deaf population is as diverse as the general population. In fact, most Deaf people are more similar to than different from people without disabilities with the exception of dealing with a hearing loss. Nevertheless, the following characteristics are relatively common among Deaf people.

Language and Deaf Culture

Most people who have severe hearing loss prefer to use American Sign Language (ASL) to communicate rather than speech. ASL is a language in and of itself with a unique grammar and structure. While hearing people can learn ASL, most never do, and thus there is a great language barrier between Deaf people and people who can hear. The use of ASL is viewed as a shared identity among Deaf people and is a big part of the Deaf culture. Many Deaf people are actually proud that they are Deaf and view their deafness as an integral part of their identity. While Deaf people will make efforts to live and work in the hearing world, they are most comfortable among other people who use ASL and are Deaf.

Behaviors and Social Skills

Deafness alone does not cause behavior problems or social skill deficits. However, not being able to readily take part in informal conversations, not being able to understand directions and instructions, and being excluded from social groups can lead to behavior problems. This is particularly true in Deaf children who are integrated into a regular school and who are trying to fit into a hearing world. Intentionally or otherwise, hearing peers can exclude and ridicule Deaf children because Deaf children cannot keep up in conversations or understand rules of games. In addition, social nuances that are learned incidentally by most hearing children (e.g., body language, appropriate social behaviors) may not be clear to Deaf children. This can further cause embarrassment and isolation.

Motor Skills

As noted earlier, children and adults who have sensorineural hearing losses may also have balance problems. Apparently, damage to the inner ear that affects hearing also affects the vestibular apparatus that is used for balance. However, it does not appear that these balance problems affect overall gross motor development or physical fitness. In other words, with the exception of balance, most children and adults with hearing loss should have similar motor skills and fitness levels compared to people without hearing loss. However, do not discount the social concerns described earlier and the affect they may have on actual motor performance. Not understanding how to do the skills correctly because they don't understand the directions or not participating in community or interscholastic sports because of fears of not being able to understand the coach or teammates or the rules of the game may prevent Deaf children from reaching their motor potential.

Teaching Golf to People With Hearing Impairments

Since the vast majority of Deaf golfers will have no physical or cognitive impairments, key teaching strategies focus on communication issues. The following suggestions, adapted from Auxter, Pyfer, and Huettig (2001), Block (2000), and Sherrill (1998), focus on communicating with Deaf golfers. The suggestions you use will depend on whether the golfer has residual hearing, is proficient at reading lips, or uses sign language.

Lip Reading

Many Deaf golfers will use lip reading as a way to pick up verbal directions and cues. The following are simple ways you can help a Deaf golfer have an easier time reading lips.

1. Speak normally. Trying to speak louder or slower can change how your lips move and may actually make it more difficult for a person to read lips. Do not chew gum while speaking. Beards and mustaches may also create difficulty in reading lips. Keep your hands away from your face when speaking so the Deaf golfer has a clear view of your lips.

2. Position the Deaf golfer close to you and in a place where she can be most successful in reading lips (the golfer will know where best to stand).

3. Position yourself so you face the sun rather than having the golfer face the sun. In addition, try to avoid giving directions where there are a lot of distractions such as people moving in the background.

4. Try to stand still when giving instructions or at least limit how much you move. When demonstrating a skill, do not try to talk at the same time or repeat the verbal cues again while facing the Deaf golfer.

5. Accentuate verbal directions by using body language, facial expressions, and gestures to get ideas across. For example, after telling the golfer about the proper grip, look at your hand, regrip several times showing the correct grip, and then repeat the verbal direction.

6. Keep instructions simple and direct, and use essential words rather than long, difficult words.

Getting the Golfer's Attention

When golfers with hearing impairments are walking the course or actively practicing on the range, it may be difficult to get their attention. The following are some suggestions to get a golfer's attention.

1. Cue the golfer to look back at you after each practice stroke when putting or hitting in case you want to give cues (most Deaf golfers naturally look up often to see if there is anything going on that they need to know about).

2. Cue peers to help you get the attention of the Deaf golfer. For example, if you want to stop practice on the range to point out a correction for all the golfers in your class, say "Stop" to the group and have the person next to the Deaf golfer wave her hand to get the golfer's attention and then point to you to cue the Deaf golfer to look to you for instruction.

3. Use visual attention getters such as raising your hand, waving a towel, or waving a flag attached to the end of an umbrella. With the golfer already looking up at you occasionally while practicing or walking the course, the golfer will quickly see the visual cue and know to stop and look to you for instruction.

Types of Communication

Each Deaf golfer will have a preferred way to receive communication and to communicate with you. The following are some simple ideas regarding communication.

1. Obviously, demonstrations work best with Deaf golfers. Try to highlight key aspects of the demonstrations by pointing or tapping that part of the body, shaking that part of the body, or putting a piece of tape on that part of the body. Also, it is perfectly acceptable to slow down your swing to highlight a key aspect. However, make sure the Deaf golfer understands that you are slowing down the swing to highlight an aspect of the swing and that the real swing should actually be faster (it is best to show a slow swing first to highlight a part of the swing and then end with a demonstration of what the swing should look like in real time).

2. Ask the Deaf golfer how he prefers to communicate and then try your best to accommodate him. Note that most Deaf golfers will use multiple forms of communication, such as sign language and lip reading to understand your cues and speech and writing to communicate with you, so you might be able to use whichever form of communication is easiest for you. However, Deaf golfers will appreciate any effort you make to accommodate their preferred communication.

3. Use a buddy system so that peers can reexplain instructions and help the golfer know where to go. This also prevents the Deaf golfer from feeling isolated.

4. Golfers with hearing impairments will often have residual hearing, and they may be able to pick up quite a bit of information from your verbal cues. Again, find out if the golfer can hear you, under what circumstances, and what you can do to enhance her ability to understand your speech.

5. Learn some simple signs (the Deaf golfer can teach you), and use these signs whenever possible during your instruction and when communicating with the Deaf golfer. The Deaf golfer will appreciate your effort to learn and use sign language.

6. Use visual materials to communicate body placement (e.g., footprints to show foot placement).

7. If you are showing videos, try to get them captioned (written words on the bottom of the screen) so the Deaf golfer can follow the verbal cues on the tape. Check your local phone directory for places that can add captions to videos.

8. Don't forget to explain golf etiquette, especially being quiet when someone is hitting (remember, Deaf golfers cannot hear the sounds they might be making). Demonstrate etiquette through "dos and don'ts" exhibitions. For example, when a golfer is getting ready to hit, move around a little, then shake your head "no" to convey that you should not move when a golfer is getting ready to hit. Then have the golfer address the ball again while you show how still to stand.

9. In some cases, especially in groups or clinics, it might be necessary to employ a sign language interpreter.

Golf Programs for People With Hearing Impairments

There is no longer a specific golf association for Deaf golfers (at one time there was the National Deaf Golfers Association). However, golf has recently become an official sport of the USA Deaf Sports Federation (USADSF, 2002). There are no sport classifications for Deaf athletes (including Deaf golfers). To qualify one has to have a hearing loss of 55 dB or greater in the better ear, and the use of hearing aids during competition is prohibited. Since Deaf athletes have no physical disabilities, there are virtually no rule modifications for any Deaf sports, including golf. For more information, contact the USADSF.

Chapter 13

Physical Disabilities

Missy was always a happy child. As a baby, she beamed at her mother and father every time they looked at her. Even when friends of her parents came to visit, Missy was ready with a big smile and a hug. This happy personality carried into preschool and later into elementary school. She loved school, she loved playing with her friends, and she loved her teachers. Every day Missy would come home excited about what she did, whom she played with, and what she learned.

Middle and high school were no different. Missy continued to do well in school, and she was very popular with her friends and teachers. She joined the orchestra, she was president of her class, and she was involved with the yearbook and school newspaper. It seemed like there was nothing Missy could not do, which was even more remarkable given that Missy was born with spina bifida. For some unknown reason, Missy's spinal cord didn't form properly before she was born. The result was that Missy was born paralyzed from the waist down. Sure, she had to learn how to use a wheelchair, how to do things in physical education a little differently than her peers, and how to deal with health issues related to her disability that resulted in 10 different surgeries by the time she was 16 years old. But Missy never used her disability as an excuse for not doing things or not excelling in everything she did. She truly was a remarkable young woman.

Missy was completing her junior year in high school, and like all high school students she was looking forward to the summer. She had recently gotten her driver's license (she used hand controls), and with her new independence she was looking forward to having some fun and finding a job so she could start saving money for college. One idea she had was to work at a country club across town. She had heard that this country club paid their waitresses well, and she knew that a few of her friends were hoping to work there this summer too. And, she was intrigued by the game of golf. Her father was an avid golfer, and Missy would occasionally sit with him on the weekends watching golf tournaments on TV. Missy even enjoyed practicing putting with him in their living room. She thought it would be fun for her and a nice surprise for her father if she worked at the country club and took advantage of the club's policy of allowing employees to take lessons, practice at the driving range, and even use the golf course for free. She figured she could practice during the week during her break time and maybe take lessons with the club pro once or twice a week before work. By the end of the summer she would surprise her father by taking him to the club (a place he talked about longingly but never played at) and playing a round of golf with him.

Fortunately for Missy, the club restaurant and golf teaching professional both were willing

(continued)

(continued)

to give her a chance. She quickly became an adept and popular waitress at the club, skillfully balancing trays of food on her lap while pushing her chair through the restaurant (to the amazement of many customers). Missy also became a regular at the driving range, whether by herself or with the club teaching professional, and she learned to be a very competent golfer by the end of the summer. The teaching professional even borrowed a single-rider golf car for Missy to use that had a pivoting seat and modified tires so she could easily drive around the course and play from the car. As promised, in late August Missy drove her father to the golf club to play a round of golf. Her father just assumed that Missy would sit in the car and watch him play. He was surprised when Missy pulled up in her single-rider golf car with her clubs to pick him up from the bag-drop area. She surprised him even more when she easily drove her car up to the tee box, addressed the ball from her car, and ripped a driver (modified to accommodate hitting from a seated position) about 125 yards (114 meters) right down the middle of the fairway. Missy and her father enjoyed playing golf together that day in August, and they are now frequently seen around town at other golf courses.

Physical disability is a broad term used to define anyone with a condition caused by a disease (e.g., cancer resulting in an amputation), traumatic injury (e.g., spinal cord injury), or neurological impairment (e.g., cerebral palsy) that affects the ability to move. Some physical disabilities result in movement with a limp or slightly different gait pattern (e.g., Casey Martin walks with a limp due to a circulation problem that affects his legs). For others, a physical disability may require the use of prosthetics or a walking aid such as a cane or crutches. Still others may require the use of a manual or motorized wheelchair to move independently. With rare exceptions, people with physical disabilities do not have cognitive impairments, so adaptations focus more on equipment and alternative ways to swing a golf club and move around the course than on different teaching styles. While there are literally hundreds of different kinds of orthopedic conditions, the focus of this chapter will be on the most common types of conditions: spinal cord injuries, amputations, and neuromuscular disorders including cerebral palsy, muscular dystrophy, and multiple sclerosis. Each disability will be defined followed by a review of common characteristics and treatments. When appropriate, common classification systems will be outlined. The chapter concludes with suggestions for golf professionals who work with people with physical disabilities.

Spinal Cord Injury

Spinal cord injuries are a class of disabilities in which the vertebrae (bones) or nerves in the spinal column are damaged. Such damage affects the ability of the central nervous system (spinal cord and nerves, which control movement and sensation) to send information to the muscles of the body. Consequently, the person has some degree of paralysis, or loss of movement as well as loss of feeling. There is nothing wrong with the muscles, it is just that the information from the brain to the muscles must travel through the spinal nerves, and the spinal nerves no longer provide information to the muscles. In addition, spinal injuries often affect the autonomic nervous system, which controls vital functions such as heart rate, blood pressure, temperature control, and bladder, bowl, and sexual activity. Thus, a person with a spinal cord injury may have trouble controlling body temperature and heart rate when participating in activity and may be incontinent (Kelly, 2005; Sherrill, 1998).

Paralysis due to spinal cord injury can be complete, meaning there is a total loss of function, or incomplete (also known as paresis), meaning there may be muscle weakness and some but not complete loss of function. A completely severed spinal cord results in a permanent loss of function because the spinal cord cannot regenerate itself. However, people who have an incomplete spinal cord injury may recover part or all of the nerves' function. The spinal cord does not regenerate itself, but functioning may be restored as the pressure on the spinal nerves eases as bruising and swelling decrease (Kelly, 2005; Sherrill, 1998).

The degree of paralysis is related to the location of the damage and the number of neural fibers that are destroyed (Kelly, 2005; Sherrill, 1998). Nerves are specified by the region of the spine (C = cervical or the area of the spine around the neck area, T = thoracic or the area of the spine from the shoulders to the upper abdomen, L = lumbar or the area of the spine in the lower abdomen, and S = sacral or the area of the spine below the waist) followed by the number of the specific nerve (see table 13.1). For example, a person breaks his back in an auto accident. Damage occurs around the 10th thoracic vertebrae (T10) and severs the spinal cord. Neural activity from the unharmed portion of the spinal cord above the injury will still take place, so the person will experience normal function in the muscles that are stimulated by those spinal nerves and thus will be able to move his arms and hands and have good trunk and abdominal control. However, since the nerves below the injury will no longer stimulate the muscles, the person will be completely paralyzed from that point downward.

Causes of Spinal Cord Injuries

Spinal cord injuries can be congenital (due to a birth defect in the formation of the spinal cord) or acquired (due to a trauma that occurs after birth). The most common type of spinal cord birth defect is spina bifida. The most severe form of spina bifida is known as meningomyelocele. With meningomyelocele, the vertebrae fail to close around the spinal cord. The child is born with a hole in the spinal column with the spinal cord exposed. There is no known cause for this defect, but the result is either partial or complete paralysis from the site of the spinal damage downward (usually around the lower thoracic vertebrae). Surgery is performed immediately after birth to close the hole, but the damage to the spinal cord cannot be repaired. In some cases (meningocele), only the spinal cord covering, or meninges, is exposed into a sac, but the spinal cord and nerves are not damaged. While surgery is still required to close the hole, children with meningocele often have no paralysis or only partial paralysis. One complication that 90 percent of the time is related to spina bifida is hydrocephalus, caused by an increase in cerebrospinal fluid in the ventricles of the brain. Left untreated, hydrocephalus can cause the brain to swell and head size to increase. Hydrocephalus is repaired with a shunt in

Table 13.1 Spinal Cord Segments and Muscles Innervated

Spinal cord section	Muscles innervated
Cervical spinal cord (C1-C7)	Neck and arm muscles and diaphragm (damage to C1 or C2 often leads to death or the need for a breathing device)
Thoracic spinal cord (T1-T12)	Chest and abdominal muscles
Lumbar spinal cord (L1-L4)	Hip and knee muscles
Lumbar and sacral spinal cord (L5- S1)	Hip, knee, ankle, and foot muscles
Sacral spinal cord (S2-S4)	Bowel, bladder, and reproductive organs

Adapted, by permission, from L. Kelly, 2005, Spinal cord disabilities. In J.P. Winnick (ed.), *Adapted physical education and sport,* 4th ed. (Champaign, IL: Human Kinetics), 277.

which a tube is inserted into the ventricles of the brain, taking the excess fluid into the abdomen (Sherrill, 1998).

Acquired or traumatic spinal cord injuries are due to trauma to the spinal cord such as that caused by automobile accidents, falls, gun shots, and sport injuries (usually diving accidents). Paralysis can be complete or partial and can affect the cervical, thoracic, or lumbar portions of the spinal cord. Damage to the cervical portion of the spinal cord resulting in loss of function to the arms, trunk, and legs is commonly known as quadriplegia. People with quadriplegia use electric wheelchairs, although people with C7 injuries often can use a manual wheelchair. Damage to the thoracic portion of the spinal cord results in loss of function to the legs only and is commonly known as paraplegia. People with paraplegia usually use a manual wheelchair, although people with T6 injuries or lower often can ambulate with leg braces and crutches.

Common Characteristics of Spinal Cord Injuries

People with spinal cord injuries usually have no cognitive or learning impairments related to their injury. The one exception is children born with spina bifida, who seem to have a greater incidence of learning and perceptual problems compared to children without spina bifida (Culatta, 1993). The main characteristics of people who have spinal cord injuries that golf professionals need to be aware of are medical and psychological.

Health Problems

People with spinal cord injuries usually have numerous health issues. One of the most common problems is pressure sores or decubitus ulcers that result from lack of blood flow and constant pressure on a part of the body. People with a spinal cord injury cannot feel pressure on their body or relieve pressure by lifting and moving their body. As a result, the skin begins to break down and get infected, particularly in the buttocks and legs when they are in constant contact with the wheel-

chair. Prevention is the key, including heavily padding wheelchairs, moving the body off of pressure spots and into different positions, and constantly inspecting the skin.

Another common problem is urinary tract infections. Most people with spinal cord injuries cannot voluntarily control their ability to urinate, so catheterization (a tube inserted into the urethra to stimulate urination) on a regular schedule is required. If this regular schedule is disrupted, causing the bladder to retain urine for long periods, then urinary tract infections can occur. Again, prevention, by drinking plenty of fluids and relieving oneself regularly, is the best treatment.

Other common problems related to spinal cord injuries are muscle spasms and contractures. Muscle spasms are strong muscle contractions that cause the legs to shake uncontrollably. They result from sudden increased muscle tone in the muscles that no longer receive input from the central nervous system. Treatment involves passively stretching the muscles often (someone moves the limbs for the person) as well as muscle-relaxing medication. Contractures, or stiffness and eventual immobility of joints, are caused by staying in one position too long over several months or years. The person's joints become frozen in one position due to lack of movement. As with muscle spasms, treatment involves regularly stretching the limbs and moving them through a full range of motion.

One final set of medical problems, particularly in people with high thoracic or cervical spinal cord injuries, is due to physiological changes in the body related to the spinal cord injury, including thermoregulation, autonomic dysreflexia, and hypotension. Thermoregulation is the body's ability to regulate internal temperature in response to outside temperature. People with higher-level spinal cord injuries seem to have difficulty with thermoregulation and thus get overheated or overly cold very easily. Golf professionals should be aware of these problems and constantly check the person's temperature. Hypotension is extremely low blood pressure that is caused by blood pooling in the legs, which reduces how much blood flows back to the heart. Vigorous exercise can cause hypotension, which in turn can cause a person to pass out due to lack of blood and oxygen reaching the brain. Warming up the body to prepare it for exercise and cooling down are important preventatives to hypotension. Finally, autonomic dysreflexia is a condition in which the heart rate and blood pressure rapidly increase to dangerous levels. Autonomic dysreflexia can be triggered by bowel or bladder problems, restrictive clothing, or skin irritations. Going to the bathroom before playing golf and monitoring heart rate and even blood pressure are important for people who are susceptible to autonomic disreflexia (Kelly, 2005).

Psychological Challenges

Not surprisingly, a traumatic injury can be devastating not only physically but psychologically. One has to learn how to cope with changes in ability (learning to use a wheelchair and other adapted equipment), changes in relationships with family members (family members may suddenly become care providers), changes in work (maybe having to find a new job), and changes in recreation (giving up some sports or learning how to do sports in a different way). Each person will handle the stress and psychological aspects of acquiring a severe disability differently. Some will find it a challenge and even an opportunity, pushing themselves to become independent as quickly as possible, while others will spin into a deep depression that can last for months and even years.

Dunn (1997) suggests that most people with acquired disabilities, including spinal cord injuries, go through stages of adjustment to their disability. First, they are in denial about the severity of the injury. In the case of a spinal cord injury, they might say they will walk again. This can actually be a positive response because they avoid being overwhelmed by the injury and are motivated to work toward improving their abilities. The second stage is a negative response to the disability. Over time, they realize that their disability is real and that they will have some real limitations. This stage is noted by anger,

depression, and self-pity. Obviously, the more severe the disability the more likely people will have trouble coping. Some may never get over the loss of independence and ability and may stay in a depressed state for years. However, most people move out of this negative response and into the third stage, positive acceptance of their disability and an interest in learning a new vocation or going back to their previous vocation; participating more in regular community activities such as going to movies, restaurants, and ball games; and learning how to become as independent as possible while at the same time learning when to ask for help. Golf professionals might work with people with a spinal cord injury who could be in any one of these stages. For example, it is not uncommon for a therapeutic recreation professional at a rehabilitation center to try to help a person recovering from a spinal cord injury shake his self-pity and depression by going to a local recreation setting such as a driving range to hit a bucket of balls. Similarly, a person who is in the last stage and accepts her disability may be interested in relearning how to play golf, an activity enjoyed before the accident, from her wheelchair or a single-rider golf car.

Treatment

Treatment for spinal cord injuries has three components. First, the injury is stabilized and surgery or other treatments are carried out in a hospital to prevent further injury. For example, after an automobile accident that results in a traumatic spinal cord injury, doctors stop any bleeding, repair any broken vertebrae, and then stabilize the spinal column through surgery or bracing. The second step of treatment involves rehabilitation and counseling. The person is taught through physical and occupational therapy how to strengthen and use the parts of the body that are still functional and how to use assistive devices such as wheelchairs and hand-control automobiles. Learning a new job that matches one's new abilities or learning new ways to perform already-mastered job skills is part of the rehabilitation program.

Counseling is also a critical part of rehabilitation, helping the person learn how to deal with the trauma, limitations, and capabilities. Part of this process usually includes recreation therapy, helping a person learn new sports and recreation pursuits or relearn activities that now require different techniques. For example, a person who played golf before his injury may be encouraged to learn how to play golf from a single-rider golf car or wheelchair. The final step in treatment is ongoing support from family members, community support groups, and medical personnel. Ongoing psychological and job counseling, medical treatment including physical and occupational therapy, and recreation therapy are all part of the support that a person will need to be reintegrated into the community (Kelly, 2005). Most important for golf instructors is to recognize their own attitudes, overcome stereotypes, and treat people with spinal cord injuries as they would treat any golfer without disabilities.

Amputation

Amputation refers to the loss of part or all of a limb. Amputations can be relatively minor resulting in the loss of a few fingers or involve more significant loss such as both legs at the level of the hip. In an effort to equalize competition based on functional ability, Disabled Sports USA (DS/USA) (2001) has created nine levels of sport classification for persons with amputations (see table 13.2). Note that the National Amputee Golf Association (NAGA) has two categories: golfers with arm amputations and golfers with leg amputations.

Causes of Amputations

Causes of amputations are often divided into two categories: congenital amputations (also known as limb deficiencies) and acquired amputations. With congenital amputations, people are born missing part of or an entire limb. In some cases the limb fails to develop past a certain point, giving the appearance of a surgical amputation. Also known as a transverse deficiency, a baby might be born

Table 13.2   Disabled Sports USA Sport Classification System for People With Amputations

Class A1	Double above-knee (AK) amputation
Class A2	Single above-knee* (AK) amputation
Class A3	Double below-knee+ (BK) amputation
Class A4	Single below-knee (BK) amputation
Class A5	Double above-elbow# (AE) amputation
Class A6	Single above-elbow (AE) amputation
Class A7	Double below-elbow^ (BE) amputation
Class A8	Single below-elbow (BE) amputation
Class A9	Combined lower- plus upper-limb amputation

* Above-knee amputation refers to loss of limb including the knee joint and above the knee.
+ Below-knee amputation refers to loss of part of limb anywhere below the knee but not including the knee joint.
# Above-elbow amputation refers to loss of limb including the elbow joint and above the elbow.
^ Below-elbow amputation refers to loss of part of limb anywhere below the elbow but not including the elbow joint.

Used with the permission of Disabled Sports USA.

missing just a hand or the arm from the elbow down. In other cases, known as longitudinal deficiencies, a single bone may be missing or does not develop normally. The baby may be born with a relatively normal hand and upper arm but may be missing the bones and muscles of the lower arm. In such cases the hand may be attached directly to the upper arm. The exact cause of congenital amputations is often unknown.

Acquired amputations are amputations due to surgery (e.g., to remove a cancerous tumor), trauma (e.g., an automobile accident or industrial accident), or disease (e.g., gangrene as a result of severe frostbite). Acquired amputations are much more common than congenital amputations and usually occur after the individual has learned how to move with the use of all limbs. For example, 80 percent of lower-extremity (LE) amputations are due to peripheral vascular disease and diabetes. Trauma, especially trauma due to auto accidents, is the second most common cause of LE amputations. Trauma due to auto accidents as well as severe injury from tools or machinery are the major causes of upper-extremity (UE) amputations (Pitetti, 2001).

Treatment

Whether congenital or acquired, the treatment of choice for people with amputations is a prosthetic device or artificial limb. Prosthetic devices are individually fitted for each person and include a socket, a connection mechanism (harness, straps, suspension device, suction apparatus, or clamp), and a terminal device such as an artificial foot or hand (Sherrill, 1998). Terminal devices can be cosmetic (a nonfunctional but normal-appearing hand or foot) or functional (a device that can grasp and release objects or a foot that can be used to run and walk with a relatively normal gait). Some people with amputations prefer to participate in sports like golf without their prosthesis while others prefer to use their prosthesis. Note that a person who loses a limb later in life often has a more difficult time learning how to move either with or without the prosthetic device compared to a person who was born without the use of a limb or lost a limb early in life and learned to compensate for the missing limb at a much younger age.

Cerebral Palsy

Cerebral palsy is a general term used to describe a variety of permanent, nonprogressive movement disorders caused by damage to the brain before, during, or after birth. The damage to the brain does not actually damage muscles or the nerves connecting the muscles to the spinal cord. Rather, the injury affects the ability of the brain to control the muscles. The term is descriptive in that *cerebral* refers to the brain and *palsy* refers to disordered movement or posture (Gersch, 1998; Porretta, 2005). The exact nature of the disability will vary depending on the part of the brain that is damaged and the extent of the damage (see table 13.3).

Causes of Cerebral Palsy

When the part of the brain that controls voluntary movement does not develop properly or is damaged, then cerebral palsy may result. Prior to birth the most common cause of cerebral palsy is failure of the brain to develop properly (developmental brain malformation). While the exact cause of these brain malformations is often unknown, genetic disorders, chromosome abnormalities, or faulty blood supply to the brain during development are a few known causes. Other causes of cerebral palsy prior to birth include lack of oxygen, bleeding into the brain, and toxic injuries or poisoning, which may result from a pregnant mother ingesting alcohol or drugs or being exposed to a disease such as rubella, for example. Causes of cerebral palsy during or after birth include premature birth; lack of oxygen; trauma to the head such as a birth injury, fall, or a car accident; or infections of the nervous system such as encephalitis (inflammation of the tissues of the brain) or meningitis (inflammation of the covering of the brain) (Gersch, 1998).

Types of Cerebral Palsy

There are many different ways to classify cerebral palsy. One of the more common ways is to note the part of the brain that is affected and the resultant movement disorder. For example, if the cerebellum, or the structure in the back part of the brain, is affected, then the person will have ataxic cerebral palsy, resulting in balance and coordination problems. Another way to classify cerebral palsy is to identify the limbs that are involved (see table 13.4). For example, a child who has spasticity (stiffness) only in the legs would be classified as having paraplegic, spastic cerebral palsy. Finally, there is a functional classification system, used by the United Cerebral Palsy Athletic Association (UCPAA), that combines type of cerebral palsy and limb involvement along with functional ability (see table 13.5).

Table 13.3　Classification of Cerebral Palsy Based on Location of Brain Damage and Movement Disorder

Neuromotor name	Characteristics
Spastic cerebral palsy	• Increased muscle tone (hypertonicity) primarily of the flexor muscles (which flex the arms and legs) and internal rotators (which help turn the arms and legs inward) • Exaggerated muscle contractions that often make people seem like they are flexing their muscles all the time, but the muscles are actually quite weak • Hyperactive stretch reflex—we all have this stretch reflex to prevent injury (e.g., the stretch reflex does not allow us to hyperextend our knee after kicking a ball), but in people with spastic cerebral palsy, this reflex is activated before it is necessary, resulting in jerky movements and often a flexed position • Difficulty generating force due to slow movements
Athetoid cerebral palsy	• Overflow of motor impulses to the muscles makes it difficult to control how much muscle force is exerted (sometimes seem to move slowly as if they have spastic cerebral palsy, and other times the muscles contract too quickly, causing movements to occur too quickly) • Muscle tone fluctuates, making it difficult to control movements • May have facial grimaces and trouble controlling saliva • May have difficulty eating, drinking, and speaking • May have difficulty controlling the head, which in turn affects balance and eye–hand coordination
Ataxic cerebral palsy	• Muscles often have very low muscle tone (hypotonicity) • Unsteady, clumsy locomotor patterns due to balance problems (may never learn how to do more complex locomotor skills such as jumping on two feet together or skipping) • Difficulty learning ball skills such as catching or striking

Modified from Porretta, D.L., 2005, Cerebral palsy, traumatic brain injury, and stroke. In J.P. Winnick (Ed.), *Adapted physical education and sport,* 4th ed., (Champaign, IL: Human Kinetics), 235-254.

Table 13.4　Classification of Cerebral Palsy by Limb Involvement

Monoplegia	Any one body part involved, usually one arm
Paraplegia	Involvement of both lower limbs only
Hemiplegia	Involvement of one complete side of the body (arm and leg on same side)
Triplegia	Involvement in any three limbs (very rare)
Diplegia	Major involvement of both lower limbs and minor involvement of both upper limbs
Quadriplegia	Major involvement of all four limbs

This classification system is used in a variety of UCPAA-sanctioned sports in order to equalize competition (note that golf is not currently a sanctioned UCPAA sport). For example, a person classified as a class-IV athlete would compete against other class-IV athletes.

Conditions Associated With Cerebral Palsy

Unlike the other conditions discussed in this chapter, people with cerebral palsy often have other disabilities associated with brain injury (see table 13.6). Not all people with cerebral palsy will have all or even one of the associated conditions, and it would be unfair to assume that a person even with severe cerebral palsy has one or more of these associated conditions. This is especially true with cognitive impairment, as many people who are unfamiliar with

Table 13.5 Functional Classification Profile for Cerebral Palsy (UCPAA)

Class description	Locomotion	Object control
I. Severe spasticity and/or athetosis with poor functional strength	Motorized wheelchair or assistance	Only thumb opposition and range of motion and strength in all extremities; one finger possible; can grasp nonexistent trunk control; only beanbag
II. Severe to moderate spasticity and/or athetoid quadriplegia; poor functional strength in all extremities; poor trunk control; classified as level II if one or both lower extremities are functional; otherwise classified as level-II upper	Propels wheelchair on level surface and slight inclines (level-II lower with legs only); sometimes may be able to ambulate short distances with assistance	Can manipulate and throw a ball (level-II upper)
III. Moderate quadriplegia or triplegia; severe hemiplegia; fair to normal strength in one upper extremity	Propels wheelchair independently but may walk a short distance with assistance or assistive device	Normal grasp of round object, but release is slow; limited extension in follow-through with dominant arm
IV. Moderate to severe diplegia; good functional strength and minimal control problems in upper extremities and torso	Assistive devices for distances; wheelchair usually used for sports	Normal grasp in all sports; normal follow-through evident when pushing wheelchair or throwing
V. Moderate to severe diplegia or hemiplegia; moderate to severe involvement in one or both legs; good functional strength; good balance when assistive devices are used	No wheelchair; may or may not use assistive devices	Minimal control problems in upper limbs; normal opposition and grasp seen in all sports
VI. Moderate to severe quadriplegia (spastic, athetoid, or ataxic); fluctuating muscle tone produces involuntary movements in trunk and both sets of extremities; greater upper-limb involvement when spasticity or athetosis present	Ambulates without aids; function can vary; running gait can show better mechanics than when walking	Spastic or athetoid grasp and release can be significantly affected when throwing
VII. Moderate to minimal spastic hemiplegia; good functional ability on nonaffected side	Walks and runs without assistive devices but has marked asymmetrical action; obvious Achilles tendon shortening when standing	Minimal control problems with grasp and release in dominant hand; minimal limitation seen in dominant throwing arm
VIII. Minimal hemiplegia, monoplegia, diplegia, or quadriplegia; may have minimal coordination problems; good balance	Runs and jumps freely with little to no limp; gait demonstrates minimal or no asymmetry when walking or running; perhaps slight loss of coordination in one leg or minimal Achilles tendon shortening	Minimal incoordination of hands

Table 13.6 Other Conditions Associated With Cerebral Palsy

Condition	Typical problems
Cognitive impairment	Can range from mild to severe, and may be unrelated to severity of motor involvement (i.e., person with severe motor problems may not have cognitive impairment while person with relatively mild motor problems may have cognitive impairment); more common in people with spastic cerebral palsy. Treatment is special education.
Seizures	About 50% of people with cerebral palsy have seizures, most commonly people with quadriplegia or hemiplegia; seizures may range from relatively mild episodes, staring, or minor involuntary movements to more severe convulsions and loss of consciousness. Often can be controlled with medications.
Learning disabilities	Most common are visual–perceptual problems (may affect ability to read and write) and developmental language disorders (difficulty producing speech). Speech problems include oral–motor movement problems (known as dysarthria). Treated with special education and speech therapy.
Attention deficits	Approximately 20% of people with cerebral palsy have some kind of attention-deficit disorder. Individuals may be easily distracted, have a hard time focusing for long periods of time, or be very fidgety and overly excited by stimulating activities. Treatment includes changing the environment, behavior management, and medication.
Vision problems	Muscle-tone problems related to damage to the brain can result in eye-muscle imbalance in about 50% of people with cerebral palsy. Most common vision problems include strabismus (crossed eyes) and refractive errors (near- or farsightedness). Most often corrected with prescriptive glasses or in rare cases surgery. A small percentage of people with cerebral palsy have cortical blindness related to damage to the visual pathways in the brain that cannot be corrected.
Hearing problems	Approximately 5-15% of children with cerebral palsy have some degree of sensorineural hearing loss (damage to the inner ear where sound is picked up by the cochlea or auditory nerve). Treatment includes hearing aids and speech therapy.

Adapted, by permission, from E. Gersch, 1998, What is cerebral palsy? In *Children with cerebral palsy: A parents' guide,* 2nd ed., edited by E. Geralis, (Bethesda, MD: Woodbine House), 1-34.

physical disabilities wrongly assume that a person who has limited movement control and poor speech must have cognitive impairment. The point is that people with cerebral palsy are more likely to have these conditions than the general public. Many of these conditions can be treated with medications (e.g., seizure medication), corrective devices (e.g., glasses to correct visual problems), or technology (e.g., voice synthesizers to compensate for limited speech).

Treatment

As noted earlier, cerebral palsy is the result of damage to the part of the brain that controls movement. This damage cannot be corrected, but early intervention can help children reach their full movement and learning potential while minimizing motor and related problems. Also, early intervention can help the nondamaged part of the brain compensate for the damaged part of the brain. This may result in a reduction of abnormal movement patterns. The most common treatments for people with cerebral palsy include early intervention and special education by trained teachers; physical and occupational therapy focusing on positioning, preventing inappropriate movements, facilitating normal movement patterns, and using assistive devices such as walkers and adaptive writing aids; orthotics such as braces and splints to maintain normal range of motion prevent contractures (stiffening of joints) and control involuntary movements that interfere with functioning; medications to control and improve muscle tone; neurosurgery to reduce spasticity in children with lower-extremity involvement; and orthopedic surgery such as releasing and lengthening tendons to increase range of motion (Pelligrino,1997).

Muscular Dystrophy

Muscular dystrophies are a group of inherited disorders characterized by progressive wasting away of muscle tissue and subsequent muscle weakness. The muscles deteriorate over time, and in turn the person experiences loss of muscular strength. While there are many types of muscular dystrophy, the most common is Duchenne muscular dystrophy (DMD). With DMD, which affects boys almost exclusively, signs of muscular weakness begin as early as three years of age. One of the telltale signs of DMD is an enlarged calf muscle, also known as pseudohypertrophy. The disease gradually weakens all the skeletal muscles in the body (arms, legs, and trunk). Doctors can determine if a child has DMD by examining family history, performing blood tests that can detect an elevated enzyme known as creatine kinase (CK) that leaks out of damaged muscles, and doing a muscle biopsy to see exactly what is happening to the muscle (MDA, 2000).

Cause of DMD

Duchenne muscular dystrophy is caused by a mutation in a gene on the X chromosome. In essence, this gene fails to make the protein dystrophin, which is necessary for proper muscle function. Without dystrophin, the muscles waste away. Females have two X chromosomes, so the flaw in the gene that is on one of the X chromosomes can be counterbalanced with a properly functioning gene on the other X chromosome. Males have one X and one Y chromosome, and because there is no second X chromosome to counterbalance the flawed gene, boys almost exclusively have Duchenne's muscular dystrophy while girls are usually unaffected.

Common Characteristics of DMD

Duchenne muscular dystrophy follows a fairly set course noted by progressive changes in movement abilities. The child does not experience any pain with these changes other than associated contractures as a result of loss of movement. In addition, there is no relationship between the muscle loss and cognitive problems (i.e., children with DMD do not experience mental retardation or learning disabilities at a higher rate than the general population). However, children with DMD are more susceptible to depression as a result of dealing with the disease and loss of function, and they may run into academic difficulties due to depression.

With regard to motor problems, initially the child will have trouble standing up, climbing stairs, and maintaining balance. The child may fall a lot and seem clumsy. In early elementary school, he may be seen walking on his toes with a waddling, unsteady gait. To aid in maintaining balance the child may stick out his belly and pull his shoulders back. Braces may be prescribed to help him walk more steadily. At this stage the child also will begin to have difficulty raising his arms above shoulder level. By late elementary school (ages 7 to 12), the child's muscular wasting and associated weakness will take away the ability to walk, requiring him to use a manual wheelchair. In addition, as the muscles of the trunk begin to degenerate, the child may show signs of scoliosis (side-to-side spinal curvature) or kyphosis (forward spinal curvature or hunchback shape). Contractures are also common at this point. By middle school, children with DMD will often be so weak they need an electric wheelchair for mobility and will have difficulty even lifting their hand to write. By late middle school into high school the muscles of the heart and respiration may also be affected, making it difficult for the child to breathe and making him more susceptible to respiratory illnesses. In fact, respiratory illnesses are often the cause of death in children with DMD, which usually occurs sometime before their 20th birthday (MDA, 2000).

Treatment

While researchers are working feverishly to prevent and treat Duchenne muscular dystrophy, to date DMD is considered an incurable disease. However, a variety of treatments and therapies are used to help children maintain their functional abilities as long as possible. Physical therapy, for example, is used to help the child stay as strong and flexible as possible and to prevent contractures. Physical therapy usually involves range-of-motion exercises to help keep the joints as fluid as possible and delay contractures. Physical therapy also can help keep the back straight.

Bracing is often used in conjunction with physical therapy to help the child maintain an upright position and maintain proper joint, tendon, and ligament function. Bracing also can help maintain a straight back. In some cases, surgery is performed to release and lengthen the Achilles tendon to treat ankle contractures and keep the child walking longer (usually around 8 to 10 years of age) or to straighten a severely curved spine (usually around 11 to 13 years of age).

Medications are often prescribed to slow down the progress of DMD or to prevent some of the associated effects of the disease. The most commonly prescribed medication is prednisone, a type of steroid that seems to slow the loss of muscle function and even increase strength in children with DMD. Research has shown that prednisone can help some children with DMD walk and have better arm function for several months longer than would be possible without the steroid. Unfortunately, prednisone has strong side effects, including significant weight gain, loss of bone, thinning of the skin, raised blood pressure and blood sugar, and depression. Parents have to weigh the benefits of prednisone with its possible side effects. Some children end up taking prednisone with a host of other supplements (e.g., calcium for osteoporosis and antidepressants) to deal with these side effects (MDA, 2000).

Multiple Sclerosis

Multiple sclerosis (MS) is a chronic and degenerative disease of the central nervous system. It is a slow, progressive disease that is caused by damage to the myelin covering of the nerve fibers in the brain and spinal cord. This myelin sheath normally protects the nerve fibers and allows for accurate and fast delivery of information from the brain to the muscles. With MS, this myelin sheath becomes damaged and scarred, which affects nerve conduction.

Causes of MS

The exact cause of MS is still unknown, although there is some speculation that it may be the result of an autoimmune problem (the body mistakes the portions of the myelin as a virus and releases a substance that destroys the myelin) (Sherrill, 1998). Onset usually occurs between the ages of 20 and 40, although in rare cases it has occurred in children and in older adults. It occurs in women more than in men and in people living in cold and temperate versus tropical climates (Beers & Berkow, 1999). Multiple sclerosis is diagnosed through a variety of tests including neurological examinations to determine the exact type and degree of motor deficit and magnetic resonance imaging (MRI) to show lesions on the myelin sheath.

Common Characteristics of MS

Multiple sclerosis usually begins slowly with subtle sensory problems such as blurred vision or muscular problems such as tremors, muscle weakness, spasticity, speech difficulties, dizziness, partial paralysis, fatigue, and motor difficulties. These problems tend to worsen over time. However, MS is notable for periods when the disease and symptoms are in remission followed by periods with moderate to severe flare-ups or exacerbations of symptoms. As the scarring continues, symptoms tend to continue without remission. However, the course of the disability varies greatly from individual to individual. In some cases there may be almost undetectable symptoms for many years after the initial diagnosis, while other individuals soon lose so much functioning that they need to use a wheelchair and require assistance for even the simplest daily care.

One important characteristic related to MS is difficulty dealing with warm weather. Many people with MS have trouble controlling their temperature and thus can get overheated quite easily. Another common characteristic related to MS is depression. Since the disease usually attacks a person in the prime of life, it can be quite difficult to deal with the loss of current function and know that the disease will get progressively worse with no cure in sight.

Treatment

There is no known cure for multiple sclerosis. Ongoing research is examining ways to regrow portions of the damaged myelin, and drug therapy to slow down the disease is being explored. To date, however, treatment focuses on physical therapy and exercise to help people maintain their range of motion, endurance, strength, and functioning. A regular exercise regimen (including golf if it is the person's exercise of choice) can be particularly helpful in maintaining fitness levels as well as improving self-esteem. However, exercise during acute periods may lead to fatigue and even injury. Therefore, exercise prescription (including how much golf a person should play or whether or not the person should use a golf car or walk the course) should be determined by the individual's physician and tolerance level. In addition to fitness training, physical therapy often includes activities to help people maintain their balance, agility, and walking gait (Porretta, 2005). Additional treatments include medications to relieve some symptoms (e.g., muscle relaxants for people experiencing spasticity). The use of walking aids or wheelchairs may be needed for more severe cases (Sherrill, 1998).

Teaching Golf to People With Physical Disabilities

Clearly the term *physical disability* describes a heterogeneous group of people ranging from those missing one limb or having mild multiple sclerosis to those with quadriplegia or severe cerebral palsy. Thus, the following teaching suggestions will have to be tailored to the individual needs of each golfer. For example, some golfers with physical disabilities will be able to walk the golf course independently but may require modified golf clubs (e.g., golfer with an upper-extremity amputation), while other golfers will need a single-rider golf car to move around the course but need no other special considerations (e.g., golfer with paraplegia).

With virtually all golfers with physical disabilities, there is no need to find different ways to communicate with or instruct them since they typically have no mental or sensory impairments. Instructional strategies instead focus on understanding the movement abilities of each golfer and then discovering ways to accommodate each person through modified movement patterns and adapted equipment. This might require you to think of a unique swing pattern to accommodate a person who is paralyzed on the right side, an adapted piece of equipment to help a person with a prosthetic arm to grip the club, and a single-rider golf car for golfers who cannot walk. The following suggestions for movement and equipment modifications for golfers with physical disabilities should help begin the process of providing the best individualized program possible for each golfer with a physical disability.

Alternative Swing Patterns

One of the greatest challenges of working with golfers with physical disabilities is determining whether or not a regular stance and swing pattern are appropriate or if a modified stance and swing pattern might be more effective. A regular stance and golf swing are preferred since they have already been proven to be an effective way to hit a golf ball. However, modified stances and swing patterns may make sense for golfers who cannot use a regulation swing effectively.

Unfortunately, there is no easy way to determine if a golfer with a physical disability should use a regular or modified stance and swing pattern. The golfer simply has to practice hitting balls using different stances and swing patterns. Check the golfer's ability to grip the club, stance, range of motion (how far the golfer can bring the club back), ability to rotate the body, consistency with contact, ball trajectory, and ball distance. A regular stance and golf swing are a learned pattern that can be awkward even for golfers without physical disabilities who are just learning the game, so do not give up on teaching the regular stance and golf swing until it is clear that such a pattern is not feasible. If it is determined through assessment that a golfer can swing without modifications, then certainly proceed with teaching that pattern.

It may be that a golfer should use the accepted method of swinging with subtle modifications such as using a wider stance for balance, gripping with the hand and swinging with the arm, taking a shorter backswing and follow-through, and limiting rotation. Again, determining modifications will be more of a trial-and-error process than following a systematic checklist. Each golfer will have different strengths and weaknesses, and modifications should highlight the strengths while minimizing the weaknesses. For example, using a wider stance might help a golfer with early muscular dystrophy or mild cerebral palsy who can stand but who has balance problems. Similarly, a golfer with a spinal cord injury who is paralyzed from the waist down may have powerful arms from using a manual wheelchair but may have weak abdominal muscles because they don't work due to the injury. Thus, the swing may need to be modified so that the golfer is using the arms more and not rotating as much. Each golfer is different and must be treated on an individual basis, and the exact modification will vary for each golfer. To become a better instructor to golfers with physical disabilities, practice swinging using various modifications. See how a swing feels from a wider stance, while leaning against the car, when using one arm, when swinging without rotating the body, or when in a seated position.

Adapted or Modified Equipment

Analyzing and then prescribing a modified swing pattern may be all that some golfers with physical disabilities need to be able to play the game. However, other golfers may need the addition of adapted equipment to be successful. Again, there is no quick and easy way to determine which equipment is best for a particular golfer. Try different adaptations and then watch the golfer's swing to see if a particular modification seems to be effective. Avoid the temptation of having the golfer take just a few swings and then give up on the equipment. How long does it take a golfer without a disability to get used to hitting a large-headed driver? It may take hundreds of practice trials before the golfer begins to feel comfortable with a particular piece of equipment. The instructor should use the adapted equipment to experience what it feels like. Following are some of the more popular golf adaptations.

Clubs

Clubs can be customized to meet the needs of golfers, such as longer clubs with flat lies and more flexible shafts for golfers who play from a seated position or clubs with wider grips or extra straps for golfers with grip problems (see figure 13.1a). Children's clubs are often shorter and lighter than adult clubs and may be more appropriate for shorter golfers, golfers who play one-handed from a seated position, or golfers who have limited strength (Paciorek & Jones, 2001).

Prosthetic Devices

A number of assistive devices for golfers with amputations are available. These devices, most of which have been approved by the USGA, help golfers with upper-extremity amputations grip the club (see figure 13.1b). They attach to a golfer's existing prosthesis and allow the golfer to use a club without any additional modifications (Paciorek & Jones, 2001) (see appendix B for information on where to find these devices).

Figure 13.1a   Golfers who play from a seated position typically use a modified golf club.

Figure 13.1b   Prosthetic devices aid golfers with amputations.

Other Adaptations

Simple devices can help golfers tee up their ball or retrieve a ball from the hole from a seated position or without bending down. The devices also can be used to pick up tees, balls, and ball markers. Another simple device used by golfers who have trouble bending over is a suction cup that fits on the grip end of the putter. To retrieve a ball, the golfer simply turns the putter over, sticks the suction cup on the ball, and pulls the ball up without ever having to bend over (Paciorek & Jones, 2001).

Single-Rider Golf Cars

Some golfers with physical disabilities such as those with spinal cord injuries and those with more advanced muscular dystrophy or multiple sclerosis will need to play golf from a golf car. Fortunately, there are newly designed golf cars that allow the golfer to play right from the car and even move onto tees and greens without causing damage. Most single-rider golf cars weigh about one-third of a traditional golf car and can move all over the golf course including onto tees, onto greens, and into sand bunkers. Golfers who can stand but are weak can move the car right next the ball and then lean on the car. Or, for golfers who cannot stand, the car can be fitted with a swivel seat and seat belt so the golfer can hit from a seated position. Some also have hydraulic or electric seats that adjust vertically. Single-rider golf cars are electric so there is no chance of oil or gas leaks on the green. In addition, single-rider golf cars are so lightweight and balanced that they provide less ground pressure than a person walking (see appendix B for more information).

Golf Programs for People With Physical Disabilities

There are many golf programs and associations specifically for people with physical disabilities. Adapted equipment such as prostheses, modified clubs, and single-rider golf cars allow golfers with physical disabilities to play with their peers without disabilities (Paciorek & Jones, 2001). For more details on rule modifications for golfers with physical disabilities, see *A Modification of the Rules of Golf for Golfers With Disabilities* (USGA, 2001), available in appendix A. This USGA publication describes official rule adjustments to make golf fairer for golfers with disabilities. Following are some golf associations and programs for golfers with physical disabilities. Contact information for these groups is located in appendix B.

• Physically Challenged Golf Association (PCGA). Founded in 1995, the PCGA is a nonprofit organization that conducts workshops, clinics, and seminars for golfers with physical disabilities. The PCGA also works with golf professionals and health care providers who are interested in working with golfers with physical disabilities. The PCGA operates several regional adaptive golf programs that offer clinics and workshops for golfers with physical disabilities as well as other interested professionals.

• National Center on Accessibility (NCA). The NCA provides information on accessibility for a variety of public and private entities from offices to restaurants to recreation facilities. With reference to golf, the NCA provides information on course modification, course design (including access to architects with expertise on accessibility), and adapted equipment.

• Amputee golf associations. There are a handful of golf associations specifically for golfers with amputations, including the National Amputee Golf Association (NAGA), Eastern Amputee Golf Association (EAGA), and Western Amputee Golf Association (WAGA). Each of these groups offers a variety of clinics and hosts various regional and national golf tournaments (Paciorek & Jones, 2001). Amputee golf tournaments use a classification system similar to that used in other amputee sport programs, dividing golfers into "flights" based on their amputation (see table 13.2 on page 132). Golfers have the choice of playing with or without a prosthetic device. Over the past several years there have been some wonderful improvements in prosthetic and adaptive devices that allow golfers with amputations to have more fluid movements. For example, new lower-limb prostheses allow pivoting and rotation during the swing, and rubber gloves and Velcro attachments used with upper-limb prosthetic devices allow better gripping (Paciorek & Jones, 2001). Caution should be used, especially with new lower-limb amputees, because excessive rubbing can cause trauma to the skin under the prosthesis.

NAGA sponsors a golf program called the First Swing Program. This program is designed to introduce golf to individuals with a variety of physical and sensory disabilities through a one- or two-day clinic. The program also helps therapists and golf professionals who work with people with disabilities.

Part IV

Developing a Full-Participation Golf Program

Chapter 14

Enhancing Playability Using Adaptive Equipment

Ben was an avid golfer until a car accident left him without the use of his legs. Before the accident, he played golf at least twice a week and had gotten his average score down to the mid-70s. He enjoyed his time on the golf course and played in many tournaments. Ben did not want to give up the game. He had heard about single-rider golf cars that would allow him to get around, so he went to the local municipal course that had some of those golf cars and gave one a try. He got his clubs on the car and proceeded to the practice facility. Ben could maneuver the car fine and was able to swing from the seated position with ease; however, he did not make very solid contact with the ball, and he got frustrated and decided to leave. As he was leaving, Ben saw Fred, the golf professional at the course. Fred asked him how things went, and Ben explained his frustration. Fred told Ben about Cheryl, a certified professional clubmaker in the area. He told Ben that Cheryl had modified golf clubs for golfers with disabilities in the past and they seemed to be extremely happy with the results.

Ben took Fred's advice and went to see Cheryl. She modified Ben's golf clubs with a bent hosel that allowed the club to sit squarely behind the ball instead of with the toe raised

© National Alliance for Accessible Golf

in the air. Cheryl also shortened and bent Ben's putter so he could putt from the single-rider golf car.

Ben was so anxious to see if his new clubs worked better that he went back to the golf course the next day. Ben went into the golf shop and told Fred he was ready to give it another try. Fred helped Ben get his clubs on the golf car and went to the practice facility with him. Although he still had some difficulties, he was hitting the ball much better. Fred, who had some experience instructing golfers

(continued)

(continued)

with disabilities, gave Ben some tips and Ben started hitting the ball better and better. By the end of the day, he was hitting golf shots better than he ever dreamed he would be able to after the accident.

Although he still doesn't score as well as he used to, Ben is back to playing at least twice a week and enjoying the game as much as ever. He is even playing in local golf tournaments. Ben is working hard on his game and is trying to improve to the point where he can compete in a national tournament for golfers with disabilities.

Golfers have been adapting and modifying equipment for years in an effort to enhance the playability of the game. Many of these modifications have become commonplace and are now mass produced for the general public. As golf has become a viable leisure pursuit for people with disabilities, more and more equipment specifically designed for them has been developed. Most of these developments also came from an individual's desire to make the game easier to play. Adapted equipment for golfers with disabilities can come in many different forms. It can be as extensive as a single-rider golf car that allows the golfer to hit while seated or as simple as a device designed to tee a ball or get a ball out of the hole for people who have trouble bending over.

Adaptive Equipment for Golfers With Physical Disabilities

More and more people with disabilities are participating in golf. There are numerous initiatives and organizations dedicated solely to facilitating golf for people with disabilities. While golfers with disabilities face many barriers, vendors in the industry are discovering new ways to assist their participation and enjoyment of the game. Equipment design is often limited only by imagination and motivation. If rock-climbing equipment can be adapted to allow paraplegics to ascend 3,000-foot (914-meter) rock faces, then surely equipment can be adapted to enhance golf experiences for people with disabilities. These pieces of adapted equipment are often designed as one-of-a-kind innovations that become more widespread over time.

Modifying Grips and Gloves

Many modifications to grips and gloves assist golfers with disabilities. The most common modification to grips is increasing their size. Grip size can be enlarged to aid golfers who have difficulty with hand strength. There are numerous ways to enlarge a golf grip, including adding tape under the grip, adding tape on top of the grip, and installing oversized grips. Golfers with reduced grip strength can also wear wrist braces or gloves on both hands to provide stabilization. Golf gloves have also been developed to assist with the clutching and proper positioning of golf clubs. Another way to modify gloves to assist golfers with disabilities is to add Velcro. The Velcro wraps around the club and attaches to the glove. This helps with stability and keeps the club from coming out of the golfer's hand during the swing.

The use of specialized prostheses designed for specific activities can significantly enhance the quality of athletic experiences for athletes with amputations. Prostheses have been developed to grip the golf club and can be customized for right- or left-handed golfers. These devices allow golfers with amputations to perform at higher levels of proficiency. Countless variations of specialized equipment have been developed, and innovation has continued to improve prosthetic devices designed for golf.

Modifying Golf Clubs

Golf clubs can be easily modified to meet specific needs of golfers with disabilities. Most modifications are designed to assist golfers who play from a seated position. Many companies produce clubs for golfers with disabilities, and some even specialize in such equipment. The following are examples of how golf clubs can be modified to meet the needs of golfers with disabilities:

- Install bent hosels that let the club sit square on the ground when soled from a seated position.

- Reshaft clubs with lightweight, flexible graphite to accommodate lower swing speeds.

- Build up the grip to allow golfers with decreased hand strength to control the club easier.

- Shorten clubs and putters to allow for one-armed swings from a seated position.

- Adjust the lie angle to a flat position to allow the club to sit square on the ground when soled from a seated position.

- Install light perimeter-weighted clubheads that allow for more forgiveness on off-center shots.

- Attach a suction device to the grip end of a putter to allow golfers to get their ball out of the hole without bending.

- Attach a teeing device to the grip end of a driver to allow golfers to tee up the ball without bending.

Using Wheelchairs or Single-Rider Golf Cars

The design of wheelchairs for specific sport needs has advanced significantly in recent years as more people with disabilities take part in athletic endeavors. There are motorized and general sport chairs that have characteristics that aid golfers who play from a seated position. They generally have no arm rests and have strong braking systems to allow for maximum range of motion while providing stability.

Most golfers who need to play from a seated position use a single-rider golf car (see figure 14.1). Due to their popularity, there are many such golf cars in development and on the market. Research has shown that they do not harm the course or greens under most conditions. They even typically have a lower psi (pounds per square inch) rating than the human foot or most greens mowers (NAAG, 2003). While features vary from car to car, most have a seat that swivels or rotates to allow the golfer to swing from a seated position or use the seat to provide support when swinging from a standing position. Some have adjustable seats that tilt forward and lift upward to allow the golfer to swing from a more natural position. Single-rider golf cars are designed so that they can be operated entirely by hand controls. The amenities on the cars vary but most have a golf bag rack, drink holder, and scorecard holder.

When purchasing a single-rider golf car, it is best to test drive each model under consideration to make sure it meets the specific needs of the golfer. Not all golf cars are the same and the cheapest or closest one might

Figure 14.1 A single-rider golf car.

not be sufficient. Here are some questions to think about:

- Is it stable during a swing from the seated position?
- Is it easy to maneuver?
- Will it adjust and adapt to meet the needs of the golfer?
- Is it safe on all terrains?
- Does it have enough power to climb hills?
- How does it handle entering and exiting sand bunkers?
- Are the batteries strong enough to make a full round of golf?
- Is it easy to travel with and store?
- Is it built well enough to last?
- Is the golf bag rack located where clubs can be reached with no trouble?
- Does it hinder the golf swing?
- How much does it cost?
- How does it look?

Adaptive Equipment and Assistance for Golfers With Visual Disabilities

Adapted equipment designed for golfers with visual disabilities typically can be categorized as either nonoptical or optical adaptive aids. An example of a nonoptical aid would be using a brightly colored golf ball that is easier to see. An example of an optical aid would be special glasses such as high-powered bifocals. More information on each of these adaptive aid categories follows.

Nonoptical Adaptive Aids

One of the most important considerations for golfers with visual impairments is protection from the sun. Golfers with visual impairments may also benefit from filters and glare-reduction devices. The most popular filters are gray and blue blockers. Gray distorts color

the least so it is best for distinguishing the topography of the land. Blue-blocking filters improve contrast and assuage light at the blue end of the light spectrum.

Modifications to equipment may also make golf easier for people with visual impairments. Sometimes using a ball in a color different than the traditional white can boost visibility. Neon yellow works well, particularly when combined with a putter head that has been painted black. Some golfers with visual impairments may benefit from a ball that emits an audible tone. Another modification is highlighting the center or sweet spot of the club with a yellow or red mark.

The ultimate adaptive aid for golfers with visual impairments is the addition of a coach or guide. This person describes the hole, gauges distances, places the club behind the ball, positions and aligns the golfer, locates the ball after shots, and reads the green. Obviously, this coach must be able to communicate effectively with the golfer. A coach does not need to have much golfing experience to assist a visually impaired golfer. However, coaches who do play golf will improve their own game by gaining a better awareness of alignment, setups, and attention to detail.

Optical Adaptive Aids

A low-vision optometrist may prescribe glasses and devices that enhance golf experiences for golfers with visual impairments. High-powered bifocals or jeweler's loupes can allow a player to record a score. The loupes clip onto glasses and can simply be swung out of the way. Telescopes might also be helpful. They are not considered artificial devices and are acceptable under the *Rules of Golf* as long as there are no range-finder attachments. Other optical adaptive aids that may help some golfers with visual impairments include a monocular that can be worn around the neck and a prescribed bioptic.

Golfers are always looking for equipment and devices that make the game easier and more enjoyable. The same can be said for golfers with disabilities. There have been several new designs in equipment for golfers with disabilities and many more become available each year. For information on companies to contact about specific adaptive golf equipment, please see the Adaptive Equipment Resources section beginning on page 179 in appendix B.

Chapter 15

Creating Community-Based Support

Larry, a therapeutic recreation specialist at the local hospital and avid golfer, heard about accessible golf programs and thought it would be a good idea for his community. He just didn't know how to get started. After attending a conference where he sat in on a session about accessible golf programs, Larry came home excited and confident that he could create an accessible golf program in his community.

Larry learned many great ideas and strategies at the conference, but perhaps most importantly he came to understand the necessity for creating community-based support for the accessible golf program. The first thing he did was get on the phone to locate others in the community who might be interested in helping out. Larry's enthusiasm was contagious, and he easily began to put together a team of golf professionals, community leaders, medical personnel, administrators from organizations that serve people with disabilities, and golfers with disabilities to organize and

plan the accessible golf program. He wanted to create as much support as possible, so he also spoke at local organization meetings, such as the Lion's Club, and contacted the media.

In a very short time, Larry had everything in place except for one thing. To sustain the accessible golf program, locating funding was going to be vital. Larry got donations from individuals and organizations in the community. He even staged a golf tournament that raised $5,000 for the program. Even with all this effort, it was still not enough. Larry didn't know what to do. Then the golf professional at

© National Alliance for Accessible Golf and National Center on Accessibility

(continued)

(continued)

his course told him about the USGA's For the Good of the Game grants program. Larry contacted the USGA to get more information and submitted an application. He was overjoyed the day he heard that his grant application was accepted. Larry knew that his dream of establishing an accessible golf program was now going to become a reality.

Formal and informal support systems have numerous benefits for people with disabilities. For example, one of the most significant determinants of health and wellness is enhanced social support from the community (Gottlieb, 1998). People with disabilities profit from organized, consistent support networks that are responsive to the complexity of their circumstances. Support networks also have the capability to generate more opportunities for community involvement and improved quality of life (Ochocka & Lord, 1998).

Importance of Creating Community Support

To develop more potential for the inclusion of people with disabilities in golf programs, human service agencies, golf professionals, golfers with disabilities, therapists, and community agencies and organizations must collaborate with each other in their efforts (Schleien, Ray, & Green, 1997). Sometimes this entails taking on new roles. For human service agencies, for example, it requires shifting emphasis away from the operation of their own recreation program to facilitating participation in community recreation golf programs. This may necessitate a willingness to learn from community agencies and golf professionals about their ways of doing things, providing consultation and technical support, providing staff assistance for people with disabilities to participate in community golf programs, and supplying funding or other resources to support the inclusion of participants with disabilities. Golf professionals who are accustomed to operating programs on their own must work in a collaborative team to ensure maximum

success of the accessible golf program. Golfers with disabilities need to provide input and help recruit other participants. Community agencies and organizations may need to take increased responsibility for the accessible golf program and provide financial and other resources to support the program (Walker, 1999).

Developing a specific approach to systematically planning for inclusion in community golf programs is vital. However, supporters must generate momentum to set the process in motion. Obstacles formerly thought to be insurmountable will dissipate as information is generated regarding community support for accessible golf programs and the accessibility of current facilities (Schleien, Ray, & Green, 1997).

Although golf professionals, therapists, and community recreation professionals may have the requisite skills and knowledge to plan and implement suitable golf programs and services for golfers with disabilities, seldom do they operate alone in this process. The key to effectively including people with disabilities in community golf programs depends to a great extent on the amount and quality of networking that is done. Mobley and Toalson (1992) note that leisure services are a vital part of the community. As such, it is imperative for accessible golf programs to involve the community in creating coalitions through which the program can accomplish its goals and mission (Toalson & Mobley, 1993). Networking and collaboration are essential for any group that seeks to enhance the quality of life for people with disabilities, because they help organize individuals and groups who are dedicated to developing accessible golf programs in the community.

Effective networking primarily includes making connections with professionals from a variety of disciplines, with people with disabilities and their families, and with other community members, all of whom have an interest in creating golf opportunities in the community for people with disabilities. Networking is a process. It requires establishing continuing and collaborative functional relationships among a variety of key players. Networking can be instigated through a contact passed along by a colleague, an introduction and exchange at a meeting, Internet searches, and personal meetings or telephone conversations. It is important to determine the potential strengths of these contacts and solicit the assistance of others in planning and delivering accessible golf programs. Information and resources needed to successfully implement accessible golf programs in the community will have to come from a variety of sources. Networking is an excellent means of identifying these sources (Schleien, Ray, & Green, 1997).

In practice, many communities continue to have difficulties implementing recreation programs for people with disabilities and rely on family members, care providers, service agencies, and specialists (e.g., allied health professionals, golf professionals) to establish, offer, and direct leisure and recreation programs for individuals with disabilities. It may be vital to have key players interested in an accessible golf program gather together on a continuing basis to address issues that arise. Establishing an accessible golf program steering committee or advisory board is a natural extension of the networking enterprise (Schleien, Ray, & Green, 1997).

Establishing an Advisory Board

The advisory board should consist of representatives from each category of key players. Members should have a personal and professional commitment to increasing golf opportunities for people with disabilities. Establishing an accessible golf program steering committee or advisory board also affirms that golf participation by individuals with disabilities is a community issue and can best be supported

through a collaborative mechanism such as an advisory board. From a practical standpoint, leaders of an accessible golf program stand to gain a great deal of valuable support and input from this voluntary representative group. To ensure that the advisory board's decisions accurately represent the wishes of the people it was founded to serve, a number of golfers with disabilities and their family members should be included.

The National Alliance for Accessible Golf's (NAAG's) Project GAIN has developed guidelines for creating an accessible golf program steering committee (see page 162 in chapter 16 for more information about NAAG and Project GAIN). They indicate that the composition of the steering committee may vary from place to place but should include people of power and position along with cause-oriented individuals. People of power in the community include PGA section administrators, the director of the local recreation and park department, media executives and personalities, administrators from local organizations representing people with disabilities, and representatives from local disability sport organizations. Project GAIN steering committees also include people representing the medical and rehabilitation fields, special education school systems, transportation systems, independent living coordinators, city and county accessibility experts, golfers with disabilities, and golf professionals who go through training and teach in the program. Due to the fact that they exercise some control over funding in the community, leaders of industry are also included. Project GAIN strives to have between 20 and 30 individuals on each of their steering committees; this gives them adequate numbers to assign subcommittees (NAAG, 2004).

The accessible golf program advisory board has the potential to be an effective agent for change within a community and can positively affect the lives of individuals with disabilities (Ray, 1991). Primary functions of the advisory board include the following:

1. Formulate and state a common vision for the accessible golf program. Board members should arrive at a universal

objective for the accessible golf program from a group and community perspective. It may be helpful to devise a mission or position statement as a guide.

2. Develop clear agendas and action plans. Be focused and reassure all members that their time is well spent. Set goals and objectives that contribute to real versus perceived outcomes for individuals with disabilities and the program as a whole.

3. Utilize the strengths of key players. The board should represent stakeholders and others who can make discernable contributions to the accessible golf program. All members should agree to be active and support the program while serving on the board.

4. Advocate for the rights of people with disabilities. Board members should advocate for the rights of people with disabilities to have full access to golf opportunities enjoyed by people without disabilities.

5. Examine and evaluate the accessible golf program. The board can provide feedback, design and administer surveys, and set up focus groups to discuss the program.

6. Meet regularly to discuss concerns and opportunities for the accessible golf program. The meetings need to be regularly scheduled and convenient for advisory board members. Use the meetings to discuss issues and strategies for improving and sustaining the program.

7. Cultivate and publicize resources and reports. The board should develop press releases, survey data, position papers, and other information to disseminate to the media and interested individuals.

8. Create an atmosphere of comfort and respect. Members should feel at ease expressing themselves and their ideas, knowing that there is mutual regard and consideration for one another. Visioning exercises and brainstorming can be integrated into agendas to foster creativity and appreciation of a team effort in confronting potentially divisive issues.

Advisory board meetings should be formal enough to focus on the issues and tasks at hand but casual enough to permit dialogue and friendly conversation among members. This openness and sharing establishes a sense of trust, awareness, belonging, empathy, shared commitment, and accountability, all of which enhance the potential for a successful accessible golf program. Monthly meetings will probably work best. The meetings will be most effective if they are one to two hours in length. Decisions should be reached by consensus. However, on occasion differences of opinion may call for some compromise (Schleien, Ray, & Green, 1997).

Speaking at Clubs and Agencies

As mentioned in chapter 3, many local organizations within your community provide or sponsor activities and programs for individuals with disabilities. Speaking to these organizations is an excellent way to demonstrate your commitment to providing golf to individuals with disabilities. Speaking to local community groups is also an excellent means of promoting the accessible golf program as well as soliciting resources to ensure the program's sustainability.

Identifying Funding Sources

In times when resources are limited and financial assistance is scarce, identifying funding to support the accessible golf program can be a challenge. Securing external funds can be necessary to sustain the program. External funds can strengthen the program to provide optimal access for the widest range of users through innovative design. Locating funding sources can be a wearisome task; however, there are useful resources that offer assistance to accessible golf projects (Shrake, 2004).

The competition for external funding is extreme. A number of things can be done to enhance the possibility of getting financial support for an accessible golf program. When searching for grant funds, petitioning organizations for donations, or conducting fundraising activities, it is crucial to spell out for prospective funding sources why they should support the accessible golf program. Potential funders are normally overwhelmed with solicitations. In almost every case, requests surpass an organization's ability to accommodate them. Before soliciting funds from any source, it is imperative to develop a strong case for the accessible golf program. This is probably the most important aspect of the fund-seeking process (Shrake, 2004).

Take a Workshop

Many times courses on fundraising or grant writing are offered through continuing education programs at universities and community colleges. In addition, several online seminars are available that provide excellent training. See the following useful Web sites: www.revisions-grants.com, www.apa.org/science/freegrantclass.html, www.thefineart offundraising.com, www.npguides.org, and www.eduplace.com/grants/help/courses.html. If raising funds to support the accessible golf program is going to be an ongoing task, these types of courses can be very useful, saving time and offering guidance to make the most of your time searching for funding (Shrake, 2004).

Get Local Support

Although often overlooked, essential funding may be available in your own community. Frequently local businesses contribute to local projects as a way to give back to the community in appreciation for its support. Sometimes businesses or corporations will want to know how the project can promote their mission or goals. It could be as simple as an acknowledgment such as a plaque signifying where the funding came from, a mention of the business in program materials, or a press release identifying their contribution. Local bank branches also usually have funds allocated for use at the discretion of the bank manager to support local programs in the

community. Another way of acquiring funding from local sources is to form partnerships with local organizations, medical institutions, schools, or agencies. Local civic clubs such as Kiwanis Club, Lions Club, Rotary International, and the Junior League also frequently look for philanthropic causes (Shrake, 2004).

Expand the Search Outside the Community

In addition to local sources, there are other resources available to utilize when trying to locate funds for an accessible golf program. Some of the more pertinent resources include the following:

1. The Internet. The Internet is a great resource when searching for financial support. There are a few Web sites in particular that offer funding opportunities, including Fundsnet Services (www.fundsnetservices.com) and the Foundation Center (www.fdncenter.org). Fundsnet Services has an array of categories including grants explicitly aimed toward disability-related projects. The Foundation Center has a Finding Funders section that contains information on grant applications. It also has an online directory of individual and foundation donors. The Foundation Center is perhaps the most authoritative source of grant and funding information on the Internet. Many university Web sites also provide information on a variety of funding resources.

2. State and national funding directories. Several directories are available that provide extensive resources for external financing. The directories are typically organized by state, region, nation, international, and topic. There are also directories that are specifically for nonprofit organizations. Directories can be purchased from a variety of locations including bookstores and organizations such as the Foundation Center (www.fdncenter.org). They are also often on hand at the reserve desk in local and university libraries.

3. University grants and contracts offices. Most universities have units or departments solely dedicated to contracts and grants. They

are a good source for locating funding opportunities. In addition to funding opportunities, university grants and contracts offices can be used as a resource for preparing proposals and answering questions about grant writing and fundraising.

4. Disability publications and newsletters. Publications such as *Disability Funding News* and *Disability Compliance Bulletin* have information about funding accessibility programs and other projects for people with disabilities. These newsletters require the purchase of a subscription and can be obtained through their publishers. *Disability Funding News* is published by CD Publications (www.cdpublications.com) and *Disability Compliance Bulletin* is published by LRP (www.lrpdartnell.com). Both can be very useful if seeking funding for an accessible golf program will be an ongoing task (Shrake, 2004).

Golf-Related Grant Programs

Two golf-specific grant programs that assist projects such as an accessible golf program are the PGA's Growth of the Game grant program and the USGA's For the Good of the Game grant program. The Growth of the Game grant program administered by the PGA Foundation supplies financial support and other resources to active PGA members and PGA sections to develop and enhance programs that grow the game of golf. This grant program provides for the cost of instruction by PGA professionals at the program's site. It also supplies golf clubs, grips, publications, and instruction equipment as required by the program. In addition, the grant program includes a one-time matching grant for new programs to provide assistance with infrastructure costs (PGA, 2003). The PGA Foundation receives several hundred grant proposals each year. It is important to have a well-thought-out and organized proposal because funding and other resources are provided to just a small percentage of the many worthy proposals. The PGA of America Grant Committee oversees the guidelines for grants. Grants are reviewed once a year, usually in October. Proposals that will introduce golf to juniors, girls, women,

minorities (including all ethnic groups), and people with disabilities are encouraged and considered. The PGA Foundation does not accept proposals for community construction projects; however, it does support community golf developmental programs. In these cases, the PGA Foundation partners with a community-based organization to provide funding for PGA professionals to deliver golf instruction (PGA, 2003).

The USGA's For the Good of the Game grant program is aimed at making the game more affordable and accessible. It targets organizations serving individuals with disabilities and youths from disadvantaged backgrounds. Grant awards are intended for instructional programs, the construction of alternative facilities, beginner-friendly golf courses, golf facilities in locations where there are obstacles to affordable and accessible introduction to the game, and caddie or other work-based curriculums. The USGA also aids with public relations, equipment, and fiscal planning. To date, the USGA Foundation has granted over $40 million to nonprofit organizations around the country (USGA, 2004).

Funding for Accessible Golf Programs

The following list of resources is not all encompassing, but it will provide a good start when searching for funding sources to help initiate and sustain the accessible golf program.

American Express: http://home3. americanexpress.com/corp/ philanthropy/default.asp

Arthur M. Blank Family Foundation: www.blankfoundation.org

Disability Compliance Bulletin: www.lrpdartnell.com

Disability Funding News: www.cdpublications.com

Fundsnet Services: www.fundsnetservices.com

The Foundation Center: www.fdncenter.org

Hasbro: www.hasbro.org

Home Depot: www.homedepot.com/ HDUS/EN_US/corporate/corp_respon/ corp_respon.shtml

Junior Leagues International: www.ajli.org

Kiwanis International: www.kiwanis.org

Lions Clubs International: www.lionsclubs.org/EN/index.shtml

Mailman Family Foundation: www.mailman.org

Robert Wood Johnson Foundation: www.rwjf.org

Rotary International: www.rotary.org/ support/clubs

Target Corporation: http://target.com/ targetcorp_group/company/index. html

Telecom Pioneers: www.telecompioneers.org

UPS: www.community.ups.com/ community/philanthropy/main.html

An accessible golf program must have community support to be successful. Operating an accessible golf program requires many talents and demands a team effort. Stakeholders must work together to ensure the best possible experience for participants in the program. Networking, a process that takes time and effort, is essential in creating support from the community. Once key players in the community have been identified, it is a good idea to establish an advisory board that consists of a variety of individuals dedicated to increasing golf opportunities for people with disabilities. The advisory board should include some golfers with disabilities to make certain that decisions truly represent the wishes of those the program was founded to serve.

Funding is another issue that must be considered to sustain the program. The first step is to utilize resources within the local community. However, this may not be sufficient to maintain the program. There are other sources, such as grants, that can be useful in securing funding for the accessible golf program. The key is to be thorough and make a detailed case for the use of the funds. There are two golf-specific grant programs that assist accessible golf programs: the USGA's For the Good of the Game grants program and the PGA's Growth of the Game program. It is a good idea to contact both of these organizations when seeking funding.

Chapter 16

Creating a Team for Program Development

Bob is a golf professional who wanted to become more active in his community. He had talked to other golf professionals who had become involved in adaptive golf programs. They told him how rewarding it was to work with golfers with disabilities, and it sounded like something he would like to try. After doing some research at the library and on the Internet, Bob realized that a golf program for people with disabilities was needed in his community, but he didn't know how to get started. Bob knew that he couldn't organize a program on his own, but he was fairly new to the area and didn't know whom to ask for help.

Then Bob met Suzanne at a neighborhood picnic. Suzanne was a therapist at the local rehabilitation hospital. She didn't know anything about golf but liked Bob's idea. She had worked with interns from an area university and knew they taught classes in adapted physical education. Together, they went to meet with the professor who directed the adapted physical education program. The professor not only wanted to get involved, she informed

© National Alliance for Accessible Golf and National Center on Accessibility

them that she had students who would like to help out, too.

They were beginning to assemble a team that could plan and implement an accessible golf program. Suzanne told her boss about their activities and she said that the hospital would provide resources and sponsor the program as long as the instruction could take place at Bob's golf course. The team met at the golf course to evaluate the facilities. They determined that with minor modifications such as widening some of the practice hitting stations and

(continued)

installing a couple of ramps, the facility would be suitable for golfers with disabilities.

Suzanne began to recruit patients from the hospital to participate in the program, and in a couple of months they held their first clinic. Today they have one of the most successful accessible golf programs in the state, and Bob has even had to recruit more golf profes- sionals to help provide instruction. Bob looks forward to each clinic and enjoys his job as a golf professional more than ever. He gets as much enjoyment and satisfaction out of the program as the individuals with disabilities. It makes him feel great to see past participants in the program come out to enjoy a round of golf. Bob sure is glad he met Suzanne.

A successful golf program for people with disabilities depends primarily on the availability of excellent human resources and the ability of involved personnel to function effectively as members of a team. People are needed to organize and administer services, fulfill technical responsibilities, perform advocacy functions, and provide instruction (Winnick, 2005). People providing direct ser- vice are the key for golf programs to ensure quality experiences.

Importance of Creating a Team

Professionals with diverse areas of expertise should be involved in designing and imple- menting accessible golf programs. Depending on the needs of individual students, the team could include golf professionals, therapeutic recreation specialists, adapted physical educa- tion teachers, community recreation experts, occupational therapists, physical therapists, communication specialists, family members, and others. No one discipline has sufficient expertise to design and implement strategies for a successful golf program for people with disabilities. The challenge is to focus the expertise of each individual team member to the joint efforts of the collaborative team. There are three essential requirements for a valuable team process: a unified philosophy, a working organizational structure, and the accomplishment of team goals (Johnson & Johnson, 1987).

Unified Philosophy

The varied opinions and methods of individ- ual team members enhance and strengthen a team. With respect to accessible golf pro- grams, however, it is important that all team members share certain beliefs. The first is that all people, including those with the most sig- nificant intellectual and physical disabilities, can enjoy and learn to participate in a variety of golf-related activities. Furthermore, golf opportunities should be offered throughout an individual's lifetime and should include activities enjoyed by people without dis- abilities in golf settings. The second facet of a unified philosophy requires that team members understand that they can achieve better outcomes by collaborating in the design and implementation of golf programs than by working alone. In other words, the whole is greater than the sum of all its parts (Schleien, Meyer, Heyne, & Brandt, 1995).

Working Organizational Structure

An organized structure for team member con- nections and program design serves to define roles, tasks, and expectations. Structure also typically includes regularly scheduled com- munication times that enable team members to work collectively, carry out joint assess- ments of student abilities in the golf environ- ment, and design and implement strategies for student improvement. Team member roles are defined both in terms of the distinctive expertise of each individual and mutual responsibilities for program design and implementation.

Accomplishing Team Goals

The final prerequisite for effective teamwork is the achievement of team goals. Collaborative cooperation is often criticized for unnecessary energy spent on team processes that minimally improve learner outcomes. To be effective, team members must establish a unified philosophy and an operational structure for exchanges of information. However, the main goal should be to increase participation in golf activities by people with disabilities and enhance their quality of life.

Potential Team Members

As mentioned earlier, team members are the key to a successful golf program for people with disabilities. These individuals include golf professionals, therapists, family members, volunteers, and others. Regarding golf professionals, instruction must be provided not only by professionals who specialize in working with people with disabilities but also by regular golf professionals. If instruction were provided only by instructors who specialize in teaching golfers with disabilities, relatively few people would get suitable instruction because too few specialists exist. To teach golf to individuals with disabilities, golf professionals must have appropriate golf instruction knowledge, skills, and values and a caring attitude. A good golf instructor emphasizes the development of positive self-esteem and exhibits an attitude of acceptance, compassion, friendship, and kindness while ensuring a safe and controlled environment.

It may be helpful to establish an advisory board to assist with the management and design of the accessible golf program. The advisory board can provide technical assistance and may also contribute considerably to developing promotions, identifying participants, and securing funding. It is a good idea to invite people with the following qualifications or affiliations to participate on the advisory board:

- Medical and health care professionals
- Area golf professionals and instructors
- Adapted physical educators and therapeutic recreation specialists
- Exercise specialists
- Media and marketing professionals
- Financial sponsors
- People with disabilities
- Representatives from local disability organizations

Responsibilities of Team Members

Each team member is responsible for contributing expertise and methods for accessible golf instruction programs to enhance student performance. Team members must share information and skills distinctive to their particular discipline with others who implement the program. For example, golf professionals are not expected to understand intricate details of particular disabilities and may need help from recreational therapists or medical personnel when designing instruction programs to meet the needs of specific individuals.

All team members should share some responsibilities in the design and implementation of adaptive golf programs. No one person should be asked to accomplish activities when others have the ability to help out. The following activities can easily be shared by all team members:

- Helping with initial assessment of participants in golf settings and involvement in golf activities
- Modifying golf activities and equipment
- Participating in team problem solving and decision making
- Contributing to increased communication and instructional methods that maximize student performance

- Monitoring participant performance through data analysis and direct interaction
- Learning from other team members so that instruction is implemented appropriately
- Collecting data and doing paperwork
- Soliciting resources needed to ensure success of the program (e.g., financial, facility, or equipment resources)
- Assisting with public relations and marketing
- Following up with past participants to ascertain if they have continued to partake in golf activities
- Participating in ongoing program evaluation

Team members will also need to carry out responsibilities that are specific to their area of expertise. Golf professionals will provide background on the game, teach rules and etiquette, instruct participants in skills needed to play the game, and develop the sequence of elements to be taught in the program. Therapists need to develop mobility strategies for the golf environment and specific activities, detect potential obstacles to participation, ensure the safety and well-being of participants, and identify prospective participants for the program. Family members and volunteers should assist in getting people to join the program, provide physical support to participants when needed, interact socially with participants and offer motivation, and assist other team members with activities in which they are comfortable. As with any organization, team members should do their part to ensure maximum success of the program.

Organizing and Meeting With the Team

Putting together a team to implement an adaptive golf program can be a daunting task. The program will not be effective if not all of the team members identified previously are included. It is also important to find team members who share the same goals and objectives. A good place to start is to contact area colleges or rehabilitation hospitals. Most universities have either a physical education or recreation department with professors who have an interest in people with disabilities. They may want to be involved, and they at least have contacts in the community who may be potential team members. They may also have students who would serve as volunteers. Therapists at rehabilitation hospitals have experience with recreation and exercise activities for patients or clients. Their experience and expertise are invaluable in organizing an adaptive golf program.

Once the team has been assembled, it is time to get together and design the program. The initial organizational meeting for the team should take place at the site of instruction, giving each team member the opportunity to inspect the facilities for possible problems or challenges. Subsequent meetings should be planned so that team members can arrange their schedules. It is imperative that all team members meet on a regular basis to evaluate the program and plan strategies to enhance the experience of participants. The absence of one team member could stall the progression of the program.

Meeting with volunteers can also be problematic. It is not easy to get everyone to show up at the same time. However, every effort should be made to have someone from the team meet with each volunteer at the instruction site before the volunteer assists with the program. The volunteers then have a better idea of their surroundings and exactly what will be expected of them. This also gives them a chance to ask questions that may help them become more comfortable assisting golfers with disabilities.

The National Alliance for Accessible Golf and Project GAIN

In the 1990s, certain organizations began meeting in a series of national forums on accessible golf, cohosted by Clemson University and the National Center on Accessibility (NCA) at Indiana University. During the sixth forum in 2000, a call to action was made to form a national alliance that could make substantial progress toward the inclusion of people with disabilities in golf (Skulski, 2003). In an attempt to address policy issues, enhance awareness, and promote participation of people with disabilities in the game of golf, the National Alliance for Accessible Golf (NAAG) was formed in July 2001. Leaders of organizations in the golf industry, representatives from disability organizations, and golfers with disabilities joined forces to create a unified group. The Board of Directors has members from organizations such as the Ladies Professional Golf Association (LPGA), the Professional Golfers' Association of America (PGA), the PGA Tour, the United States Golf Association (USGA), the Club Managers Association of America (CMAA), the Golf Course Superintendents Association of America (GCSAA), the National Golf Course Owners Association (NGCOA), the American Therapeutic Recreation Association (ATRA), the National Therapeutic Recreation Society (NTRS), the First Tee, Clemson University, the University of Utah, the City of Las Vegas, the University of Missouri, the University of Chicago, and the NCA at Indiana University.

The vision of the National Alliance for Accessible Golf is for individuals with disabilities to become vigorously engaged in the social fabric of a community and gain health benefits that enrich quality of life through participation in the game of golf. The fundamental ideas compelling NAAG are the beliefs that

- all persons are entitled to participate in the game of golf regardless of their ability, socioeconomic circumstance, or experience;
- the game of golf contributes directly to social inclusion in the community;
- golf must be accessible and affordable for all who desire to participate;
- real health benefits are derived from playing golf; and

- information regarding the benefits of golf for people with disabilities and the golf industry must be publicized to the media, the general public, and health, rehabilitation, recreation, and golf professionals on an ongoing basis (Skulski, 2003).

NAAG is focused on increasing opportunities for people with disabilities to play golf, raising the golf industry's awareness of the needs of golfers with disabilities, furthering scientific understanding of the benefits of golf for people with disabilities, and offering technical assistance to golfers with disabilities and community recreation programs. One of the first projects of the alliance was the creation of a toolkit for golf course owners and operators that gives background information and answers frequently asked questions. Another toolkit has been developed for golfers with disabilities (Skulski, 2003).

The second major initiative of NAAG is Project GAIN (Golf: Accessible and Inclusive Networks). This national research and development project organizes and develops community-based models of inclusive networks among golf professionals, golf course operators, public recreation departments, rehabilitation and therapeutic recreation specialists, advocacy organizations, and individuals with disabilities. The objective of the project is to impart opportunities for people with disabilities to become involved in golf. Project GAIN not only offers lessons on how to hit the ball and play the game but also seeks to involve individuals with disabilities in the social and community aspects of the game as well. Project GAIN also serves as a research project investigating the potential for golf as a medium to maximize opportunities for integrating people with disabilities into the fabric of the local community. Project GAIN is funded by grants from the USGA Foundation, the PGA Tour, and the PGA of America Foundation (Skulski, 2003).

Project GAIN has been initiated in five U.S. cities since November 2002: Salt Lake City, Sacramento, Baltimore, Chicago, and Toledo. Roughly 100 golfers with and without disabilities participate at each site. At the beginning of each project, all golfers are screened and their golf skills are assessed. They engage in a series of lessons given by golf professionals who have been trained by NAAG and who also participate in social inclusion activities. Participants are sometimes partnered with mentors who work with them during the lessons, but more significantly, contact them between lessons. They may call or e-mail each other to discuss the latest professional tournament and how well their favorite players performed, they may go out and practice together, or they may even play a round of golf (Skulski, 2003).

By the time Project GAIN is completed in each of the cities, the community-based network model will be evaluated for effectiveness. From this assessment, further guidance ought to emerge for other accessible golf programs interested in developing similar models (Skulski, 2003). For further information regarding NAAG and Project GAIN, visit their Web site at www.accessgolf.org.

In order for an accessible golf program to thrive and be successful over the long term, it is imperative that a group of individuals be assembled that works effectively as a team. This team should include professionals with diverse areas of expertise so all phases of the accessible golf program can be designed and implemented appropriately. Each member of the team should focus their expertise toward collaboratively attaining the goals and objectives of the program. Putting together the team can sometimes be a daunting task. A good place to start when looking for team members is the local rehabilitation hospital or university. People at these two locations may want to be included or at least have contact with others in the community who would like to be involved with an accessible golf program.

Appendix **A**

A Modification of the Rules of Golf for Golfers With Disabilities

Preface

This publication contains permissible modifications to the Rules of Golf for use by disabled golfers. This is not intended to be a revision of the Rules of Golf as they apply to able-bodied players. As is the case for the Rules of Golf themselves, these modifications, along with the philosophy expressed herein, have been agreed upon by the United States Golf Association and the Royal and Ancient Golf Club of St. Andrews, Scotland.

A Modification of the Rules for Golfers With Disabilities

In modifying the Rules of Golf for golfers with disabilities, the desired result should allow the disabled golfer to play equitably with an able-bodied individual or a golfer with another type of disability. It is important to understand that this critical objective will occasionally result in a modification to a Rule which may seem unfair at first glance because a more simplified answer may appear to exist when two golfers with the same disability are playing against one another.

From a practical standpoint, it is useful to subdivide disabled golfers into groups, each one of which has a need for somewhat different Rules modifications. Five such groups are easily identified. They are blind golfers, amputee golfers, golfers requiring canes or crutches, golfers requiring wheelchairs, and mentally handicapped golfers.

Blind Golfers

Definition of "Coach"

The status of the coach and the duties which he may perform should be defined clearly. Without such clarification, it would be difficult, for example, to determine how a blind golfer must proceed if his ball were to strike his or another player's coach after a stroke. Therefore, the following definition is recommended:

Coach

A "coach" is one who assists a blind golfer in addressing the ball and with alignment prior to the stroke. A coach has the same status under the Rules as a caddie.
Note: A player may ask for and receive advice from his coach.

Rule 6-4 (Caddie)

There is nothing in the Rules which would prohibit the coach of a blind golfer from functioning as his caddie. For a variety of reasons, however, a coach may not be able to perform the duties of a caddie. Therefore, it is permissible for a blind golfer to have both a coach and a caddie. In such circumstances, however, the coach may not carry or handle the player's clubs except in helping the player take his stance or align himself prior to making the stroke, or in assisting him as permitted by analogy to Decision 6-4/4.5. Otherwise, the player would be subject to disqualification for having more than one caddie.

Rule 8-1 (Advice)

In view of the Definition of "Coach," it is recommended that Rule 8-1 be modified as follows:

8-1. Advice

During a stipulated round, a player shall not give advice to anyone in the competition except his partner. A player may ask for advice during a stipulated round from only his partner, either of their caddies, or, if applicable, their coaches.

Rule 13-4b (Grounding Club in Hazard)

The following additional Exception under Rule 13-4 is permissible:

Exceptions:

3. Provided nothing is done which constitutes testing the condition of the hazard or improves the lie of the ball, there is no penalty if a blind golfer grounds his club in a hazard preparatory to making a stroke. However, the player is deemed to have addressed the ball when he has taken his stance.

Rule 16-1f (Position of Caddie or Partner)

Due to the complexities involved in aligning a blind golfer on the putting green, it may be difficult or unreasonable to expect the blind golfer and his coach to comply with Rule 16-1f. Therefore, there is no penalty if a player's coach positions himself on or close to an extension of the line of putt behind the ball during a stroke played from the putting green provided the coach does not assist the player in any other manner during the stroke.

However, given the intent of Rule 16-1f, it may be appropriate to prohibit a coach from remaining in a position which contravenes this Rule if he is performing the duties of a coach or a caddie for two different players simultaneously.

Amputee Golfers

At the present time, the only significant issue with respect to amputee golfers is the status of prosthetic devices. Decision 14-3/15 clarifies the USGA's position on such devices and is included herein for reference.

14-3/15 Artificial Limbs

An artificial leg or arm is not an artificial device within the meaning of the term in Rule 14-3, even if an artificial leg has been modified to aid the player in playing the game or an artificial arm has a fitting specially designed for gripping a golf club. However, if the Committee believes that an artificial limb so modified would give a player an undue advantage over other players, the Committee has authority to deem it to be an artificial device contrary to Rule 14-3.

Clubs used by a player with an artificial arm must conform with Rule 4-1 except that an attachment may be fitted to the grip or shaft to assist the player to hold the club. However, if the Committee believes that the use of a club modified in this way would give the player an undue advantage over other players, it should deem the attachment an artificial device contrary to Rule 14-3.

The USGA Rules of Golf Committee is in the process of examining the much larger issue of medical devices and their conformance under Rule 14-3. While that analysis has not been completed, the position expressed in Decision 14-3/15 is not likely to change. A potential issue for some lower extremity amputee golfers who wear a prosthesis is their inability to climb into or out of bunkers, a situation which probably occurs rather infrequently. On that basis, Rule 28 (Unplayable Ball) should govern without further modification.

Golfers Requiring Canes or Crutches

Definition of "Stance"

The use of assistive devices raises the question of what constitutes taking the stance. This is a critical element in determining relief from an immovable obstruction (Rule 24-2) and abnormal ground conditions (Rule 25-1) and whether or not a player is subject to penalty if his ball moves prior to his playing a stroke. The following Definition is recommended:

Stance

Taking the "stance" consists in a player who is using an assistive device placing the device and, if applicable, his feet in position for and preparatory to making a stroke. The assistive device is deemed to be part of the player's stance.

Rule 6-4 (Caddie)

By analogy to Decision 6-4/4.5, someone, including another caddie or player, who assists a player with the retrieval of his ball is not acting as the player's caddie. Such an act does not constitute a breach of Rule 6-4, which prohibits a player from having more than one caddie at any one time under penalty of disqualification.

Rule 13-2 (Improving Lie, Area of Intended Swing, or Line of Play)

The interpretation of what constitutes a player "fairly taking his stance" is one of the most difficult judgment calls in golf. Whereas most of the Rules of Golf are objective, this Rule is highly subjective. Decision 13-2/1 (Explana-tion of "Fairly Taking His Stance") lends some clarification to this phrase, but significant gray areas remain. The disabled golfer who is using an assistive device is entitled to bend or even break the branches of a tree or bush in order to fairly take his stance. However, he may not use the device to deliberately hold back branches which would otherwise interfere with the area of his intended swing or line of play. There is not, nor will there probably ever be, a substitute for the judgment required to interpret this Rule.

Rule 13-3 (Building Stance)

The use of assistive devices by disabled golfers does not constitute building a stance within the meaning of the term in Rule 13-3. However, there may be an issue with regard to assistive devices which may be adjusted to various positions during a stipulated round. The USGA Rules of Golf Committee is considering this issue in the course of reviewing medical devices and their conformance under Rule 14-3.

Another issue relating to this Rule concerns the following query:

> If a player builds a stance so that his supporting crutch does not slip during the swing, is he in breach of this Rule? This is an interesting question, because the answer is also dependent on the concept of "fairly taking his stance" (Rule 13-2).

A player who "builds a stance" by creating a raised mound of soil against which he braces his crutch would be in breach of Rule 13-3 for building a stance. However, a certain amount of "digging in" with the feet is permitted. By analogy, this would allow for some "digging in" with an assistive device in an effort to prevent slipping, but there is a point beyond which the player would be in violation of "fairly taking his stance." As noted in the discussion of Rule 13-2, this is a very subjective determination which the Committee must make after considering all of the circumstances.

Rule 13-4a (Testing the Condition of the Hazard) and Rule 13-4b (Touching the Ground in the Hazard)

By analogy to Decision 13-4/22 (Rake Handle Stuck in Bunker Before Stroke), it could be argued that a disabled golfer who enters a bunker with a cane or crutches is testing the condition of that hazard and, therefore, is subject to penalty. However, the intent of Decision 13-4/22 is to clarify that a player may not gain additional information about the condition of a hazard through actions other than those which are necessary to allow him to reach his ball and take his stance. Therefore, a player who enters a hazard with canes or crutches would not be in breach of Rules 13-4a or 13-4b provided his actions are not intended to test the condition of the hazard.

Rule 14-2 (Assistance)

Prior to the stroke, it is permissible for a disabled golfer to accept physical assistance from anyone for the purpose of positioning himself or any assistive device which he is using. The provisions of this Rule apply only while the player is making a stroke.

Rule 14-3 (Artificial Devices and Unusual Equipment)

Assistive devices are considered artificial devices or unusual equipment under Rule 14-3. Nevertheless, a Committee may allow a disabled golfer to use such an assistive device, even if it has been modified to aid the player in playing the game. However, if the Committee believes that an assistive device so modified would give the player an undue advantage over other players, the Committee has the authority to prohibit its use under Rule 14-3.

Rule 16-1e (Standing Astride or on Line of Putt)

In view of the proposed Definition of "Stance," it is recommended that Rule 16-1e be modified to read:

e. Standing Astride or on Line of Putt

The player shall not make a stroke on the putting green from a stance astride, or with either foot or any assistive device touching, the line of putt or an extension of that line behind the ball.

Rule 17-3b (Ball Striking Flagstick or Attendant)

The language in Rule 17-3b makes it clear that if a ball strikes an assistive device which is being used by any person while he is attending the flagstick with the player's authority or prior knowledge, the player incurs a penalty for a breach of this Rule.

Rule 20-1 (Lifting)

See same entry under Golfers Requiring Wheelchairs.

Rule 22 (Ball Interfering With or Assisting Play)

See same entry under Golfers Requiring Wheelchairs.

Rule 24-2 (Immovable Obstruction) and Rule 25-1 (Abnormal Ground Conditions)

The amended Definition of "Stance" would entitle a player to relief from an immovable obstruction or an abnormal ground condition if, in fairly taking his stance, the obstruction or the ground under repair interfered with the positioning of his assistive device. However, the Exceptions under Rules 24 and 25 would preclude relief for a player who has interference from these conditions as a result of placing his assistive device in an unnecessarily abnormal position for the required shot or using an unnecessarily abnormal direction of play.

Rule 28 (Ball Unplayable)

It is a fact that one able-bodied golfer may attempt and successfully execute a stroke with a ball which another able-bodied golfer may have declared unplayable. It is also a fact that the disabled golfer who requires the use of canes, crutches, or any other type of assistive device may occasionally be unable to play a stroke at a ball which the able-bodied golfer could play. For example, a player using crutches may need to declare a ball which lies on a steep slope of wet grass unplayable in an effort to eliminate the possibility of injury from a fall. However, this situation is not any different than a case where the balls of two able-bodied golfers lie on a gravel cart path which has been declared an integral part of the golf course, and one player plays the stroke and the other player declares his ball unplayable, thus obviating any chance of an injury from flying gravel.

One might argue that because the situations noted above are potentially dangerous, Decision 1-4/10 (Dangerous Situation; Rattlesnake or Bees Interfere with Play) should apply, and the player should be entitled to free relief as prescribed by that Decision. While the situations described in the preceding paragraph are potentially dangerous, they are not analogous to the circumstances contemplated or the answer offered in Decision 1-4/10. That Decision concerns the player who encounters a dangerous situation which is both totally out of his control and unrelated to conditions normally encountered on the course. Additionally, it presupposes that the player's ball is in a playable position. If this were not the case, the player would have to proceed under the unplayable ball Rule incurring a penalty of one stroke, rather than obtaining free relief as prescribed by the Decision. Ultimately, all players must exercise their best judgment in determining whether they are placing themselves at risk by playing a particular stroke. If they are, then their best option may be to declare the ball unplayable. Rule 28 must govern in these situations. Providing free relief in any instance in which there may be a potential for injury will create an unmanageable situation ripe with the potential for abuse.

Golfers Requiring Wheelchairs

Definition of "Stance"

See same entry under Golfers Requiring Canes and Crutches.

Rule 1-2 (Exerting Influence on the Ball), Rule 13-1 (Ball Played As It Lies), and Rule 18-2a (Ball at Rest Moved by Player)

Prior to making a stroke, golfers who play from a wheelchair have traditionally moved the ball a short distance to facilitate positioning it in their stance before address, a maneuver often referred to as "bumping" the ball. Increasing the pace of play and decreasing turf damage by not having to precisely position their chair are the reasons which are often cited to justify this practice. Everyone would like to increase the pace of play while simultaneously decreasing turf damage. Consequently, the rationale for "bumping" the ball is not without some merit. However, such an action violates one of the two most fundamental principles of the game—playing the ball as it lies.

Drafting language which would permit such a procedure is more difficult than it might seem. For example: By what means may the player "bump" the ball? How far may he "bump" it? When is the ball back in play? If the ball moves after it has been "bumped," must it be replaced, played as it lies, or may the player "re-bump" it? If the ball moves after it has been "bumped," is the player subject to penalty? Must the ball remain on the same part of the golf course (teeing ground, through the green, hazard, and putting green) after it has been "bumped"? If it must remain on the same part of the golf course, may a player who is "bumping" the ball only several inches through the green move it from high rough to short rough or to the fairway? If the original ball had come to rest in a divot hole, may the player "bump" the ball out of the divot hole?

With respect to the next-to-the-last question, it seems logical to conclude that, at a particularly crucial point in his round, the player who has the opportunity to move his ball from tall grass to short grass is much less likely to make a concerted effort to precisely position his chair than the player who would have to move his ball from short grass to tall grass.

Ultimately, "bumping" the ball becomes a mechanism by which "preferred lies" are endorsed. Certainly, this is not a desired result. Therefore, this practice should be discouraged, realizing that there is and will continue to be a marked difference in how strictly the Rules of Golf are applied by and to recreational and competitive golfers.

Rule 6-4 (Caddie)

See same entry under Golfers Requiring Canes or Crutches for additional considerations regarding this Rule.

In addition, it would be permissible for a wheelchair golfer to employ both a caddie and an aide to assist him provided the aide does not carry or handle the player's clubs (see Rule 8-1 below). Depending on his responsibilities, the status of the aide would need to be clarified (see discussion of "Coach" under Blind Golfers; see also discussion of "Supervisor" under Mentally Handicapped Golfers).

Rule 8-1 (Advice)

If a wheelchair golfer employs both a caddie and an aide (see Rule 6-4 above), the aide would be prohibited from giving advice to the player.

Rule 13-2 (Improving Lie, Area of Intended Swing, or Line of Play)

See same entry under Golfers Requiring Canes or Crutches.

Rule 13-3 (Building Stance)

See same entry under Golfers Requiring Canes or Crutches.

Rule 14-2 (Assistance)

See same entry under Golfers Requiring Canes or Crutches.

Rule 14-3 (Artificial Devices and Unusual Equipment)

See same entry under Golfers Requiring Canes or Crutches.

Rule 16-1e (Standing Astride or on Line of Putt)

See same entry under Golfers Requiring Canes or Crutches.

Rule 17-3b (Ball Striking Flagstick or Attendant)

See same entry under Golfers Requiring Canes or Crutches.

Rule 20-1 (Lifting)

Rule 20-1 states in part:
If a ball or ball-marker is accidentally moved in the process of lifting the ball under a Rule or marking its position, the ball or the ball-marker shall be replaced. There is no penalty provided the movement of the ball or the ball-marker is directly attributable to the specific act of marking the position of or lifting the ball. Otherwise, the player shall incur a penalty stroke under this Rule or Rule 18-2a.

This Rule requires no modification for use by disabled golfers. However, because physical limitations and assistive devices, especially chairs, may restrict access to the ball, the Rule should be interpreted loosely enough to give the disabled golfer the benefit of the doubt in cases where directly attributable becomes an issue.

Rule 20-2a (Dropping and Re-dropping; By Whom and How)

Rather than have a disabled golfer who uses a wheelchair hold the ball above his head and drop it or throw the ball upwards to what shoulder height would be if he were able to stand erect, and in an effort to provide some uniformity, the following modification to Rule 20-2a is recommended:

20-2. Dropping and Re-dropping

a. BY WHOM AND HOW
A ball to be dropped under the Rules shall be dropped by the player himself. He shall either

stand or sit erect, hold the ball at shoulder height and arm's length, and drop it. If a ball is dropped by any other person or in any other manner and the error is not corrected as provided in Rule 20-6, the player shall incur a penalty stroke.

Rule 20-3 (Placing and Replacing)

While a player may give another person the authority to retrieve or lift his ball, only the player or his partner may place a ball under the Rules. Because of physical limitations, it may be difficult or impossible for the disabled golfer playing from a wheelchair to place a ball as provided in Rule 20-3a. The solution to this issue is not very straightforward. Rather than suggesting that another person be authorized by the player to place the ball for him or that the player simply do his best, even if this means dropping the ball a few inches, it seems reasonable to wait and see whether or not this concern becomes a real issue.

Replacing the ball should rarely pose any difficulty, as Rule 20-3 allows for replacement not only by the player or his partner but also by the person who lifted it.

Rule 22 (Ball Interfering With or Assisting Play)

Disabled golfers using assistive devices may be inclined not to lift their ball on the putting green in an effort to reduce the potential for damage to the putting green surface. This is not the problem it may seem to be, as the player may authorize another person to lift and mark his ball. The development of assistive devices which minimize the load per square inch will also help eliminate this concern.

Rule 24-2 (Immovable Obstruction) and Rule 25-1 (Abnormal Ground Conditions)

See same entry under Golfers Requiring Canes or Crutches.

Rule 28 (Ball Unplayable)

See same entry under Golfers Requiring Canes or Crutches for additional considerations regarding this Rule.

Obviously, the most significant issue here is how this Rule should be applied to the disabled golfer who is using a wheelchair and cannot get to his ball when it lies in a bunker. At present, the wheelchair golfer often moves the ball close to the edge of the bunker and plays it, without penalty, or drops a ball outside of the bunker under penalty of one stroke.

This procedure creates the potential for a very definite inequity. Consider the case in which two wheelchair golfers are playing against one another, and the balls of both players come to rest in a bunker. If one of the balls is playable and the other ball is truly unplayable, both players are handled identically—a decidedly advantageous result for the player whose ball was unplayable.

Before suggesting a solution to this problem, another potential inequity must be examined. Consider the available options for the able-bodied golfer when he plays a stroke and the ball comes to rest in a bunker. He may play the ball as it lies. If the player deems his ball to be unplayable, he shall, under penalty of one stroke,

a. play a ball as nearly as possible at the spot from which the original ball was last played; or

b. drop a ball within two club-lengths of the spot where the ball lay, but not nearer the hole; or

c. drop a ball behind the point where the ball lay, keeping that point directly between the hole and the spot on which the ball is dropped, with no limit to how far behind that point the ball may be dropped.

If the unplayable ball lies in a bunker the player may proceed under Clause a, b, or c. If he elects to proceed under Clause b or c, a ball must be dropped in the bunker.

Therefore, the able-bodied golfer may play his next stroke from outside of the bunker, but instead of simply dropping a ball just outside of the bunker, he must go back to the spot from which he last played. In some instances, this may result in his having to play a full shot just to get back to the area of the bunker—the equivalent of a two-stroke penalty and a very definite inequity.

Keeping in mind the goal of allowing able-bodied and disabled golfers to play against one another on an equitable basis, the following modification to the language of Rule 28 is recommended:

If a disabled golfer deems his ball to be unplayable in a bunker, he shall

    a. proceed under Rule 28a, b or c; or

    b. add an additional penalty of one stroke and play a ball outside the bunker, keeping the point where the ball lay directly between the hole and the spot on which the ball is dropped.

While this modification eliminates the inequity for the able-bodied golfer, it appears to create one for the disabled golfer. However, it is anticipated that future refinements in the USGA Handicap System will resolve this concern by allotting proportionally more handicap strokes to the disabled golfer who is playing from a wheelchair as the number and the severity of the bunkers increase from one golf course to another.

Mentally Handicapped Golfers

Modification of the Rules of Golf for the mentally handicapped golfer appears unnecessary. If it is elected to play by the Rules, this group of individuals should be able to do so, although some players may require on-course supervision to facilitate some or all aspects of play, including etiquette. In that regard, the on-course supervisor would, in some cases, be somewhat analogous to the coach used by a blind golfer. In other situations, the supervisor might function more like an observer, helping one or more groups of golfers on an as needed basis. In that case, he would be considered an outside agency. In defining the status and the duties of a "supervisor," potential conflicts with Rules 6-4 (Caddie) and 8-1 (Advice) will need to be considered by the Committee.

The relatively abbreviated experience with mentally handicapped golfers precludes addressing their needs under the Rules of Golf more specifically at this time. However, as these individuals become more involved in the game, it will be necessary to insure that the Rules are being properly adapted to accommodate any special requirements which interfere with their playing of the game.

Miscellaneous Issues

Golfers With Other Disabilities

There are many golfers who have physical limitations which may result in some degree of disability and which may have a significant impact on their ability to play the game. Examples include visually impaired golfers and golfers who cannot grip a club because of severe arthritis or missing digits. The foregoing Rules modifications do not specifically apply to these individuals. However, in cases where an artificial device, such as a brace or a gripping aid, will allow these individuals to play, the USGA will review and issue a decision, on a case-by-case basis, as to whether or not the use of such a device constitutes a breach of Rule 14-3 (Artificial Devices and Unusual Equipment). Any player may request a ruling on an assistive device which they wish to use by submitting a written request to the USGA.

Etiquette—Courtesy on the Course Pace of Play

This section in The Rules of Golf states:

> In the interest of all, players should play without delay. If a match fails to keep its place on the course and loses more than one clear hole on the players in front, it should invite the match following to pass.

Both able-bodied and disabled golfers should make their best effort to maintain their pace of play and their position on the course. No one deserves special consideration with regard to this point.

Etiquette—Care of the Course

Through the green, the player should repair any damage caused by spikes, tires, and any other type of assistive device. On the putting green, such damage should be repaired after all players in the group have completed the hole. Due to certain weather or turfgrass conditions, disabled golfers may be precluded, most often temporarily, from using certain types of assistive devices.

It is hoped that current research will result in the development of assistive devices which have minimal effect on agronomic conditions and that the Golf Course Superintendents Association of America (GCSAA), the Professional Golfers' Association of America (PGA) and the United States Golf Association (USGA) will lead the effort to re-educate the public regarding the true, rather than the perceived, impact of these devices on turfgrass.

Rule 6-7 (Undue Delay)

The interpretation and application of this particular Rule provides more than enough difficulty in dealing with able-bodied golfers. To suggest a mechanism by which this Rule should be applied to disabled golfers is equally as difficult. Clearly, there is enough subjectivity in determining what constitutes undue delay that considerable Committee discretion is required. In that regard, a slightly liberal interpretation of what constitutes undue delay is suggested when dealing with golfers with disabilities. Ultimately, each Committee must establish what it considers to be reasonable parameters in defining undue delay, taking into account the difficulty of the golf course, weather conditions, and the quality of the field. To offer more specific guidance to the Committee than that is probably unrealistic.

Handicapping

In establishing handicaps for disabled golfers, several issues manifest themselves imme-diately. As an example, consider the discrepancy in Handicap Indices which could arise when a disabled golfer establishes his handicap at a golf course with no bunkers while another disabled golfer of equal ability establishes his handicap at a golf course which is heavily bunkered. The solution to this problem may necessitate determining a maximum number of unplayable penalty strokes allowable during a stipulated round based on the player's Handicap Index and the Hazard Rating of the golf course which he is playing.

Another issue concerns the type of Handicap Index that the disabled golfer should be given once the above modifications to the Rules of Golf and the USGA Handicap System have been fully integrated with one another—regular, provisional, local, or some other restricted designation which has yet to be determined? The answer will depend, at least in part, on how closely the procedures used by disabled golfers follow the Rules of Golf. Prior to establishing permissible modifications to the Rules of Golf for disabled golfers, it was not possible to address handicapping issues because there was no foundation upon which to base the mathematical calculations that are critical in attempting to achieve accurate Handicap Indices. Having created a logical set of Rules modifications, which have been agreed upon with the Royal and Ancient Golf Club of St. Andrews, Scotland, discussions have now been initiated with members of the USGA Handicap Research Team and the USGA Handicap Committee.

Summary

This modification of the Rules of Golf for disabled golfers is intended to provide a means by which they may play equitably with non-disabled golfers or other golfers with disabilities. Hopefully, all of the issues have been addressed, although it is anticipated that continued analysis and further modification will be necessary, as is the case for the Rules of Golf.

Appendix B

Resources

Publications

The increase in recreation activities, and in particular golf participation, by people with disabilities in recent years has been accompanied by the development of several publications devoted to the subject. Among the most relevant are the following:

Amputee Golfer Magazine
National Amputee Golf Association
11 Walnut Hill Road
Amherst, NH 03031

Phone: 800-633-6242
E-mail: info@nagagolf.org
Web site: www.nagagolf.org/
Magazine1.shtml

Access to Recreation
8 Sandra Court
Newbury Park, CA 91320

Phone: 800-634-4351
E-mail: dkrebs@accessstr.com
Web site: www.accessTR.com

Etiquette Seminar on Golf and Players With Disabilities
Available from the National Center on Accessibility
501 North Morton Street, Suite 109
Bloomington, IN 47404-3732

Phone: 812-856-4422
TTY: 812-856-4421
Fax: 812-856-4480
E-mail: nca@indiana.edu
Web site: www.indiana.edu/~nca/

Feeling Up to Par: Medicine Tee to Green
Cornelius N. Stover, John R. McCarroll, and William J. Mallon, eds. 1994. Philadelphia: F.A. Davis.

From Bag Drop to 19th Hole: **Tips for Accommodating a Golfer With a Disability**
Available from the United States Golf Association (USGA) or the National Center on Accessibility (NCA)

Resource Center, USGA
1631 Mesa Avenue
Colorado Springs, CO 80906

Phone: 908-234-2300
E-mail: resourcecenter@usga.org

National Center on Accessibility (NCA)
501 North Morton Street, Suite 109
Bloomington, IN 47404-3732

Phone: 812-856-4422
TTY: 812-856-4421
Fax: 812-856-4480
E-mail: nca@indiana.edu
Web site: www.indiana.edu/~nca/

Golf and ADA: A Winning Twosome
by Greg Jones
Available from National Golf Foundation
1150 South US Highway One, Suite 401
Jupiter, FL 33477

Phone: 561-744-6006
Fax: 561-744-6107
E-mail: general@ngf.org
Web site: www.ngf.org/cgi/home.asp

*Golfers With Disabilities: A Primer
for Golf Course Personnel*
Available from the National Center on
Accessibility (NCA)
501 North Morton Street, Suite 109
Bloomington, IN 47404-3732
Phone: 812-856-4422
TTY: 812-856-4421
Fax: 812-856-4480
E-mail: nca@indiana.edu
Web site: www.indiana.edu/~nca/

***Interacting With People Who Have
Disabilities***
Available from the National Center on
Accessibility (NCA)
501 North Morton Street, Suite 109
Bloomington, IN 47404-3732
Phone: 812-856-4422
TTY: 812-856-4421
Fax: 812-856-4480
E-mail: nca@indiana.edu
Web site: www.indiana.edu/~nca/

New Mobility Life
No Limits Communications
P.O. Box 220
Horsham, PA 19044
Phone: 215-675-9133
Fax: 215-675-9376
Web site: www.newmobility.com/
magazine.cfm

***Paraplegia News
Sports 'n Spokes***
PVA Publications
2111 E. Highland Avenue, Suite 180
Phoenix, AZ 85016-4702
Phone: 888-888-2201
E-mail: suzi@pnnews.com
Web site: www.pvamagazines.com/pnnews

USGA Modified Rules of Golf
Resource Center, USGA
1631 Mesa Avenue
Colorado Springs, CO 80906
Phone: 908-234-2300
Fax: 908-234-9687
E-mail: resourcecenter@usga.org
Web site: www.resourcecenter.usga.org/
TeeOff/CurPlayers/ModifiedRules.cfm

Video Resources

There have also been a few videos produced
that are geared toward golfers with disabilities.
They include the following titles:

***Adaptive Golf Workshop
by J.E. Hanger***
Hanger Prosthetics and Orthotics
P.O. Box 406
Alpharetta, GA 30239
Phone: 800-779-4923

Kathy Corbin's *Never Say Never*
7141 N 16th Street, #223
Phoenix, AZ 85020
Phone: 602-678-1832

Peter Longo's *Challenge Golf* (1987)
Access to Recreation
8 Sandra Court
Newbury Park, CA 91320
Phone: 800-634-4351
E-mail: dkrebs@accesstr.com
Web site: www.accessTR.com

Periodicals

The increase in knowledge about and greater
attention to adapted sports in recent years
have been accompanied by the development
of several periodicals devoted to the subject.
Among the most relevant are the following:

Adapted Physical Activity Quarterly
Publisher: Human Kinetics
P.O. Box 5076
Champaign, Illinois 61825-5076
Phone: 217-351-5076
E-mail: info@hkusa.com
Web site: www.humankinetics.com/
APAQ/journalAbout.cfm

Palaestra
Publisher: Challenge Publications, Ltd.
P.O. Box 508
Macomb, IL 61455
Phone: 309-833-1902
Fax: 309-833-1902
E-mail: challpub@macomb.com
Web site: www.palaestra.com

Other periodicals that publish relevant information from time to time include the following:

American Annals of the Deaf
Publisher: Gallaudet University Press
800 Florida Avenue, NE
Washington, DC 20002

Phone (v/tty): 202-651-5488
Fax: 202-651-5489
E-mail: Valencia.simmons@gallaudet.edu
Web site: http://gupress.gallaudet.edu/annals/

American Journal of Mental Retardation
Publisher: Allen Press
P.O. Box 1897
Lawrence, KS 66044-8897

Phone: 866-730-2267
Fax: 785-843-1274
E-mail: AJMR@allenpress.com
Web site: http://aamr.allenpress.com/
    aamronline/?request = index-html

Clinical Kinesiology
Publisher: American Kinesiotherapy
    Association
P.O. Box 1390
Hines, IL 60141

Phone: 800-296-2582
E-mail: ccbkt@aol.com
Web site: www.akta.org

Journal of Learning Disabilities
Publisher: Sage Publications
2455 Teller Road
Thousand Oaks, CA 91320

Phone: 800-818-7243
E-mail: webmaster@sagepub.com
Web site: www.sagepub.com/
    journal.aspx?pid = 251

Journal of Physical Education, Recreation and Dance
Publisher: American Alliance for Health,
    Physical Education, Recreation and
    Dance
1900 Association Drive
Reston, VA 20191

Phone: 703-476-3400
E-mail: info@aahperd.org
Web site: www.aahperd.org/aahperd/
    template.cfm?template = johperd_
    main.html

Journal of Special Education
Publisher: Pro-Ed
8700 Shoal Creek Boulevard
Austin, Texas 78757-6897

Phone: 800-897-3202
Fax: 800-397-7633
Web site: www.proedinc.com/jse.html

Journal of Visual Impairment & Blindness
Publisher: American Foundation for the
    Blind
11 Penn Plaza, Suite 300
New York, NY 10001

Phone: 212-502-7600
E-mail: afbinfo@afb.net
Web site: www.afb.org/jvib.asp

Research Quarterly for Exercise and Sport
Publisher: American Alliance for Health,
    Physical Education, Recreation and
    Dance
1900 Association Drive
Reston, VA 20191

Phone: 703-476-3400
E-mail: info@aahperd.org
Web site: www.aahperd.org/aahperd/tem
    plate.cfm?template = rqes_main.html

Strategies
Publisher: American Alliance for Health,
    Physical Education, Recreation and
    Dance
1900 Association Drive
Reston, VA 20191

Phone: 703-476-3400
E-mail: info@aahperd.org
Web site: www.aahperd.org/naspe/
    template.cfm?template = strategies_
    main.html

Teaching Exceptional Children
Publisher: The Council for Exceptional
    Children
1110 North Glebe Road, Suite 300
Arlington, VA 22201

Phone: 800-232-7733
TTY: 866-915-5000
Fax: 703-264-9494
E-mail: service@cec.sped.org
Web site: www.cec.sped.org/bk/
    abtec.html

Therapeutic Recreation Journal
Publisher: National Recreation and Park
   Association
22377 Belmont Ridge Road
Ashburn, VA 20148-4150

Phone: 703-858-0784
Fax: 703-858-0794
E-mail: dvaira@nrpa.org
Web site: www.nrpa.org/content/default.
   aspx?documentId=511

Programs and Clinics

There are numerous established programs
and clinics for golfers with disabilities
throughout the country, and new programs
are continually developed. A few of them are
included here:

Challenge Golf Program (Edwin Shaw Hospital)
Edwin Shaw Hospital Main Campus
1621 Flickinger Road
Akron, OH 44312-4495

Phone: 330-784-5400
E-mail: communityrelations@
   edwinshaw.com
Web site: www.edwinshaw.com/
   patientcare/challengegolf.htm

Eagle Mount Adaptive Golf Program
2822 3rd Avenue North, Suite 203
Billings, MT 59101

Phone: 406-245-5422
Fax: 406-245-4390
E-mail: samc@eaglemount.us
Web site: www.eaglemountbillings.org/
   html/Golf.htm

Fore All!
P.O. Box 2456
Kensington, MD 20891-2456

Phone: 301-881-1818
Fax: 301-881-2828
E-mail: fore_all@juno.com
Web site: www.paralysis.org/
   ActiveLiving/ActiveLiving.cfm?ID=
   26214&c=19

Fore Everyone (Walton Rehabilitation Hospital)
1355 Independence Drive
Augusta, GA 30901

Phone: 706-823-8691
E-mail: jthompson@wrh.org
Web site: www.wrh.org/news_events/
   rec_events.html

Fore Golf Sacramento
3645 Fulton Avenue
Sacramento, CA 95821

Phone: 916-481-4653
Fax: 916-575-2523
E-mail: lovetogolf@mortongolf.biz
Web site: www.capitalcitygolf.com/Mg/
   mortongolf.htm

Fore Hope
925 Darby Creek Drive
Galloway, OH 43119

Phone: 614-870-7299
Fax: 614-870-7245
E-mail: info@forehope.org
Web site: www.forehope.org

Golf4Fun
P.O. Box 27595
Denver, CO 80227

Phone: 303-905-9912
E-mail: Mgr8ful@comcast.net
Web site: www.golf4fun.org

Golf Alive
1220 McMinn Avenue #115
Santa Rosa, CA 95407

Phone: 707-545-3011
Fax: 707-545-3011
E-mail: winwingolf@webtv.net

Golf Without Handicap (Cleveland Sight Center)
1909 East 101st Street,
   University Circle
P.O. Box 1988
Cleveland, OH 44106

Phone: 216-791-8118
Web site: www.clevelandsightcenter.
   org

Helen Hayes Hospital GolfAbility Program
David Wickes, GolfAbility Coordinator

Phone: 845-786-4200
E-mail: wickesd@helenhayeshosp.org
Web site: www.helenhayeshospital.org/
golfability.htm

Kernan Hospital Golf Clinics
2200 Kernan Drive
Baltimore, Maryland 21207

Phone: 410-448-6320
E-mail: pcauley@kernan.umm.edu
Web site: www.kernanhospital.com/
kernan/index.html

Maine Adaptive Golf (Portland Humanities Committee)
100 Commercial Street, Suite 320
Portland, ME 04101

Phone: 207-774-8711
Fax: 207-774-9711
E-mail: info@portlandhumanities.org
Web site: www.porthc.org

Marianjoy Rehabilitation Hospital and Clinic Therapeutic Golf Program
26 W. 171 Roosevelt Road
Wheaton, IL 60187

Phone: 630-462-4039
E-mail: golf@marianjoy.org
Web site: www.marianjoy.org/stellent/
groups/public/documents/www/mj_
057879.hcsp

Flint Adaptive Golf (McLaren Regional Rehabilitation Center)
401 S. Ballenger Highway
Flint, MI 48532

Phone: 810-342-2360
E-mail: monicah@mclaren.org
Web site: www.mclaren.org/
body.cfm?id=541

Project GAIN
501 North Morton Street, Suite 109
Bloomington, IN 47404

Phone: 812-856-4422
TTY: 812-856-4421
Fax: 812-856-4480
E-mail: naag@indiana.edu
Web site: www.accessgolf.org

Sister Kenny Institute's Golf Program
800 E. 28th Street
Minneapolis, MN 55407

Phone: 612-863-5712
E-mail: Susan.Hagel@allina.com
Web site: www.allina.com/ahs/ski.nsf/
page/golf

Adaptive Equipment Resources

ATC Golfers
Product: Tee-Stick
P.O. Box 361
Moonee Ponds, 3039
Victoria, AUSTRALIA

Phone: 866-840-8900
Email: info@atcteestick.com
Web site: www.achievableconcepts.
com.au/

Access to Recreation
Product: golf clubs
8 Sandra Court
Newbury Park, CA 91320

Phone: 800-634-4351
E-mail: dkrebs@accesstr.com
Web site: www.accessTR.com

Achievable Concepts
Products: adaptive golf gloves, single-rider golf cars, tee aid

Phone: (61) 3 9370 0217 (Australia)
E-mail: sales@achievableconcepts.
com.au
Web site: www.achievableconcepts.
com.au/

Arthra Grip
Product: gripping strap
Phone: 302-734-0602

Branside Associates
Product: Tee-EZ Plus
1086 West Galbraith Road
Cincinnati, OH 45231

Phone: 513-522-3408

Club Car
Product: 1-pass single-rider golf car
P.O. Box 204658
Augusta, GA 30917-4658
Phone: 800-258-2227
Fax: 706-863-5808
Web site: www.clubcar.com

DRA Products
Product: Pick-It-Up ball retriever
P.O. Box 290924
Kerrville, TX 78029-0924
Phone: 830-896-1598
E-mail: info@easiergolfing.com
Web site: www.EasierGolfing.com

E-Car Corporation
Product: single-rider golf cars
8673 Grovemont Circle
Gaithersburg, MD 20877
Phone: 800-890-4251
Fax: 301-208-8691
E-mail: usoffice@e-caramerica.com
Web site: www.e-caramerica.com

Electric Mobility
Product: single-rider golf cars
Electric Mobility Corporation
World Headquarters
591 Mantua Boulevard
Sewell, NJ 08080
Phone: 800-662-4548
Fax: 856-468-3426
Web site: www.electricmobility.com

EZ Grip Glove
Product: securing glove
4090 Post Road, Suite A
Warwick, RI 02886
Phone: 401-885-0214

Fairway Golf Cars
Product: single-rider golf cars
3225 Gateway Road, Suite 300
Brookfield, WI 53045
Phone: 888-320-4850
Fax: 262-790-9396
Web site: www.fairwaygolfcars.com

Flex-Grip
Product: prosthetic arm attachment
Phone: 480-733-7833
E-mail: r-dilly@cox.net

Genesis Golf
Product: single-rider golf cars, ball suction
100 Snake Hill Road
West Nyack, NY 10094
Phone: 888-456-2468
E-mail: golf@genesisny.net
Web site: www.genesisny.net

Get-A-Grip
Product: prosthetic arm attachment
Phone: 763-374-2886
E-mail: vikingwoman84@aol.com

Gibas Golf Products
Product: clubs
16182 Gothard Street, Suite I
Huntington Beach, CA 92647
Phone: 800-783-2255
Fax: 714-842-7460
E-mail: info@gibasgolf.com
Web site: www.gibasgolf.com

Golf Around the World
Product: grip wrap and gripping aids
1396 N. Killian Drive
Lake Park, FL 33403
Phone: 800-824-4279
Fax: 561-848-0870
E-mail: info@golfaroundtheworld.com
Web site: www.golfaroundtheworld.com

Golf Country
Product: Adapt-a-club
Phone: 888-860-9160
E-mail: info@golf-country.com
Web site: www.golf-country.com

Golf Xpress
Product: single-rider golf cars
Phone: 989-846-6255
E-mail: Mitch@GolfXpress.com
Web site: www.golfxpress.com

Grip Mate Products, Inc.
Product: gripping device
4850 Oak Arbor Drive
Valdosta, GA 31602
Phone: 800-941-4505
Fax: 229-241-1114
E-mail: info@gripmate.com
Web site: www.gripmate.com

Jimmy Jammz Motorsports
Product: single-rider golf cars
123 Camden Avenue
West Elkton, OH 45070

Phone: 937-787-9966
E-mail: jimjammz@siscom.net
Web site: www.jimmyjammz.com

Joe's Original BACKTEE
Product: teeing device

Phone: 319-268-9039
E-mail: jim.egli@cfu.net

LaJolla Golf Clubs
Product: lightweight and children's golf
   clubs
1390-A Engineer Street
Vista, CA 92081

Phone: 800-468-7700
Fax: 760-599-9359
Web site: www.ljcgolf.com

Madentec
Product: virtual golf (on the course) for
   quadriplegia
3022 Calgary Trail South
Edmonton, Alberta
Canada T6J 6V4

Phone: 780-450-8926
Fax: 780-988-6182
E-mail: sales@madentec.com
Web site: www.madentec.com/
   downloads/ra2000press.pdf

Matzie Golf Co.
Product: EZ Swinger clubs

Phone: 800-783-2255
E-mail: info@gibasgolf.com
Web site: www.matzie.com

Mdek
Product: single-rider golf cars
900 Dutchess Turnpike
Pougnkeepsie, NY 12803

Phone: 305-787-5880
Fax: (718) 921-6078
Web site: www.mdek.com

Next Step Orthotics and Prosthetics
Product: prosthetic arm attachment

Phone: 800-572-7938
Web site: www.nextstepoandp.com

No-Bend Teeing Device
Product: teeing aid
P.O. Box 30
Swanton, OH 43558

Phone: 419-867-1421
E-mail: CONCO2000@compuserve.com
Web site: http://ourworld.compuserve.
   com/homepages/conco2000

One Putz Putter
Product: putter

Phone: 877-785-2870
E-mail: sales@oneputz.com

Ortho-Kinetics Incorporated
Product: Teestick and single-rider golf cars

Phone: 888-320-4850

Pat Ryan Golf
Product: adaptive golf clubs
14900 Highway 7 West
Minnetonka, MN 55345

Phone: 800-922-6924
Fax: 952-930-1888
E-mail: patryangolf@aol.com
Web site: www.patryangolf.com

Power Glove
Product: grip aid
P.O. Box 2323
Princeton, NJ 08543

Phone: 800-836-3760
Fax: 609-688-9814
E-mail: info@powerglove.com
Web site: www.powerglove.com

Precision Pick Up Putter
Product: putter

Phone: 800-242-8463
E-mail: pikupputtr@aol.com
Web site: www.pickupputter.com

Pride Healthcare
Product: single-rider golf cars
182 Susquehanna Avenue
Exeter, PA 18643

Phone: 800-800-8586
Fax: 800-800-1636
Web site: www.pridemobility.com

Professional Clubmakers Society
Product: custom clubs
70 Persimmon Ridge Drive
Louisville, KY 40245

Phone: 800-548-6094
Fax: 502-241-2817
E-mail: pcs@proclubmakers.org
Web site: www.proclubmakers.org

Really Cool Golf Stuff
Product: EZ-OUT ball retriever, EZT
    no-bending golf accessory

Phone: 800-553-6472

Scientific Golfers, Inc.
Product: short putters

Phone: 800-433-1574
E-mail: infous@scientificgolfers.com

Scoobug
Product: single-rider golf cars

Phone: 866-694-0444
Web site: http://electroline4u.com/shopsite_
    sc/store/html/scoobugYT107.html

Solorider Industries
Product: single-rider golf cars
7315 S. Revere Parkway, Suite 604
Centennial, CO 80112

Phone: 800-898-3353
Fax: 303-858-0707
Web site: www.solorider.com

Spinlife.com
Product: single-rider golf cars
1108 City Park Avenue
Columbus, OH 43206

Phone: 800-850-0335
Web site: www.spinlife.com

Tee-Stick
Product: teeing device

E-mail: info@teestick.com
Web site: www.teestick.com

That's Clever, Inc.
Product: golf ball grabber
655 Pullman Avenue
Rochester, NY 14615

Phone: 888-736-3220
Fax: 585-254-2367
E-mail: info@thatscleverinc.com
Web site: www.thatsclever.com

Therapeutic Recreation Services, Inc.
Product: amputee golf grip
3090 Sterling Circle, Studio A
Boulder, CO 80301-2338

Phone: 800-279-1865
Fax: 303-444-5372
Web site: www.oandp.com/trs

ToT'in Bone'z Golf
Product: clubs for seated position
2069 Archer Circle
Rocklin, CA 95765

Phone: 877-HIT-HARD
Fax: 916-415-1660
E-mail: JstGolfin@aol.com (California);
    ClubWizard1@aol.com (New York)
Web site: www.totinbonezgolf.com

USA Golf Products, Inc.
Product: single-rider golf cars, grip aids,
    static chair, teeing devices
21417 Brewer Road
Grass Valley, CA 95949

Phone: 530-268-6813
Fax: 530-268-0901
E-mail: usagolf@foothill.net
Web site: www.usagpi.com

U.S. Kids Golf Clubs
Product: golf clubs
3040 Northwoods Parkway
Norcross, GA 30071

Phone: 888-3-US KIDS (888-387-5437)
Fax: 770-448-3069
E-mail: webmaster@uskidsgolf.com
Web site: www.uskidsgolf.com

Wheelin' Canada
Product: single-rider golf cars and tee
    devices
P.O. Box 14a, Section A
Toronto, ON M8V 3R9

Phone: 800-722-7977
E-mail: wcanada@cogeco.ca
Web site: www.wheelincanada.com

Wheels To Go Electric Carts
Product: single-rider golf cars
131 Progressive Drive
Ottoville, OH 45876

Phone: 800-452-2495
Fax: 419-453-2278

Organizations and Associations

Adaptive Golf Association of Texas
661 Harvest Hill
Lewisville, TX 75067

Phone: 214-222-4624
E-mail: bbromley@airmail.net

Adaptive Golf Foundation
E-mail: webmaster@adaptivegolffoundation.
    com
Web site: http://adaptivegolffoundation.
    com/index.html

Alberta Deaf Golf Club
E-mail: ahhaas@shaw.ca
Web site: www.deafalberta.org/ADSA/
    Pages_ADSA/AltaDeafGolfClub.html

American Blind and Disabled Golf Association
7634 Benassi Drive
Gilroy, CA 95020

Phone: 504-891-4737
E-mail: abdga@charter.net
Web site: www.abdga.org

Bay State Deaf Golf Association
E-mail: POLASKA1954@aol.com

Canadian Amputee Golf Association (CAGA)
P.O. Box 6091, Section A
Calgary, Alberta
Canada T2H 2L4

Phone: 403-256-1884
E-mail: canamps@caga.ca
Web site: www.caga.ca

Carolina Deaf Golfers Club
TTY: 919-662-8512
E-mail: CEnsley48@aol.com

Central Illinois Deaf Golf Association
E-mail: cidga@aol.com
Web site: www.deaf-center.org/cidga.htm

Children's Golf Foundation
7301 N. Haverhill Road
West Palm Beach, FL 33407

Phone: 561-842-0066
Fax: 561-842-0304
E-mail: info@childrensgolf.org
Web site: www.childrensgolf.org/staff.htm

Colorado Physically Handicapped Golf Association
6030 Hoyt Street
Arvada, CO 80004

Phone: 303-421-3823

Connecticut State Deaf Golf Association
E-mail: seanpatrick77@msn.com
Web site: www.ctdeafgolfer.com/
    19thHole/Admin/SiteSettings/tabid/39/
    ctl/Login/Default.aspx

Division for Learning Disabilities (DLD), the Council for Exceptional Children (CEC)
1110 North Glebe Road, Suite 300
Arlington, VA 22201-5704

Phone: 703-620-3660
E-mail: cec@cec.sped.org
Web site: www.dldcec.org

Eastern Amputee Golf Association (EAGA)
2015 Amherst Drive
Bethlehem, PA 18015-5606

Phone: 888-868-0992
Fax: 610-867-9295
E-mail: info@eaga.org
Web site: www.eaga.org

Eastern Pennsylvania Golf Association of the Deaf
E-mail: Mnelson634@aol.com
Web site: http://hometown.aol.com/
    ace265/epgad.htm

Empire State Deaf Golf Association
E-mail: RDFISH4@yahoo.com

Far West Golf Association of the Deaf
E-mail: jshayes72@comcast.net
Web site: www.fwgad.org

Florida Deaf Golfers Association
E-mail: RDEM930244@aol.com
Web site: www.fdga.info

Georgia Deaf Golfers' Association
529 Staghorn Lane NW
Suwanee, GA 30024

TTY: 770-271-7994
Fax: 678-623-8105
Web site: www.gdga.org

Golf Association of Florida
720 DS. Sapodilla Avenue, Suite 313
West Palm Beach, Florida 33401

Phone: 561-655-8749
Fax: 561-655-9712
E-mail: fredcorc@aol.com
Web site: www.gafgolf.org

HandiGolf Foundation
Stone Cottage
Launton Road
Stratton Audley
Oxon OX6 9BW

Phone: 01869 277369
E-mail: kirbys@keyingham51.fsnet.co.uk
Web site: www.handigolf.org

Heartland Disabled Golfers Association
12750 Coachlight Square Drive
Florissant, MO 63033-5120

Phone: 314-355-2697
Fax: 314-355-5117

International Blind Golf Association
Phone: 0118-940-1959
E-mail: Derrick@Sheridan25.freeserve.
    co.uk
Web site: www.internationalblindgolf.
    com/text%20only/contact_text.htm

International Dyslexia Association
    (formerly the Orton Dyslexia Society)
Chester Building, Suite 382
8600 LaSalle Road
Baltimore, MD 21286-2044

Phone: 800-222-3123
E-mail: info@interdys.org
Web site: www.interdys.org

LDOnline (online only)
Web site: www.ldonline.org

Kentucky Deaf Golfers Association
113 Silvercreek Road
Danville, KY 40422

E-mail: president@kdga.org
Web site: www.kdga.org

Ladies Professional Golf Association
100 International Golf Drive
Daytona Beach, FL 32124-1092

Phone: 386-274-6200
Fax: 386-274-1099
E-mail: feedback@fans.lpga.com
Web site: www.lpga.com

Learning Disabilities Association of
    America (LDA)
4156 Library Road
Pittsburgh, PA 15234-1349

Phone: 888-300-6710
E-mail: info@ldaamerica.org
Web site: www.ldanatl.org

Mason Dixon Deaf Golfers Association
Web site: www.mddga.org

Michigan Amputee Golf Association
52065 Pulver Road
Three Rivers, MI 49093

Phone: 269-279-5131
Fax: 269-273-1230
E-mail: pineview@net-link.net
Web site: www.pineviewgolf.com/
    page8.html

Michigan Wolverine Deaf Lady Golfers
E-mail: MichDLGA@aol.com
Web site: http://members.aol.com/michdlga/

Middle Atlantic Blind Golf Association
P.O. Box 27
Valley Forge, PA 19481-0027

Phone: 215-745-2323
Web site: www.mabga.org

Midwest Amputee Golf Association
Phone: 708-460-8706
E-mail: onegun@ameritech.net

Midwest Deaf Golfers Association
TTY: 317-576-9849
E-mail: kinggotcha@aol.net
Web site: www.mdga1947.org

Midwest Deaf Ladies Golfers
    Association
TTY: 317-852-6926
E-mail: dekacat@aol.com
Web site: www.mdga1947.org

National Alliance for Accessible Golf
    (NAAG)
501 North Morton Street, Suite 109
Bloomington, IN 47404

Phone: 812-856-4422
TTY: 812-856-4421
Fax: 812-856-4480
E-mail: naag@indiana.edu
Web site: www.accessgolf.org

National Amputee Golf Association (NAGA)
11 Walnut Hill Road
Amherst, NH 03031

Phone: 800-633-6242
E-mail: info@naga-golf.org
Web site: www.nagagolf.org

National Center on Accessibility (NCA)
501 North Morton Street, Suite 109
Bloomington, IN 47404-3732

Phone: 812-856-4422
TTY: 812-856-4421
Fax: 812-856-4480
E-mail: nca@indiana.edu
Web site: www.ncaonline.org

National Center for Learning Disabilities (NCLD)
381 Park Avenue South, Suite 1401
New York, NY 10016

Phone: 888-575-7373
Web site: www.ld.org

National Center on Physical Activity and Disability (NCPAD)
1640 W. Roosevelt Road
Chicago, IL 60608-6904

Phone: 800-900-8086 (voice and TTY)
Fax: 312-355-4058
E-mail: ncpad@uic.edu
Web site: www.ncpad.org

New Jersey Deaf Golf Association
Web site: www.deafgolf.com

North American One-Armed Golfer Association
8406 Cloverport Drive
Louisville, KY 40228

Phone: 502-964-7734
E-mail: naoaga@yahoo.com
Web site: http://naoaga.com

PGA of America
100 Avenue of the Champions
Palm Beach Gardens, FL 33410

Phone: 407-624-8400
E-mail: hthrower@pgahq.com
Web site: www.pga.com

Physically Challenged Golf Association, Inc.
Avondale Medical Center
34 Dale Road, Suite 001
Avon, CT 06001

Phone: 860-676-2035
Fax: 860-676-2041
E-mail: pcga@townusa.com
Web site: www.townusa.com/pcga

Physically Limited Golfers Association
2018 County Road 19
Maple Plain, MN 55359

Phone: 763-479-6419
E-mail: info@mngolf.org
Web site: www.mngolf.org/allied_plga.cfm

Recording for the Blind and Dyslexic
20 Roszel Road
Princeton, NJ 08540

Phone: 609-452-0606
E-mail: nbraman@rfbd.org
Web site: www.rfbd.org

South Carolina Deaf Golfers Association
E-mail: MWBates@aol.com
Web site: www.scdga.org

Southeastern Deaf Golfers Association
E-mail: president@sedga.org
Web site: www.sedga.org

Southern Amputee Golf Association
1300 Woodmere Creek Trail
Vestavia, AL 35226

Phone: 205-978-4586
E-mail: golfer22@mindspring.com

Special Olympics
1133 19th Street, NW
Washington, DC 20036

Phone: 202-628-3630
Fax: 202-824-0200
E-mail: info@specialolympics.org
Web site: www.specialolympics.com

Texas Amputee Golf Association
502 Quail Creek Drive
Round Rock, TX 78664

Phone: 512-431-2861
E-mail: rmccoy2@austin.rr.com
Web site: http://amputee_
    golf.tripod.com/

**United States Adaptive Golf
    Association**
E-mail: golfpro@usagas.org
Web site: www.usagas.org

United States Blind Golf Association
3094 Shamrock Street North
Tallahassee, FL 32309

Phone: 904-893-4511
E-mail: USBGA@blindgolf.com
Web site: www.blindgolf.com

United States Deaf Golf Foundation
Phone: 301-464-9581
E-mail: jhynesjr@aol.com
Web site: www.usdgf.org

United States Golf Association (USGA)
Resource Center, USGA
1631 Mesa Avenue
Colorado Springs, CO 80906

Phone: 908-234-2300
TTY: 800-659-2656
E-mail: resourcecenter@usga.org
Web site: www.resourcecenter.usga.org

West Coast Deaf Golf Club
Web site: www.bcdeafsports.bc.ca/golf/

**Western Amputee Golf Association
    (WAGA)**
Phone: 800-592-9242
E-mail: rmartin@wagagolf.com
Web site: www.wagagolf.org

**Western Canada Blind Golf
    Association**
Phone: 250-723-2726
E-mail: dougstoutley@shaw.ca

Wisconsin Deaf Golf Association
E-mail: jotis@wi.rr.com
Web site: http://home.wi.rr.com/wdga/
    wdga.html

Accessible Golf Architects

Some golf course architects have experience and expertise in designing golf courses that are accessible for golfers with disabilities, including the following architects:

D.J. DeVictor
DeVictor Langham, Inc.
10896 Crabapple Road, Suite 100
Roswell, GA 30075

Phone: 770-642-1255
Fax: 770-642-0925
E-mail: dvl@devictorlangham.com

Dick Phelps
P.O. Box 3295
Evergreen, CO 80439

Phone: 303-670-0478

Online Seminars

www.apa.org/science/freegrantclass.html

www.eduplace.com/grants/help/
    courses.html

www.npguides.org

www.revisions-grants.com

www.thefineartoffundraising.com

Etiquette Tips for Golfers With Disabilities and Golf Course Operators

Robb, G. *Golf Etiquette and Players with Disabilities,* 1996, (Bloomington, IN: National Center on Accessibility-Indiana University). Adapted with permission from the National Center on Disability.

Preparation for Play

Suggestions for Golfers With Disabilities

1. Call ahead. Set a tee time. If special accommodations are required, inform the golf course of the services that might be requested.

2. Get the names of the golf professional and green superintendent.

3. If applicable, ask specific questions about golf course policies, such as the following:

   • Course policy on bringing private or single-rider golf cars (trail fees)

   • Course accessibility (e.g., bag drop, parking, pro shop)

   • Policies for coaches (for blind golfers) or personal care attendants

   • If this will be first time playing the course, check it out for accessibility before playing

   • If applicable, you may wish to ask what information the golf course personnel would like to have about your assistive devices

4. Become familiar with the golf course and layout.

5. Arrive early to ensure plenty of time to check in, warm up, and answer any questions that golf course personnel may have.

6. If you are being paired with strangers, introduce yourself early and discuss playing conditions and so on.

7. Determine what the policies for golf car and assistive-device access are for that day. If available, go to the practice range to warm up and test course conditions.

8. Know your limitations and determine the level of course difficulty you feel comfortable with well in advance of teeing off.

Suggestions for Golf Course Operators

1. Determine what, if any, information you would like to have regarding the special needs of golfers with disabilities so that you can address their questions appropriately. Any questions to golfers with disabilities should be asked in the

context of making it easier for the golfer to be prepared to play the course upon arrival.

2. Where possible and appropriate, disperse accessible parking to nearest points of access to the pro shop, clubhouse, and practice facilities.

3. Appropriate and accessible signs will save time and prevent inconvenience for you, your staff, and the golfer with a disability.

4. As much as possible, determine what your course policies are regarding private golf car use, assistive devices, access points on the course for cars and assistive devices, and so on. Policies should be nondiscriminatory and should be clearly indicated to all golfers.

5. Provide assistance in bag-drop area if you know a golfer with limited mobility will be arriving at a predetermined time.

Teeing Ground

Suggestions for Golfers With Disabilities

1. Know ahead of time where the most appropriate access is to the teeing ground of choice and which tees are accessible.

2. Know your playing capabilities and choose the tee most appropriate for your game if it is accessible.

3. Get to the designated teeing ground as quickly as possible. If it is on the forward tees, tee off first if it is safe and maintain a good pace of play.

4. Ensure that your playing partners know and are ready to assist, if requested, in getting to the teeing ground, placing and picking up tees, and so on. (New players may need reminding.)

5. Always try to position yourself so that you are ready to play when it is your turn.

6. Be aware of course policy regarding golf cars and assistive devices on teeing grounds. (Certain access routes may be preferred.)

7. Always carry two balls to the teeing ground in case a provisional ball is appropriate or a ball is deemed out of play from the tee.

Suggestions for Golf Course Operators

1. If possible, provide the golfer information on tees that are most accessible.

2. If possible, at teeing grounds where barriers are present (e.g., curbs, ropes) leave openings for golfers using assistive devices to independently access the teeing ground.

Through the Green

Suggestions for Golfers With Disabilities

1. Always be aware of golf car policy and exceptions before teeing off.

2. Be familiar with access points to and from the fairways.

3. Determine areas that should be avoided such as sensitive natural areas or newly planted or seeded areas.

4. When golf cars are taken to various areas of the course because of access needs, be sensitive to where your car is parked in relation to other golfers as well as to the proximity of their next play.

5. Good judgment should always be used. Golf cars and assistive devices can do damage. Sensitive areas should be avoided.

6. It is helpful to know where the accessible restrooms are before beginning play.

7. Always be prepared to move as fast as your playing partners, if not faster.

8. Play "ready golf" (be ready to hit the ball when it is your turn).

9. Be sure to have the right clubs with you when preparing to play the next shot.

10. Be prepared to move the ball to maintain the pace of play of your partners.

Suggestions for Golf Course Operators

1. Predetermine course policy on exceptions to be made for golfers with dis-

abilities, such as car flagging, access areas, and conditions under which golf cars are banned.

2. Attempt to eliminate as many barriers as possible, such as ropes and curbs.

3. Mark access areas clearly and have a plan to inform both course personnel and other golfers that a specific designation is for golfers with disabilities and may not be available to all golfers.

Hazards and Bunkers

Suggestions for Golfers With Disabilities

1. Use discretion when the ball comes to rest in a hazard. Often it is wiser to drop out of the hazard as allowed by the rules rather than risk injury or indignation.

2. Determine how you will treat hazards and bunkers before playing. Inform your playing partners of your intent.

3. Play "ready golf" (be ready to hit the ball when it is your turn).

Suggestions for Golf Course Operators

1. Try to have at least one access point for all bunkers so a golfer using an assistive mobility device may enter and exit.

Greens

Suggestions for Golfers With Disabilities

1. Where possible, predetermine the best and shortest access points to the green.

2. Avoid turning on the green when using a car or assistive device.

3. Ask a playing companion to pick the ball out of the hole if necessary. Picking the ball out of the cup with the putter blade may damage the area around it.

4. If desired, suction-cup devices that attach to the end of the putter are available for retrieving the ball from the cup.

5. Always carry divot or green repair tools.

6. If necessary, ask your playing partner to repair ball marks and to mark your ball.

7. Be certain that you have done everything that you can to ensure that your assistive device does not damage greens (e.g., properly inflated tires and so on).

8. Where possible, keep wheeled devices off the intended putting line of other golfers.

9. Position your assistive device appropriately for exiting the green in the shortest possible route.

10. Don't drive on the green until you're ready to putt.

11. Move away from the green as quickly as possible and directly to the most accessible route.

12. Wear shoes or have tires and devices that will not damage the greens.

13. If you determine that your pace is holding up play, let groups behind you play through.

14. Pick up the ball when you reach your maximum stroke allowable for handicap stroke purposes.

Suggestions for Golf Course Operators

1. Try to have at least one access point at all greens so a golfer using an assistive mobility device may enter and exit.

Making Your Facility Accessible

The following section summarizes accessibility guidelines for specific elements commonly found in golf course facilities (ADA Accessibility Guidelines, 2002).

Courtesy of the ADA Accessibility Guidelines, www.accessboard.gov/adaag/html/adaag.htm.

Parking

• Accessible parking spaces for a particular building shall be located on the shortest accessible route of travel to an accessible entrance. In parking facilities that do not serve a specific building, accessible parking shall be situated on the shortest accessible route of travel to an accessible pedestrian entrance of the parking facility. In buildings with multiple accessible entrances, accessible parking spaces shall be dispersed and located as close as possible to the accessible entrances. There should be at least one accessible parking space for every 25 regular parking spaces.

• Accessible parking spaces shall be at least 96 inches (244 centimeters) wide. Accessible parking spaces for cars must have an access aisle that is at least 5 feet (153 centimeters) wide. Van-accessible parking spaces must have an access aisle at least 8 feet (244 centimeters) wide (see figure D.1).

• Parking spaces and access aisles shall be level with surface slopes and not exceed a grade of 1:48 (2 percent) in all directions.

• Accessible parking spaces shall be designated as reserved by a sign showing the symbol of accessibility. Accessible parking

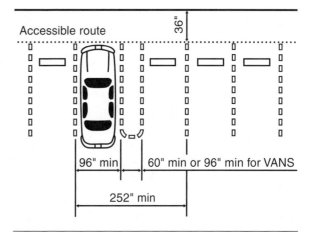

Figure D.1 Sizes and access aisles for accessible parking spaces.

Courtesy of the ADA Accessibility Guidelines, www.accessboard.gov/adaag/html/figures/fig9.html.

spaces for vans shall have an additional sign reading "Van Accessible" located under the symbol of accessibility. These signs shall be located where a vehicle parked in the space will not hide them.

• Accessible passenger loading zones shall have a vertical clearance of at least 114 inches (290 centimeters) and provide an access aisle at least 60 inches (153 centimeters) wide and 20 feet (6.1 meters) long parallel to the vehicle pull-up space. A curb ramp shall be provided if a curb is present between the access aisle and the vehicle pull-up space.

• If only one accessible parking space is provided, it must be a van-accessible space.

• If multiple accessible parking spaces are provided, at least one in six must be van accessible.

Entrance

- Accessible entrances shall be part of an accessible route and be connected to accessible parking, passenger loading zones, and public streets and sidewalks if available.

- A service entrance shall not be the sole accessible entrance.

- If there are two public entrances, only one must be accessible. However, a sign must be placed at the nonaccessible entrance indicating location of the accessible entrance.

- When a ramp is added to make available an accessible entrance, the slope of the ramp ought to be as shallow as possible but not more than a grade of 1:12. Handrails must be provided if the slope is more than 1:20 (5 percent).

Doors

- Revolving doors shall not be the only means of passage at an accessible entrance or along an accessible route.

- Doorways shall have at least 32 inches (82 centimeters) of clearance with the door open 90 degrees, measured between the face of the door and the opposite stop.

- Thresholds at doorways shall not exceed 0.75 inch (2 centimeters) in height for exterior sliding doors or 0.5 inch (1.3 centimeters) for other styles of doors. Raised thresholds at accessible doorways shall be beveled with a slope no greater than 1:2.

- Handles, pulls, latches, and locks on accessible doors shall have a shape that is easy to grasp with one hand and does not require tight grasping, pinching, or twisting of the wrist to operate. Hardware for accessible doors shall be mounted no higher than 48 inches (122 centimeters) above the floor.

Shelves and Maneuvering Space

- An accessible route of at least 36 inches (92 centimeters) wide must be provided to fixed shelves and displays.

- If a 180-degree turn is required for exit of an area, then a 60-inch (153-centimeter) diameter turning area or a 36-inch-wide (92-centimeter-wide) T is needed. The space for a T-turn has to be at least 36 inches (92 centimeters) wide for each segment of the T and it must fit within an area 60 by 60 inches (153 by 153 centimeters).

- If a significant reduction in selling space would be required to make the area accessible, alternative services such as staff assistance can be substituted for accessibility.

- Sales items may be placed at any height, but staff should provide assistance to reach items for customers.

Accessible Route

- At least one accessible route within the facility shall be provided from accessible parking, accessible passenger loading zones, and public streets or sidewalks to the accessible building entrance. The accessible route shall coincide as much as possible with the route for the general public.

- At least one accessible route shall unite all accessible buildings, facilities, and spaces that are on the same site.

- The minimum clear width of an accessible route shall be 36 inches (92 centimeters) except at doors.

- If an accessible route has less than 60 inches (153 centimeters) of clear width, then passing spaces at least 60 by 60 inches shall be located at intervals not to exceed 200 feet (61 meters). A T-intersection of two corridors is an acceptable passing place.

- The accessible route should not be a slope of more than 1:20 (5 percent).

Drinking Fountains and Water Coolers

- Spouts shall be no higher than 36 inches (92 centimeters), measured from the floor or ground surface to the spout outlet.

- The spouts of drinking fountains shall be at the front of the unit and direct the water flow in a trajectory that is parallel to the front of the unit.

- The spout shall provide a flow of water that allows the placing of a cup or glass under the flow of water (at least 4 inches, or 10 centimeters, high).

- For drinking fountains with a round or oval bowl, the spout must be positioned so that the flow of water is within 3 inches (8 centimeters) of the front edge of the fountain.

- Unit controls shall be mounted on the front or side near the front edge.

- Wall- and post-mounted cantilevered units shall have a clear knee space between the bottom of the apron and the floor at least 27 inches (69 centimeters) high, 30 inches (76 centimeters) wide, and 17 to 19 inches (43 to 49 centimeters) deep. These units shall also have a minimum clear floor space of 30 by 48 inches (76 by 122 centimeters) to allow a person in a wheelchair to come up to the unit while facing forward.

- Free-standing or built-in drinking fountains without a clear space underneath them shall have unobstructed floor space at least 30 by 48 inches (76 by 122 centimeters) that allows a person in a wheelchair to make a parallel approach to the unit.

Water Closets

- The height of the water closets shall be 17 to 19 inches (43 to 49 centimeters), measured to the top of the toilet seat. Seats shall not be fixed to return to a lifted position.

- The grab bar located behind the water closet shall be at least 36 inches (92 centimeters) long. There must also be a wall-mounted grab bar on the side wall.

- Flush controls shall be hand operated or automatic. Controls for flush valves shall be mounted on the wide side of the toilet no more than 44 inches (112 centimeters) above the floor.

- Toilet paper dispensers shall be installed within easy reach. Dispensers that control delivery and do not allow continuous paper flow shall not be used.

Toilet Stalls

- Accessible toilet stalls shall be on an accessible route.

- Standard toilet stalls with a minimum depth of 56 inches (143 centimeters) shall have wall-mounted water closets. If the depth of a standard toilet stall is increased at least 3 inches (8 centimeters), then a floor-mounted water closet may be used.

- In standard stalls, the front and at least one side partition shall have a toe clearance of at least 9 inches (23 centimeters) above the floor. If the depth of the stall is 60 inches (153 centimeters) or more, then a toe clearance is not required.

- If the toilet stall approach is from the latch side of the stall door, the clearance between the door side of the stall and any hindrance may be reduced to a minimum of 42 inches (107 centimeters).

Urinals

- Urinals can be stall type or wall hung with an elongated rim and can be no more than 17 inches (43 centimeters) above the floor.

- A clear floor space of 30 by 48 inches (76 by 122 centimeters) shall be provided in front of urinals to allow forward approach. This clear space must adjoin or overlap an accessible route.

- Flush controls must be hand operated or automatic and shall be mounted no more than 44 inches (122 centimeters) above the floor.

Lavatories and Mirrors

- Lavatories shall be mounted with the rim or counter surface no higher than 34 inches (86 centimeters) above the floor and provide a clearance of at least 29 inches (74 centimeters) above the floor to the bottom of the apron.

- A clear floor space of 30 by 48 inches (76 by 122 centimeters) shall be provided in front of a lavatory to allow forward approach. This space must adjoin or overlap an accessible route and shall extend 19 inches (49 centimeters) underneath the lavatory.

• Pipes underneath lavatories shall be insulated or otherwise arranged to protect against contact. There shall be no sharp or rough surfaces under lavatories.

• Mirrors shall be mounted with the bottom edge of the reflecting surface no higher than 40 inches (102 centimeters) above the floor.

Shower Stalls

• Shower stalls should be 36 inches square (92 centimeters).

• A seat shall be provided in shower stalls 36 inches square (92 centimeters). The seat shall be mounted 17 to 19 inches (43 to 49 centimeters) from the bathroom floor and shall extend the entire depth of the stall. In a shower stall 36 inches square, the seat shall be on the wall opposite the controls. Where a fixed seat is provided in a stall that is at least 30 by 60 inches (76 by 153 centimeters), it must be a folding type and shall be mounted on the wall adjacent to the controls.

• A shower spray unit that can be used as both a fixed showerhead and as a hand-held shower with a hose at least 60 inches (153 centimeters) shall be provided.

• If provided, curbs in shower stalls 36 inches square (92 centimeters) shall be no higher than 0.5 inch (1.3 centimeters). Shower stalls that are at least 30 by 60 inches (76 by 153 centimeters) long shall not have curbs.

• If enclosures for shower stalls are provided, they shall not obstruct the controls or transfer from wheelchairs.

Signs

• Letters and numbers on signs shall have a width-to-height ratio between 3:5 and 1:1.

• Signs that are suspended or projected overhead shall have a minimum character height of 3 inches (8 centimeters).

• Raised and Braille characters and pictorial symbol signs shall have letters and num-

bers raised at least 1/32 inch (0.8 millimeter). Raised characters must be at least 5/8 inch (1.6 centimeters) but no more than 2 inches (5 centimeters).

• The characters and background of signs shall have a nonglare finish. Characters and symbols shall contrast with their background (either dark characters on a light background or light characters on a dark background).

Symbols of Accessibility

• Facilities and areas required to be identified as accessible shall use the international symbol of accessibility.

• A sign containing a depiction of a telephone handset with radiating sound waves shall identify telephones required to have a volume control.

• Text telephones (TTYs) shall be identified by the international TTY symbol. If a facility has a public TTY, directional signs indicating the location of the nearest TTY shall be placed next to all banks of telephones that do not contain a TTY. This directional sign shall include the international TTY symbol.

Telephones

• A clear floor space at least 30 by 48 inches (76 by 122 centimeters) that allows either a forward or parallel approach by a person using a wheelchair shall be provided at telephones. Telephones shall not have bases, enclosures, or fixed seats that encumber approaches to telephones by people who use wheelchairs.

• The highest operable parts of the telephone shall be no more than 48 inches (122 centimeters) for forward reach and 54 inches (137 centimeters) for side reach.

• Telephones shall be compatible with hearing aids.

• Volume controls capable of at least 12 dBA but no more than 18 dBA shall be provided.

• Telephones shall have push-button controls.

- The cord from the telephone to the handset shall be at least 29 inches (74 centimeters) long.

Sales and Service Counters

- In areas used for transactions where counters have cash registers, the counter length shall be at least 36 inches (92 centimeters) and the height shall be no more than 36 inches (92 centimeters) above the floor. In alterations where it is infeasible to provide an accessible counter, a secondary counter meeting these requirements may be provided.
- All accessible sales and service counters shall be on an accessible route.

Examining Your Facility

To determine deficits in golf programs and barriers to participation that result in discrimination against people with disabilities, staff at golf facilities can initiate a self-analysis. The golf staff should examine all programs to determine the best ways to accommodate golfers with disabilities. Not only can this be financially rewarding in the long run by attracting more customers, but it is also the right thing to do. Any architectural, communication, or service barriers should be identified and reasonable measures should be taken to eliminate them. Interested people with disabilities or representatives from advocacy organizations can provide valuable assistance in the self-analysis process. To be most effective, self-analysis should be ongoing and available for public review. The self-analysis should include interested persons consulted, descriptions of the areas examined, problems identified, and modifications made.

When a golf facility is obligated to remove barriers, it should follow the design require-ments of the ADA Accessibility Guidelines. The ADA Accessibility Guidelines are minimum requirements, and golf facilities are encouraged to go beyond them when possible. However, some proprietors of courses may just want to make their facilities more accessible for people with disabilities. The following examples of steps to remove barriers may assist in this effort:

- Installing ramps
- Removing barriers to tee boxes and greens
- Providing accessible hitting stations at the practice range
- Making curb cuts in sidewalks, entrances, and golf car paths
- Rearranging tables, chairs, shop fixtures, vending machines, and other furniture
- Widening paths in the clubhouse and on the course to make them more accessible
- Installing grab bars
- Repositioning telephones
- Installing accessible hardware on doors
- Creating parking spaces designated as accessible
- Providing paper cups at inaccessible drinking fountains

Staff at golf facilities have a legal and ethical responsibility to make the facility accessible to people with disabilities. Modifications to golf courses and facilities that provide accessibility are typically not very difficult to achieve. If in doubt about proper procedures and guidelines, consult the Department of Justice, the Americans with Disabilities Act, or the Access Board rulings. Golf is a game for everyone, and staff at golf facilities must do their part in making the game accessible to all.

References

Chapter 1

Americans with Disabilities Act of 1990 (ADA). (1990). PL 101-336. 42 U.S.C. § 12101 *et seq.*

Appenzeller, T. (2000). *Youth sport and the law: A guide to legal issues.* Durham, NC: Carolina Academic Press.

Block, M.E. (1994). Americans with Disabilities Act: Its impact on youth sports. *Journal of Physical Education, Recreation and Dance, 66*(1), 28-32.

Carpenter, L.J. (2000). *Legal concepts in sport: A primer* (2nd ed.). Reston, VA: AAALF.

Epstein, R.S., McGovern, J.N., & Moon, M.S. (1994). The impact of federal legislation on recreation programs. In M.S. Moon (Ed.), *Making school and community recreation fun for everyone: Places and ways to integrate* (pp. 87-96). Baltimore: Brookes.

Fried, G.B. (1998). ADA and sport facilities. In H. Appenzeller (Ed.), *Risk management in sport* (pp. 253-265). Durham, NC: Carolina Academic Press.

Hypes, M.G., Himmelstein, C., & Falardeau, J. (2002). Athletic eligibility and the Americans with Disabilities Act. *Journal of Physical Education, Recreation and Dance, 73*(1), 11-14.

Imber, M., & van Geel, T. (2001). *A teacher's guide to education law* (2nd ed.). Mahwah, NJ: Erlbaum.

Lane, C. (2001, March 30). Disabled pro golfer wins right to use cart. *Washington Post,* A01.

National Alliance for Accessible Golf (NAAG). 2003. *National Alliance for Accessible Golf: Toolkit for golf course owners and operators.* Available: www.accessgolf.org/alliance/Golf-Toolkit-final-2-03.pdf. Accessed March 2005.

Paciorek, M.J., & Jones, J.A. (2001). *Disability sport and recreation resources* (3rd ed.). Traverse City, MI: Cooper.

Stein, J.U. (1993). The Americans with Disabilities Act: Implications for Recreation and Leisure. In S.J. Grosse (Ed.), *Leisure opportunities for individuals with disabilities: Legal issues* (pp. 1-11). Reston, VA: AAHPERD.

Sullivan, K.A., Lantz, P.J., & Zirkel, P.A. (2000). Leveling the playing field or leveling the players? Section 504, the Americans with Disabilities Act, and Interscholastic sports. *Journal of Special Education, 33,* 258-267.

United States Department of Justice. (2001). *A guide to disability rights.* Retrieved July 25, 2002, from www.usdoj.gov/crt/ada/cguide/htm.

United States Department of Justice. (2002). *Americans with Disabilities Act: Questions and answers.* Retrieved July 25, 2002, from http://usdoj.gov/crt/ada/qandaeng.htm.

United States Golf Association (USGA). (2001). *A modification of the rules of golf for golfers with disabilities.* Retrieved July 25, 2002, from www.usga.org/rules/golfers_with_disabilities.html.

Walsh, M. (2001, June 6). Ruling on disabled golfer could be applied to schools. *Education Week,* 29.

Chapter 2

Miller, P.D. (1995). *Fitness programming and physical disability.* Champaign, IL: Human Kinetics.

U.S. Access Board. n.d. www.access-board.gov. Accessed May 4, 2005.

Chapter 3

DePauw, K.P., & Gavron, S.J. (2005). *Disability and sport* (2nd ed.). Champaign, IL: Human Kinetics.

Chapter 4

Bandura, A. (1994). Self-efficacy. In V.S. Ramachaudran (Ed.), *Encyclopedia of human behavior* (Vol. 4, pp. 71-81). New York: Academic Press.

Bohlig, M. (1991). Recreational programming for women. *NIRSA Journal, 16*(1), 8-10.

Bullock, C.C., & Mahon, M.J. (2001). Introduction to recreation services for people with disabilities: A person-centered approach. Champaign, IL: Sagamore.

DePauw, K.P., & Gavron, S.J. (2005). *Disability and sport* (2nd ed.). Champaign, IL: Human Kinetics.

Hayden, M., Lakin, K.C., Hill, B., Bruininks, R., & Copher, J. (1992). Social and leisure integration of people with mental retardation in foster homes and small group homes. *Education and Training in Mental Retardation, 27,* 187-199.

Mactavish, J. (1995). Why is a family focus imperative to inclusive recreation? In S.J. Schleien, J. Rynders, L. Heyne, & C. Tabourne (Eds.), *Powerful partnerships: Parents and professionals building inclusive recreation programs together* (pp. 8-13). Minneapolis, MN: Institute on Community Integration, University of Minnesota.

Roggenbuck, J.W., Loomis, R.J., & Dagostino, J.V. (1991). The learning benefits of leisure. In B.L. Driver, P.J. Brown, & G.L. Peterson (Eds.), *Benefits of leisure.* State College, PA: Venture.

Schleien, S., Meyer, L., Heyne, L., & Brandt, B. (1995). *Lifelong leisure skills and lifestyles for persons with developmental disabilities.* Baltimore: Brookes.

The Harris Poll. (2000). Many people with disabilities feel isolated, left out of their communities and would like to participate more. Retrieved February 28, 2004, from www.harrisinteractive.com/harris_poll/index.asp?PID=97.

Chapter 5

DePauw, K.P. & Gavron, S.J. (2005). *Disability and sport* (2nd ed.). Champaign, IL: Human Kinetics.

Goodman, S. (1993). *Coaching athletes with disabilities: General principles.* Canberra, Australia: Australian Sports Commission.

Ladies Professional Golf Association (LPGA). (2004). *National education program series instruction manual.* Daytona Beach, FL: Ladies Professional Golf Association.

Chapter 6

National Center on Accessibility (NCA). (2003). *Golf etiquette and players with disabilities.* Retrieved June 4, 2003, from www.accessgolf.org/projectgain-CD/general_etiquette.htm.

United States Golf Association (USGA). (2001). A modification of the rules of golf for golfers with disabilities. Retrieved June 4, 2003 from www.usga.org/playing/rules/golfers_with_disabilities.html.

Chapter 7

Batt, M.E. (1992). A survey of golf injuries in amateur golfers. *British Journal of Sports Medicine, 26,* 63-65.

Dattilo, J. (1999). *Leisure education program planning.* State College, Pennsylvania: Venture.

McCarroll, J.R., & Gioe, T.J. (1982). Professional golfers and the price they pay. *The Physician and Sportsmedicine, 10,* 64-70.

McCarroll, J.R., Rettig, A.C., & Shelbourne, K.D. (1990). Injuries in the amateur golfer. *The Physician and Sportsmedicine, 18,* 122-126.

McNicholas, M.J., Neilsen, A., & Knill-Jones, R.P. (1998). Golf injuries in Scotland. In M.R. Farrally & A.J. Cochran (Eds.), *Science and golf III: Proceedings of the world scientific golf congress* (pp. 65-73). Champaign, IL: Human Kinetics.

Milton, J. (2001). Minimizing golf injuries: The physician's perspective. In the *Sixth National Forum on Accessible Golf Proceedings,* 13-18.

Raskin, R.J., & Rebecca, G.S. (1983). Posttraumatic sports-related musculoskeletal abnormalities: Prevalence in a normal population. *American Journal of Sports Medicine, 11,* 336-339.

Chapter 8

Block, M.E. (2000). *A teacher's guide to including students with disabilities in general physical education* (2nd ed.). Baltimore: Brookes.

Clements, A. (2000, March). *Emergency action plans.* Presentation at the American Alliance for Health, Physical Education, Recreation and Dance (AAHPERD). Orlando, FL.

Owens, D.D. (1984). *Teaching golf to special populations.* New York: Leisure Press.

Chapter 9

American Psychological Association (APA). (1994). *Diagnostic and statistical manual of mental disorders* (4th ed.). Washington, D.C.: Author.

The Arc. (1998). *Introduction to mental retardation.* Silver Spring, MD: Author.

Auxter, D., Pyfer, J., & Huettig, C. (2001). *Principles and methods of adapted physical education and recreation* (9th ed.). Boston: McGraw Hill.

Bierne-Smith, M., Patton, J.R., & Ittenbach, R. (1994). *Mental retardation* (4th ed.). Columbus, OH.: Merrill/Prentice Hall.

Block, M.E. (2000). *A teacher's guide to including students with disabilities in general physical education* (2nd ed.). Baltimore: Brookes.

Centers for Disease Control (CDC). (1999, July). *Physical activity and health: A report of the Surgeon General—Persons with disabilities.* Retrieved March 11, 2004, from www.cdc.gov/nccdphp/sgr/disab.htm.

Luckasson, R., Coulter, D.L., Pollaway, E.A., Reiss, S., Schalock, R.L., Snell, M.E., Spitalnik, D.M., & Stark, J.A. (1992). *Mental retardation: Definition, classification, and systems of supports.* Washington, D.C.: AAMR.

McConaughy, E.K., & Salzberg, C.L. (1988). Physical fitness of mentally retarded individuals. In N.W. Bray (Ed.), *International review of research in mental retardation* (pp. 227-258). New York: Academic Press.

National Information Center for Children and Youth with Disabilities (NICHCY). (2002). *Mental retardation fact sheet* (FS8). Washington, D.C.: Author.

Rimmer, J.H. (1994). *Fitness and rehabilitation programs for special populations.* Madison, WI: Brown & Benchmark.

Sherrill, C. (1998). *Adapted physical activity, recreation, and sport* (5th ed.). Madison, WI: WCB/McGraw-Hill.

Special Olympics. (2002a). *About Special Olympics.* Retrieved August 1, 2002, from www.specialolympics.org/about_special_olympics/index.html.

Special Olympics. (2002b). *Golf.* Retrieved August 1, 2002, from www.specialolympics.org.

Special Olympics. (2002c). *Official Special Olympics summer sports rules* (pp. 165-180). Washington, D.C.: Author.

Turnbull, R., Turnbull, A., Shank, M., Smith, S., & Leal, D. (2002). *Exceptional lives: Special education in today's schools* (3rd ed.). Columbus, OH: Merrill/Prentice Hall.

Chapter 10

American Psychiatric Association (APA). (2000). *Diagnostic and statistical manual of mental disorders* (4th ed.). Washington, D.C.: American Psychiatric Association.

Attwood, T. (1998). *Asperger's syndrome: A guide for parents and professionals.* London: Jessica Kingsley.

Auxter, D., Pyfer, J., & Huettig, C. (2001). *Principles and methods of adapted physical education and recreation* (9th ed.). Boston: McGraw Hill.

Bashe, P.R., & Kirby, B.L. (2001). *The OASIS guide to Asperger syndrome.* New York: Crown.

Berkeley, S.L., Zittel, L.L., Pitney, L.V., & Nichols, S.E. (2001). Locomotor and object control skills of children diagnosed with autism. *Adapted Physical Activity Quarterly, 18,* 405-416.

Beyer, R. (1999). Motor proficiency of boys with attention deficit hyperactivity disorder and boys with learning disabilities. *Adapted Physical Activity Quarterly, 16,* 403-414.

Fowler, M. (1994). *Attention-deficit/hyperactivity disorder* (revised edition). Washington, D.C.: NICHCY.

Groft, M., & Block, M.E. (2003). Asperger's syndrome: Implications for physical education and sport. *Journal of Physical Education, Recreation and Dance, 74*(3), 38-43.

Hallahan, D.P., & Kauffman, J.M. (1997). *Exceptional children: Introduction to special education* (7th ed.). Boston: Allyn and Bacon.

Harvey, W.J., & Reid, G. (1997). Motor performance of children with attention deficit/hyperactivity disorder: A preliminary investigation. *Adapted Physical Activity Quarterly, 14,* 189-202.

Holmes, D.L. (1997). *Autism through the lifespan: The Eden model.* Bethesda, MD: Woodbine House.

Individuals with Disabilities Education Act (IDEA). (1997). *Individuals with Disabilities Education Act, Amendments of 1997.* Washington, D.C.: GPO.

Kadesjo, B., & Gillberg, C. (1998). Attention deficits and clumsiness in Swedish 7-year-old children. *Developmental Medicine and Child Neurology, 40,* 796-804.

Kirby, B.L. (2003). What is Asperger Syndrome? *Online Asperger Syndrome Information and Support (OASIS).* Retrieved January 21, 2003, from www.udel.edu/bkirby/asperger.

Lazarus, J.C. (1994). Evidence of disinhibition in learning disabilities: The associated movement phenomenon. *Adapted Physical Activity Quarterly, 11,* 57-70.

Manjiviona, J., & Prior, M. (1995). Comparison of Asperger syndrome and high-functioning autistic children on a test of motor impairment. *Journal of Autism and Developmental Disorders, 25,* 23-39.

Miyahara, M. (1994). Subtypes of students with learning disabilities based on gross motor function. *Adapted Physical Activity Quarterly, 11,* 368-382.

Moffitt, T.E. (1990). Juvenile delinquency and attention deficit disorder: Boys' developmental trajectories from age 3 to age 15. *Child Development, 61,* 893-910.

National Center for Learning Disabilities (NCLD). (2003). *LD Basics.* Retrieved January 13, 2003, from www.ld.org.

National Information Center for Children and Youth with Disabilities (NICHCY). (2001, December). *NICHCY fact sheet #19: Attention-deficit/hyperactive disorder.* Washington, D.C.: Author.

Piek, J.P., Pitcher, T.M., & Hay, D.A. (1999). Motor coordination and kinaesthesis in boys with attention deficit-hyperactivity disorder. *Developmental Medicine and Child Neurology, 41,* 159-165.

Powers, M.D. (1989). What is autism? In M.D. Powers (Ed.), *Children with autism: A parent's guide* (pp. 1-29). Bethesda, MD: Woodbine House.

Savel, A.J. (1993). *Hot tips: A tip sheet for physical educators.* Cedar Rapids, IA: Grant Wood Education Agency.

Shapiro, B. (2001). Specific learning disabilities. In M.L. Batshaw (Ed.), *When your child has a disability* (revised) (pp. 373-390). Baltimore: Brookes.

Sherrill, C. (1998). *Adapted physical activity, recreation, and sport* (5th ed.). Madison, WI: WCB/McGraw-Hill.

Sherrill, C., & Pyfer, J. (1985). Learning disabled students in physical education. *Adapted Physical Activity Quarterly, 2,* 283-291.

Sigman, M., & Capps, L. (1997). *Children with autism: A developmental perspective.* Cambridge, MA: Harvard University Press.

Slavoff, G. (1997). *Motor development in children with autism.* Unpublished doctoral dissertation, University of Virginia, Charlottesville.

Smith, I.M. (2000). Motor functioning in Asperger syndrome. In A. Kim, F.R. Volkmar, & S.S. Sparrow (Eds.), *Asperger syndrome*. New York: The Guilford Press.

Smith Myles, B., & Simpson, R.L. (2001). Effective practices for students with Asperger syndrome. *Focus on Exceptional Children, 34*, 3, 1-14.

Stein, M.A., & Batshaw, M.L. (2001). Attention deficit/hyperactivity disorder. In M.L. Batshaw (Ed.), *When your child has a disability* (revised edition) (pp. 355-372). Baltimore: Brookes.

TEACCH. (2002). Structured teaching. *TEACCH Program*. Retrieved on December 1, 2002, from www.unc.edu/depts/teacch/strucur.htm.

Towbin, K.E. (2001). Autism spectrum disorders. In M.L. Batshaw (Ed.), *When your child has a disability* (revised ed.) (pp. 341-353). Baltimore: Brookes.

Towbin, K.E., Mauk, J.E., & Batshaw, M.L. (2001). Pervasive developmental disorders. In M.L. Batshaw (Ed.), *Children with disabilities* (5th ed.) (pp. 365-387). Baltimore: Brookes.

Tucker, E. (Ed.). (2000). Asperger syndrome guide for teachers. *Online Asperger Syndrome Information and Support* (OASIS). Retrieved March 21, 2003, from www.udel.edu/bkirby/asperger/teachers_guide.html.

Werry, J.S., Elkind, G.S., & Reeves, J.C. (1987). Attention deficit, conduct, oppositional, and anxiety disorders in children: III. *Journal of Abnormal Child Psychology, 15*, 409-428.

Wodrich, D.L. (1994). *Attention deficit hyperactivity disorder*. Baltimore: Brookes.

Yan, J.H., & Thomas, J.R. (2002). Arm movement control: Differences between children with and without attention deficit hyperactivity disorder. *Research Quarterly for Exercise and Sport, 73*, 10-18.

Chapter 11

Auxter, D., Pyfer, J., & Huettig, C. (2001). *Principles and methods of adapted physical education and recreation* (9th ed.). Boston: McGraw-Hill.

Block, M.E. (2000). *A teacher's guide to including students with disabilities in general physical education* (2nd ed.). Baltimore: Brookes.

Holbrook, M.C. (1996). What is visual impairment. In M.C. Holbrook (Ed.), *Children with visual impairments* (pp. 1-20). Bethesda, MD: Woodbine House.

Lieberman, L. (2005). Visual impairments. In J.P. Winnick (Ed.), *Adapted physical education and sport* (4th ed.) (pp. 221-234). Champaign, IL: Human Kinetics.

Lieberman, L.J., & Cowart, J.F. (1996). *Games for people with sensory impairments*. Champaign, IL: Human Kinetics.

Sherrill, C. (1998). *Adapted physical activity, recreation and sport* (5th ed.). Madison, WI: WCB/McGraw-Hill.

Stiles, S., & Knox, R. (1996). Medical issues, treatments, and professionals. In M.C. Holbrook (Ed.), *Children with visual impairments* (pp. 21-48). Bethesda, MD: Woodbine House.

Chapter 12

Auxter, D., Pyfer, J., & Huettig, C. (2001). *Principles and methods of adapted physical education and recreation* (9th ed.). Boston: McGraw-Hill.

Block, M.E. (2000). *A teacher's guide to including students with disabilities in general physical education* (2nd ed.). Baltimore: Brookes.

Lieberman, L. (2005). Deafness and deafblindness. In J.P. Winnick (Ed.), *Adapted physical education and sport* (4th ed.) (pp. 221-234). Champaign, IL: Human Kinetics.

National Information Center for Children and Youth with Disabilities (NICHCY). (2001). *Fact Sheet 3: Deafness and hearing loss*. Washington, D.C.: Author.

Paciorek, M.J., & Jones, J.A. (2001). *Disability sport and recreation resources* (3rd ed.). Traverse City, MI: Cooper.

Sherrill, C. (1998). *Adapted physical activity, recreation, and sport* (5th ed.). Madison, WI: WCB/McGraw-Hill.

USA Deaf Sports Federation (USADSF). (2002). *USA Deaf Sports Federation*. Retrieved August 5, 2002, from www.usadsf.org/about.html.

Chapter 13

Beers, M.H., & Berkow, R. (1999). *The Merck manual of diagnosis and therapy*. Rahway, NJ: Merck Research Laboratories.

Culatta, B. (1993). Intervening for language-learning disabilities. In F.L. Rowley-Kelly & D.H. Reigel (Eds.), *Teaching students with spina bifida* (pp. 171-191). Baltimore: Brookes.

Disabled Sports USA (DS/USA). (2001). *Classification in Disabled Sports USA sponsored events*. Retrieved March 5, 2004, from www.dsusa.org.

Dunn, J.M. (1997). *Special physical education* (7th ed.). Madison, WI: Brown & Benchmark.

Gersch, E. (1998). What is cerebral palsy? In E. Geralis (Ed.), *Children with cerebral palsy: A parents' guide* (2nd ed.) (pp.1-34). Bethesda, MD: Woodbine.

Kelly, L. (2005). Spinal cord disabilities. In J.P. Winnick (Ed.), *Adapted physical education and sport* (4th ed.) (pp. 275-305). Champaign, IL: Human Kinetics.

Muscular Dystrophy Association (MDA). (2000, April). *Facts about Duchenne and Becker Muscular Dystrophies*. Retrieved March 10, 2004, from www.mdausa.org/publications/fa-dmdbmd-what.html.

Paciorek, M.J., & Jones, J.A. (2001). *Disability sport and recreation resources* (3rd ed.). Traverse City, MI: Cooper.

Pelligrino, L. (1997). Cerebral palsy. In M.L. Batshaw (Ed.), *Children with disabilities* (4th ed.) (pp. 499-528). Baltimore: Brookes.

Pitetti, K. (2001). Epidemiology and pathophysiology of amputations. The National Center on Physical Activity and Disability. Retrieved March 11, 2004, from http://ncpad.cc.uic.edu/whtpprs/Amputations%20 and%20Exercise.htm.

Porretta, D.L. (2005). Cerebral palsy, traumatic brain injury, and stroke. In J.P. Winnick (Ed.), *Adapted physical education and sport* (4th ed.) (pp. 235-254). Champaign, IL: Human Kinetics.

Sherrill, C. (1998). *Adapted physical activity, recreation, and sport* (5th ed.). Madison, WI: WCB/McGraw-Hill.

United States Golf Association (USGA). (2001). *A modification of the rules of golf for golfers with disabilities.* Retrieved July 25, 2002, from www.usga.org/rules/golfers_with_disabilities.html.

Chapter 14

National Alliance for Accessible Golf (NAAG). (2003). *Toolkit for golf course owners and operators.* Retrieved February 28, 2004, from www.accessgolf.org.

Chapter 15

Gottlieb, B. (1998). Support groups. In H.S. Friedman (Ed.), *Encyclopedia of mental health.* San Francisco: Academic Press.

Mobley, T.A., & Toalson, R.F. (1992). The 21st century: Part I. *Parks & Recreation, 27*(9), 100-105.

NAAG (2004). Suggestions for creating a Project GAIN steering committee. Retrieved May 29, 2005, from www.accessgolf.org/projectgain-CD/gain_selecting.htm.

Ochocka, J., & Lord, J. (1998). Support clusters: A social network approach for people with complex needs. *Journal of Leisurability, 25*(4), 14-22.

Professional Golfers' Association of America (PGA). (2003). *Play golf America.* Palm Beach Gardens, FL: PGA of America.

Ray, M.T. (1991). *SCOLA leisure activity fun guide.* St. Paul, MN: Arc Ramsey County.

Schleien, S.J., Ray, M.T., & Green, F.P. (1997). *Community recreation and people with disabilities: Strategies for inclusion.* Baltimore: Brookes.

Shrake, A. (2004). Funding accessibility projects: In search of the money tree. *Access Today.* Retrieved March 1, 2004, from www.ncaonline.org/monographs/11funding.shtml.

Toalson, R.F., & Mobley, T.A. (1993). The 21st century: Part II. *Parks & Recreation, 28*(5), 56-61.

United States Golf Association (USGA). (2004). *Grants initiative and fellowship program.* Retrieved March 1, 2004, from www.usga.org/aboutus/annual_report/2004/grants_and_fellowship.html.

Walker, P. (1999). Promoting inclusion in recreation and leisure activities: An information packet. *National Resource Center on Supported Living and Choice.* Retrieved February 26, 2004, from http://soeweb.syr.edu/thechp/recreation.html.

Chapter 16

Johnson, D.W., & Johnson, F.P. (1987). *Joining together: Group therapy and group skills* (3rd ed.). Englewood Cliffs, NJ: Prentice Hall.

Schleien, S.J., Meyer, L.H., Heyne, L.A., & Brandt, B.B. (1995). *Lifelong leisure skills and lifestyles for persons with developmental disabilities.* Baltimore: Brookes.

Skulski, J.K. (2003). Golf: An update on the movement toward full inclusion of people with disabilities. *Access Today.* Retrieved February, 26, 2004, from www.indiana.edu/~nca/monographs/10golf.shtml.

Winnick, J.P. (2005). *Adapted physical education and sport* (4th ed.). Champaign, IL: Human Kinetics.

Appendix A

United States Golf Association (USGA). (2001). *A modification of the rules of golf for golfers with disabilities.* Retrieved July 25, 2002, from www.usga.org/rules/golfers_with_disabilities.html.

Appendix C

Robb, G. (1996). *Golf etiquette and players with disabilities.* Bloomington, IN: National Center on Accessibility—Indiana University.

Appendix D

ADA Accessibility Guidelines. (2002). *ADA accessibility guidelines for buildings and facilities.* Retrieved June 4, 2003, from www.access-board.gov/adaag/html/adaag.htm.

About the LPGA

The **Ladies Professional Golf Association (LPGA)** is the longest-running women's sports association in the world, having celebrated its 50th anniversary in the year 2000. Dedicated to the worldwide promotion and advancement of golf, the organization has grown from its roots as a playing tour into a nonprofit organization involved in every facet of golf. The LPGA maintains a strong focus on charity through its tournaments, its grassroots junior and women's programs, its affiliation with the Susan G. Komen Breast Cancer Foundation, and the formation of the LPGA Foundation.

The **LPGA Tour** and the **LPGA Teaching & Club Professional (T&CP) Membership** make up the backbone of this organization. The LPGA Tour season includes 34 events with total prize money in excess of $45 million. The LPGA Teaching & Club Professional (T&CP) Membership, founded in 1959, has enjoyed unprecedented growth in recent years and with nearly 1,200 members, boasts the largest membership of female golf professionals in the country. LPGA T&CP is dedicated to the advancement of golf through teaching, managing golf facilities, and coaching future stars. Its member programs include national programs and conferences in entrepreneurial and business skills training, tournaments, sponsor and licensee benefits, employment services, golf clinics, and junior golf programs. Considered an industry leader in its teacher education programs, the LPGA T&CP Membership also administers the LPGA's various grassroots programs that are vital to the continued growth of the game, including the Ronald McDonald House Charities LPGA Tour Junior Golf Clinics, LPGA-USGA Girls Golf, and the LPGA Clinics for Women.

The LPGA Foundation was established in 1991. Junior golf programs, scholarships, research, and financial assistance are among the major programs supported through the LPGA Foundation, which has four main goals: to develop and maintain junior golf programs across the country; to develop and maintain scholarship programs for junior golfers; to maintain a financial assistance fund for those in the golf industry; and to conduct research and develop educational activities related to golf instruction. The LPGA-USGA Girls Golf program, the Dinah Shore, Marilynn Smith, and RMHC scholarships are some of the programs that have helped to establish the LPGA Foundation as a leader in youth initiatives.

The LPGA is under the guidance of Commissioner Carolyn Bevins and is headquartered in Daytona Beach, Florida. For more information about the LPGA, visit www.lpga.com. Proceeds from the sale of *Accessible Golf* will be donated to the LPGA Foundation's DeDe Owens Education and Research Fund.

About the Authors

Dan Drane, PhD, is coordinator of the Coaching and Sport Management program at the University of Southern Mississippi. Dr. Drane has been a member of the PGA of America since 1994 and currently serves on the education committee for the National Alliance for Accessible Golf. Before coming to Southern Mississippi, he was director of the Professional Golf Management program at Clemson University. His research interests include sport marketing, youth sports, service learning, and golf. Dr. Drane has written articles for many peer-reviewed journals and made numerous national and international academic presentations. He currently resides in Petal, Mississippi, with his wife, Kara, and two sons, Hogan and Ian.

Martin E. Block, PhD, is an associate professor in the kinesiology program at the University of Virginia, where he has been the director of the masters program in adapted physical education for 12 years. From 1988 to 1999, he served as the consultant to and director of the Special Olympics Motor Activities Training Program, creating assessment tools and adapted equipment for athletes with severe disabilities. Block was the chair for the Adapted Physical Activity Council of the American Association for Active Lifestyles and Fitness (AAALF) and American Alliance for Health, Physical Education, Recreation and Dance (AAHPERD). He also chaired the Motor Development Academy of the National Association for Sport and Physical Education (NASPE) and AAHPERD. Block is a member of the Council for Exceptional Children (CEC) and The Association for Persons with Severe Handicaps (TASH), and he most recently received the Virginia AAHPERD College Professor of the Year Award in 2004. Block, his wife, Vickie, and their daughters reside in Charlottesville, Virginia.